Government by Contract

Also by John D. Hanrahan

Lost Frontier:
The Marketing of Alaska
(with Peter Gruenstein)

John D. Hanrahan

Government by
Contract

W·W·Norton & Company

New York · London

The text of this book is composed in Times Roman, with display type set in
Mominante Bold.
Composition and manufacturing by The Haddon Craftsmen, Inc.
Book design by Clint Anglin.

First Edition

Library of Congress Cataloging in Publication Data

Hanrahan, John, 1938–
    Government by contract.

    Bibliography: p.
    Includes index.
    1. Pubic contracts—United States. 2. Government
consultants—United States. I. Title.
HD3858.H36   1983   353.0071′1   82–24639

ISBN 0-393-01717-6

W. W. Norton & Company, Inc., 500 Fifth Avenue, New York, N.Y. 10110
W. W. Norton & Company Ltd., 37 Great Russell Street, London WC1B 3NU

1 2 3 4 5 6 7 8 9 0

For Deborah, Frank, Timothy,
and Frances Hanrahan

Contents

Acknowledgments

While writing a book may be a very personal endeavor, it could not be done without the help of a number of other people. Especially vital to the making of this book was Fritzi Cohen, director of the Military Audit Project (MAP) in Washington, D.C., who conceived the idea for such a project six years ago. Initially, I researched and wrote a report on government contracting that was issued by MAP in 1978. This book is a complete revamping and updating of that earlier effort. I am particularly grateful to Fritzi for her wise suggestions as to areas of contracting that needed looking into and for her initiative in seeking publication of *Government by Contract.*

I also wish to thank many friends and the dozens of people in government, in public interest groups, in labor unions, in the contracting industry, and in other organizations who provided interviews, information, and leads or otherwise assisted in some aspect of the preparation of *Government by Contract.* Especially helpful were Doug McDaniel, Till Bartels, Brinton Dillingham, James Rosa, Rebecca Moore, Fielding McGehee, A. Ernest Fitzgerald, Fred Small, L.M. Pellerzi, and Edward Norton.

My agent, Robert Roistacher, showed a tenacious spirit in dealing with potential publishers and lent me much encouragement, for which I thank him. Also, Starling Lawrence, senior editor at Norton, offered invaluable advice and steered me out of many ruts. He has my heartfelt thanks.

Finally, I express my loving thanks to my wife, Deborah, and children, Frank and Timothy, for putting up with my mess and my crabby moods. Also, Deborah's typing help and her suggestions for improving the manuscript saved me many days of additional work.

There are many others who provided help along the way, and to them I apologize for not listing their names here. Responsibility for this book's content is mine entirely, and not that of the people who so graciously assisted me.

Government by
Contract

1 · The Role
of Contracting in
Government

One snowy morning in the nation's capital in the winter of 1979, Senator David Pryor hailed a taxi to get to his office on Capitol Hill. Sharing the cab with the Arkansas Democrat were two men who asked to be dropped off at the federal Department of Health and Human Services.

Unaware that they were being overheard by a United States Senator, the two men began discussing the consulting contract they were about to negotiate with the federal agency. One man said they should ask for $25,000; the other argued they could get $50,000 just as easily. Neither was concerned with what the work was actually worth, but rather what they could get away with. By the time the two men were dropped off, they had agreed to ask for the higher amount. After the men exited, the driver remarked to Pryor, "I'll be working a long time to make the difference in the two amounts they were talking about."

It was at that moment, Pryor recalled in an interview in early 1982, that he began to sense something was amiss in the federal government's contracting policies.

For William Coleman, secretary of Transportation under the Ford administration, a similar reaction concerning government contracting came when he was asked by an agency official to look over "a proposal for two or three hundred thousand dollars to study the advantages of walking to work. I said, 'For Chrissake, why spend three hundred thousand dollars on that?' "

Brock Adams, Coleman's successor at Transportation under the Carter administration, also wondered what was going on in his department's contracting practices when one of his top aides informed him that the agency was spending almost $2 million a year on public relations contracts—even though the agency had its own information staff of more than 300 persons who had the time and expertise to do the work. Among the contracts subsequently ordered canceled were ones for $678,000 to Grey Advertising and for $518,000 to the J. Walter Thompson Agency to publicize the 55 mile-per-hour speed limit, seatbelt use, and safe driving.

Congressional staff aide Norman G. Cornish recalled an eye-opening moment during a House subcommittee investigation of energy contracts when he had to call for information to an official of the Energy Research and Development Administration. Cornish said the subcommittee needed the data as part of its probe into whether TRW, Inc., and other major contractors were exerting policymaking and managerial control over the agency. The energy official told Cornish there was no one who could answer his question, but cheerily said, "Hold on for a minute, let's call TRW and find out."

The kinds of contracting practices that concerned Pryor, Coleman, Adams, Cornish, and other officials abound in the files of federal agencies. For example, early in 1982 the Federal Highway Administration was seeking a contractor to determine how people react when traffic lights turn yellow. Also in early 1982, a study prepared by a contractor for the Department of Energy recommended that, following a nuclear attack, people over the age of forty be sent out of fallout shelters first to scout around to obtain food and water (presuming any that was uncontaminated could be found), and to dispose of human waste and garbage. People over forty have less to lose from radiation poisoning, the researchers contended, because they have a shorter life expectancy than people under forty.

Also in the futuristic vein, it was disclosed in 1982 that the government had contracted with the prestigious think-tank, the Rand Corporation, to determine "the economics of strikes and revolts during early space colonization." Rand analyst Mark Hopkins looked at the possibilities of labor problems during the construction and operation of giant solar satellite stations and suggested that the space colonists working on the stations might develop their own identity, separate from their United States citizenship, and could revolt and seize the station. "If the initial seizure were successful," Hopkins said, the "obvious U.S. counter-strategy would be to threaten to destroy the colony and its inhabitants unless the seized assets were returned unharmed."

Rand was also given a $75,000 Pentagon contract in 1982 to study back issues of *Le Monde,* the French newspaper, and *The Economist,* the British magazine, to determine how these publications "have projected the strategic arms balance" since 1979. Rand previously did a similar study covering the years 1948–72 and suggested to the Defense Department that it authorize an update. A department official said the study would help the Pentagon learn how the British and French "upper-level elite" view the arms race.

An example of another type of contracting practice occurred in the White House under President Jimmy Carter when General Services Administration (GSA) janitors were replaced by contract workers. When it was discovered that the contract employees lacked security clearances and couldn't go into certain sensitive areas of the White House to clean up, GSA workers with clearances were quickly brought back to accompany the contract employees on their rounds and watch them as they did their cleaning chores.

Then, there was the case in 1980 when a firm in the Washington, D.C., area billed to the government as overhead items on its management support contract with the Small Business Administration such apparent personal luxuries as private school tuition for the children of company officials, office liquor, a Jaguar, and the use of a tennis court and pool at the home of the company's president.

In bigger cost contracts, there was the disclosure in early 1982 that the army's innovative and expensive M-1 tank, because of a delicate transmission, could not do what other less less sophisticated tanks can —namely, dig itself into a battlefield position. So the army had to come up with a fast-moving bulldozer, the Armored Combat Earth-mover (ACE) to keep up with the high-speed M-1 to assist it in digging in. Each ACE had a pricetag of $200,000 in fiscal 1978, when it was first proposed. By 1981, when Congress finally approved funds for the ACE, the price had risen again, to about $1.1 million. By March 1982, its anticipated cost stood at $1.6 million, and army officials told a reporter they were unsure the contractor would actually provide the machines at that price.

The ACE cost escalation was following the same pattern as that of the M-1 itself. In 1972 the cost for an order of 3,312 M-1 tanks was $4.8 billion, or $1.4 million per tank. By mid-1981, the cost had risen to $18.6 billion for 7,058 tanks, or $2.6 million each: a per-unit increase of 85 percent. The General Accounting Office, the investigative arm of Congress, reported in late 1981 that the program's costs could be expected to escalate even more in the coming years. Besides the high costs of the tanks and the bulldozers, there were other problems: the tanks get only 3.86 miles to the gallon of fuel and require repairs every 43 miles. All these factors led some critics in 1982 to call for a reconsideration of plans to produce the 7,058 tanks by 1987.

Back on the lighter side, the Pentagon in 1982 also decided to contract with Atari, a major manufacturer of electronic videogames, to modify its Battlezone videogame for use in improving marksmanship of gunners for the army's new M-2 personnel transport vehicle. According to one news account, "Soldiers win points for knocking out the tanks and helicopters of the Warsaw Pact countries on the screen, but if they hit a 'friendly' war machine, they are penalized to the tune of the '1812 Overture.' " Also in 1982 the army was seeking bids on a contract to teach cosmetic use and grooming to women recruits at Fort Jackson, South Carolina.

On a more serious note, Representative Tom Corcoran, R-Illinois, expressed concern over the increased reliance by the Defense Department on contractors for such things as mobilization planning and determining army support unit requirements. He said that this increasing use of contractors raises "in my mind, the question of whether or not we have the capacity in time of emergency or in time of war to move quickly to respond to the situation" because of a depressed in-house capacity to do vital military work.

And finally, there is what should be everybody's favorite government contracting tale, which took place at the Department of the Interior's National Visitors Center inside Washington, D.C.'s, Union Station. It is a perfectly circular story: the government in the early 1970s spent upwards of $100 million on contracts, with massive cost overruns, to convert part of the lovely old train station into a visitors' center. As the years went by, few people actually visited the center. Then, the roof crumbled and heavy rains poured in, forcing closure of the center. This led Congress in 1981 to approve a plan to spend at least $80 million to turn the entire facility back into what it had been, for free, a decade earlier—merely a train station.

These examples of federal contracting practices are just a small part of a very big picture. In fact, contracting for goods and services could be considered the major activity of the United States government, given the volume of dollars and work generated by federal contracts. By the early 1980s, the government was awarding annually more than eighteen million contracts totaling more than $150 billion: about one-fifth of the entire federal budget (and rapidly closing in on one-fourth). Put another way, every second of every day the government was paying out $5,000 to the contractors. And over half of this money was being awarded without competition for the contracts.

So dependent had the government become on contractors that by 1982 it was estimated that contractor employees doing government work outnumbered civil service employees by ratios of between two to one and four to one. More than 130,000 government employees— about one in every twenty on the Federal payroll—were needed to administer the vast array of contracts. In some agencies or units within agencies, the major parts of their budgets were being spent on contractors. The Department of Energy, for example, had spent between 80 percent and 94 percent of its budgets on contracts in the late

1970s and early 1980s. Also, many agencies such as the Defense Department and the Energy Department were giving contractors more control over planning, policymaking, and other important operations.

Federal contractors constitute a bureaucracy that parallels the official civil service bureaucracy, yet many of their activities are largely hidden from public view. This quasifederal contractors' bureaucracy consists of the millions of employees of giant corporations, small businesses, think-tanks, colleges and universities, and the large and small consulting firms that have sprung up by the thousands around the nation's capital and in other areas of the country.

The contractors' bureaucracy builds, repairs, and maintains the nation's spacecraft and military ships, aircraft, weapons, and equipment; provides a vast array of goods to military and civilian agencies; operates missile test ranges; manages government research facilities and units of federal agencies on a day-to-day basis; works with intelligence agencies on supersecret projects; drafts agency budgets, legislation, regulations, testimony, letters to legislators, and official reports to Congress; organizes new agencies and reorganizes old ones; oversees the awarding of federal contracts and monitors other contractors' performances; serves as attorneys for government employees in civil suits; formulates or influences agencies' programs on such key issues as energy policy, troop deployment, and development of weapons systems through the various studies and reports it produces and through its positions on agency advisory committees; maintains official files for government agencies; paints and repairs federal facilities; provides security and cleanup services for government buildings, as well as performing hundreds of other white-collar and blue-collar jobs that at one time were done almost exclusively by civil service employees.

While the contractors' bureaucracy has been growing over the last few decades, the civil service bureaucracy—contrary to popular perception—has been shrinking. And this shrinkage in the civil service bureaucracy had begun long before the successful campaigns of Jimmy Carter and Ronald Reagan, both of whom won the presidency on pledges to cut "big government" down to size.

In 1969, eight years before President Carter took office, federal civilian employees totaled almost 3.1 million. By the time Carter began his term, the figure was under 3 million. When Reagan was inaugurated in 1981, federal employment stood at just under 2.9 million. By the end of Reagan's first year in office, the employment figure had declined to about 2.85 million, according to the Office of Personnel Management.

As a percentage of federal budget outlays, the government employees' payroll dipped from a post–World War II high of 17.7 percent in 1951, to 12.5 percent in 1975, to about 9.5 percent at the end of fiscal year 1981. In 1968 federal civilian employment accounted for 3.8 percent of the total United States work force; by 1982 the figure had fallen to under 2.6 percent. While government contractors were expected to be paid more than $160 billion in fiscal year 1982, the federal civilian employee payroll for the same year was projected to be only 40 percent of that figure.

All these statistical comparisons strongly suggest that the increase in "big government" in recent decades has not been due to any expansion of the civil service bureaucracy, but rather is linked to the ascendancy of the contractors' bureaucracy. This rise of what Professor H.L. Nieburg has referred to as "the contract state" has sparked alarm in some quarters and rejoicing in others. Unquestionably, it has produced sweeping changes in the way the government has conducted its business over the last forty years.

As Professor Victor K. Heyman prophetically observed more than two decades ago (using words that are just as applicable today), "There has occurred in federal government operations since World War II a revolutionary change that has gone virtually unnoticed by the citizenry—namely, a decisive trend toward government by contract." Heyman further noted that "The time appears to be rapidly approaching when the employees of the federal government, like the classic iceberg, are nine-tenths invisible" because they are not working as civil service personnel but rather "are obtained by contracts, grants and similar instruments."

More recently, political science Professor Ira Sharkansky has warned that government contractors "to a great extent . . . run themselves, independent of serious control by elected officials or core agencies of government." Yet, he said, few politicians, political scientists, or journalists had examined the implications of the increasing use of contractors and other nongovernment entities to perform basic functions of government. This increasing reliance on contracting, according to Sharkansky, raises the key questions of who rules and who gets what.

In the same vein, former United States Representative Herbert E. Harris II, D-Virginia, a leading critic of government contracting, sees federal contractors as forming a "fourth branch of government" that is financially wasteful and virtually uncontrolled by the federal agencies awarding the contracts, or by the White House and its Office of Management and Budget, or by Congress. "I would think," Harris said in an early 1982 interview, "that students of government would have all kinds of serious questions about people who aren't government employees, but who do the government's work and yet are not subject to the same controls and standards as government employees. . . . What does this mean for our governmental system?"

Along the same lines, Daniel Guttman, a Washington, D.C., attorney and the foremost critic of federal contracting policies, contends that federal agencies, through contracts, have "let out the management of government lock, stock and barrel." Guttman, coauthor of a book examining the role of consultants in government, says that the "contract bureaucracy has elevated invisibility, conflict of interest and unlawful delegation of power to governing principles." He terms it an "illusion that the contract bureaucracy is a cure for the ills of 'big government.' "

Contractors, for their part, see their role in government as a valuable one and discount the criticisms regarding waste and abuse. While acknowledging that some problems have occurred, they usually attribute these to inept management by federal contracting officers, rather than seeing any serious fault within their own ranks.

Typical of those expressing this view is Russell W. Richardson, chairman of the steering committee of the Committee on Contracting Out, a nationwide coalition of twenty-three contractor associations representing thousands of companies that have federal contracts. The organization supports the increased use of contractors to perform services for the government and works to oppose any legislation designed to limit or restrict federal contracting. Richardson said that contractors are "convinced that private sector know-how and private sector efficiency could, through greater contracting-out of government work, save the government and taxpayers a lot of money."

George Monroe, president of the National Council of Professional Services Firms, which also supports increased government contracting, acknowledges that some limited federal contracting abuses exist, but that "the press and others have been rather clever in taking advantage of anecdotal examples." As for contracting critics' assertions that the government exercises inadequate monitoring of its contractors, Monroe said that in his thirty-five years of experience "I know of no example . . . where there are no checks and balances."

Although the government has reliable, current figures on how many civil service employees there are and how much they are costing United States taxpayers, no one in the federal bureaucracy has up-to-date, accurate information on how many government contracts there are, the total dollar amounts of those contracts, the number of contractor employees doing government work, the number of person-hours contracted for, the cost per person-hour for contractor employees, the amounts saved or lost through contracting-out, the exact extent of competition in federal contracting, the amount of duplication in contracts, or a reliable breakdown of just what kinds of goods and services all these contractors are providing. There are also no reliable figures on how much waste there is in government contracts; some private estimates place the figure as high as $20 billion a year.

An individual shopper who didn't know exactly how many products or services he was buying, or how much he was paying for them, or didn't do comparison shopping to get the best deal, or didn't know whether he even needed some of the products or services he was paying for would not be considered a very wise consumer. Yet that is exactly the position in which the government finds itself regarding its contracting policies.

Improvements have been made by the government in recent years in obtaining information on the number and dollar amounts of contracts and the extent of competition, thanks to the creation of the Federal Procurement Data System, which compiles records on federal contractors. Yet because of errors within the system itself or in the data submitted to it by the various federal agencies, the system as late as April 1982 was found by the General Accounting Office to contain "numerous, widespread and potentially significant inaccuracies." The congressional watchdog agency estimated that almost one-half of the contract actions entered into the system "had one or more errors, such as inaccurate dates, dollars obligated, or extent of competition." The accounting office also found that some noncompetitive contracts had not been entered into the system at all. In addition, the system does not include any breakdown on contracts for less than $10,000, which means, for example, that the government in fiscal year 1981 had no clear idea what it was getting for the $11.1 billion it spent on contracts under $10,000. What was known for 1981 is that the government, on purchases of more than $10,000, spent more than 55 percent of the dollars on equipment and supplies, and about 25 percent on "various services" (excluding research and development and architect and engineer services), 13 percent on research and development, 5 percent on construction and 1 percent on architects and engineers.

In recent years, politicians and citizens across the political spectrum have grown increasingly vocal in their criticisms of the way the federal government is run and the way it spends money. To President Reagan and his conservative supporters and supply-side economists, the target has been what they see as a bloated bureaucracy and waste in social programs. To those of more liberal views, it is military spending that draws the most fire as being wasteful of taxpayers' money. People of varying points of view are likely to use the catchall term "big government" to criticize those aspects of the federal bureaucracy they object to. In all its various meanings, "big government" has become the premier political issue of the decade. But while discussions of the subject focus often on social programs, or military spending, or the civil service bureaucracy, little attention has been devoted to the largely hidden contractors' bureaucracy, which itself receives almost one-fourth of the federal budget each year and through its recommendations, followup proposals, and involvement in federal agencies' activities influences the spending of many billions more.

This book is an attempt to bring the contractors' bureaucracy into the debate over "big government" and wasteful federal spending. Much of the book concentrates on the Defense and Energy departments because, as the notorious criminal Willie Sutton once answered when he was asked why he robbed banks, "That's where the money was." The Pentagon, with more than 70 percent of all contracting dollars, spends far more money on contracting than any other federal department, while the Energy Department has spent more on contracting than any other civilian agency. Finally, in examining federal contracting, the book attempts to answer Professor Sharkansky's questions: Who rules? and Who gets what?

2 · How the System Works (or Doesn't)

If a modern-day Diogenes set out in search of one honest man, he might find him in the person of Carl E.R. Black, a consultant in the Washington, D.C., area. In late 1979 Black went public with his insider's account of how the federal contracting system really works.

It is a world, according to Black, in which the government receives perhaps fifty cents in value for every dollar spent on consulting contracts; in which sole-source, rather than competitive, contracts are awarded in the majority of cases, and often without justification; in which more than two-thirds of all contracts offered for competitive bids are already "wired," that is, a predetermination has been made as to who will get the contract; in which the government exercises only minimal, ineffective oversight of contractors; in which contractors charge off flashy cars, expensive equipment, and employee bonuses to the government.

Black, testifying before the Civil Service and General Services Subcommittee of the Senate Governmental Affairs Committee, made it clear that most contractors were honest and did quality work. His aim was not to hurt the industry from which he earned his living, but rather to clean up the widespread abuses so that "a new, more perfect system [can] be established and utilized."

At first glance, Black seemed an unlikely person to blow the whistle on contractors' questionable practices. Before entering the consulting industry, he had been a Marine lieutenant colonel naval aviator and had served on the staff of the Joint Chiefs of Staff in the Pentagon. Upon retiring in 1975 Black, like thousands of his fellow officers, immediately went to work for a small consulting firm. Eight months later, he became general manager of the firm and was allowed to buy 10 percent of the business. He then became a vice president and director of the firm. After three and a half years, he left to form a consulting firm partnership.

In his first four years in business, Black said he was involved in about 70 contracts and smaller awards, known as purchase orders, totaling nearly $5 million. All but about 15 of these were with the Defense Department. In only 5 of these did his companies have to bid competitively.

Although sole-source contracts are supposed to be awarded only to companies that have unique expertise in an area, or are the only firms capable of doing a particular job at a particular time, Black readily acknowledged this was not true in his company's case. "I would be less than truthful and candid to state that our company had the only personnel in the Washington area who could adequately perform the contracted effort," Black said. "Rather, it was a case of getting there 'firstest with the mostest,' so to speak."

Black's testimony on the lack of competitive contracting is borne out by statistics showing that, despite long-standing government policy favoring competition, the heavy majority of federal contracts and contract dollars are awarded sole-source. In recent years, advertised competitive bidding has occurred in less than 10 percent of all Pentagon contracts. Some agencies have even awarded all of their contracts in given years without any competition. In fiscal year 1976, for example, the Energy Research and Development Administration, one of the forerunners of the Department of Energy, initiated or renegotiated 426 consulting contracts—and not one involved competitive bidding.

In fiscal year 1980, about $59 billion—more than half of all contract dollars reported governmentwide by the Office of Management and Budget—was awarded noncompetitively. In fiscal year 1981, 54 percent of the contract dollars were awarded noncompetitively. OMB's Office of Federal Procurement Policy estimated in late 1981 that "For every $1 billion that is converted from noncompetitive to competitive, there is a potential saving of up to $250 million." If this were true, competitive bidding could have produced government savings of up to $18 billion in fiscal 1981.

Of contract awards of more than $10,000, only 35 percent of the contracting dollars were awarded competitively in 1980; 38 percent, in 1981. The Defense Department, with 7.6 percent of its contract dollars offered competitively in 1980 and 7.3 percent in 1981, and the Energy Department, with 23 and 19 percent, respectively, for the two years, were by far the worst of the major agencies. Among the best for the two years were the Department of Agriculture, 95 and 96 percent; Department of Transportation, 72 percent for both years; the Tennessee Valley Authority, 66 and 84 percent, and the National Aeronautics and Space Administration, 66 and 65 percent.

But the figures on competitive bidding, as bad as they are, are still misleadingly high. Several government studies have shown that the degree of competition is often limited to a few firms, when many more are actually qualified to provide the goods or services. Also, in many instances, a contract is advertised for bids but it is well known that the contract, because of the way the proposal is advertised, is earmarked for a particular company. Such "wired" contracts are an accepted, but certainly questionable, part of the federal contracting system. A federal agency contracting officer "specifies that there are certain criteria regarding office location, company background experience, personnel experience, etc. which will be used to evaluate the proposal, all the time knowing that only one company can meet the criteria. This . . . appears on the surface to be honest competition but . . . is, in reality, a thinly veiled sole source."

In the process, contractors themselves often write their own solesource justifications, which are accepted unquestioningly by agency contracting officials and put in the official contracting file as the basis for awarding the noncompetitive contracts. Agencies like to use solesource actions because they speed up the awarding of the contract and lessen the paperwork, which often bogs down an agency that issues a great number of contracts.

Another common abuse in both competitive and noncompetitive contracts is the practice by which a contractor "buys in"—that is, deliberately submits a low money proposal in order to get the contract. In such situations, the contractor hopes to make up his initial loss either through follow-up business or by being allowed to add additional work to the contract—at a later date and a higher price.

Another way to get smaller amounts of government money and avoid red tape, is through "purchase orders," which provide for specific limited tasks for a company in an area of expertise in which a contract is later to be awarded. The purchase orders then can be used by the contractor and contracting agency to justify giving the same firm an eventual sole-source contract, on the ground that the firm's personnel are uniquely familiar with the subject area.

Because of government regulations, contracts exceeding $100,000 are subject to much more scrutiny and red tape than those for lesser amounts. So contractors and federal agencies often agree to break up the proposed contract into several smaller awards under $100,000, with "options" for additional work priced in; the options are almost always exercised.

Another questionable practice that drives up the costs of contracts unnecessarily is the "cost-plus" arrangement, under which a contractor is reimbursed for all allowable costs plus a reasonable profit. Agencies are often quite lenient in their interpretations of what are justifiable costs. Because the contractor is assured of reimbursement, Carl Black noted, "he tends not to deny himself any of the niceties such as luxury automobiles, bonuses, retirement plan, insurance, and a generous salary, in that these cost him nothing because they will be paid for" by the government.

If, as the contract year is nearing its end and the contractor is not close to spending the dollar amount allotted under the contract, he will spend more to "remain very close to what was bid, even if it means leasing more space, a word processor or even another Cadillac." A cost-plus contract "does not necessarily encourage the contractor to exercise thrift or restraint like a fixed-price contract does. . . . The generous nature of a cost-plus contract lends itself to the contractor providing gratuities such as fishing trips, expensive lunches, tickets to social functions, coffee for the customers' office, and other niceties . . . for which the government will ultimately pay."

Some government contracting officials develop close relationships with contractors in the hope of winning future employment with the contractor when they retire from government work. In such situations, contracting officials provide the contractor with certain information that is not available to other potential bidders, thus allowing the favored firm to tailor its proposal in such a way as to enable it to win the contract. On other occasions, Black said, contracting officials "will tell the contractor that if he hires a certain person either as an employee or as an independent consultant, then the contract will go his way."

Many of these questionable or illegal practices occur despite government regulations to the contrary regarding competitive bids, conflicts of interest, and the like. Black made it clear that he feels there is a vital role for contractors to play in government, but he feared there was much "weeding out" to be done in order to make sure that contracts were absolutely necessary and the government was getting quality work at the best possible price.

The contractor also cited the special problem of retired regular military officers contracting with their former military departments, despite a law barring them for three years after retirement from contracting with the Defense Department and prohibiting them for life from "selling to the military department from which they retired." Although "this has been on the books for many years," Black said, "to my knowledge, no one has been successfully prosecuted under it," even though "there are literally thousands of retired military officers in the consulting business right here in the Washington area."

In this regard, a 1981 study by the Council on Economic Priorities found that a total of 1,672 former civilian and military employees of the Defense Department (between 1971 and 1979) and the National Aeronautics and Space Administration (between 1974 and 1979) went to work for the eight leading defense contractors: Boeing, Northrop, Lockheed, General Dynamics, Rockwell, McDonnell Douglas, Grumman, and United Technologies. In the same period, 270 employees left these same companies to work for Defense and the space agency. This "revolving door" situation provides the temptation for direct conflicts of interest as well as further blurring of the lines between contractors and government. As the report noted, the "revolving door" provides favored contractors with information on current and future agency plans, especially in research areas; gives them "access to key offices in federal agencies, technical expertise for weapons development and marketing, [and] skilled personnel with an intimate knowledge of both sides of contracting."

As with military personnel leaving government, there are federal statutes restricting civilian employees who leave federal agencies from using their influence to win contracts for themselves or their companies until they have been out of government for at least two years. However, the Council on Economic Priorities found in its 1981 report that these, as with the similar statutes covering former military personnel, "have not been firmly enforced."

In his testimony, Black observed that when layoffs occur in the federal government, or personnel ceilings are imposed on agencies, contractors thrive. Senator David Pryor, D-Arkansas, the subcommittee chairman, had asked Black, "How do people in the consulting business respond when the Congress adopts personnel ceilings? When we put a ceiling on personnel, say, for this department or that department, what is the response out in the consulting industry?" "Joy," answered Black. "Why?" asked Pryor. "Well," said Black, "because the requirement is not going to get less or go away. The same amount of questions or more are going to be asked and agencies will have to respond. Now, if they have fewer people to respond, then they have to get outside help to dig up answers. So we respond with joy by knowing it is going to be a fruitful year." So heavily are consulting firms involved in the basic functions of government, said Black, that if they were told to stop work, "I think the federal government would grind to a screeching halt, or at least many of the programs would."

Many adherents of personnel ceilings, including all recent presidents and key congressional leaders, claim to see them as a tool for controlling the growth of the federal bureaucracy. President Carter, as had presidents before him, affirmed his faith in the ceilings in a fireside chat within two weeks after he took office. President Reagan and his top budget aides regularly proclaim the virtues of holding down the size of the federal workforce.

In the absence of growth elsewhere—for example, in the number of functions the government is required to perform, in the budgets of federal agencies, or in the contract bureaucracy—personnel ceilings would, indeed, hold down the size and cost of government. But in practice, as a number of recent studies by congressional committees and the General Accounting Office have shown, the size of the "hidden government" has continued to mushroom as personnel ceilings have been increasingly used as a subterfuge to contract-out jobs traditionally performed by Civil Service employees. As former Rep. Porter Hardy, D-Virginia, a staunch opponent of indiscriminate contracting-out, observed more than a decade ago regarding the increasing use of contract employees by government: "The government's personnel ceilings are merely fooling the American taxpayer." Former Senator Frank E. Moss, D-Utah, likewise observed that "reducing the federal work force without reducing the workload creates a dangerous and misleading illusion of control. It controls the number of federal workers, all right, but it does not control costs, does not produce efficiency, and often forfeits accountability." Or as William R. Cater, president of the National Association of Supervisors, Federal Government, has noted, "It looks good for public officials to beat their breasts in self-praise by citing declining federal employment. Total labor dollars expended are never mentioned. The public is given the impression that a decline in federal employment is great, that the costs of government have gone down; but the taxpayers are never told that the actual costs of labor have gone up" because of contracting out.

A June 1977 study by the General Accounting Office contends that arbitrary personnel ceilings prevent federal managers from improving productivity by barring them from using the best possible mix of government and contractor employees. The report makes several key points concerning the way personnel ceilings adversely affect government operations:

- services to the public and other agencies are reduced;
- essential work is deferred or canceled, and work backlogs are increased;
- imbalances between clerical and professional staff and shortages in certain skills occur; and
- managers become more concerned with the number of persons actually employed on one particular day of the year (the final day of the fiscal year, for which annual official personnel figures are submitted) than with getting essential work performed

through the most effective, efficient, and economical use of people.

If government agencies are barred from directly hiring enough people to carry out their assigned functions, they must, in order to get the job done, either pay overtime to their employees or obtain additional people to do the work by means of contracts with private firms or through grants to institutions and state and local governments. People who work under contracts or grants are not included in agency employment ceilings and are not counted as part of the federal work force, even though they are paid from federal funds. Also, as the GAO report observes, the "emphasis on limiting the number of persons on the federal payroll may obscure the reality that the government incurs the cost of all manpower resources devoted to federal programs even though many of the people are not on the federal payroll."

The most effective way to hold down governmental costs is not through personnel ceilings but rather through funding or program limitations on the number of persons an agency can pay, be they federal or contract employees. In other words, if the agency does not have the money, it can hire neither more government employees nor more contract workers. The General Accounting Office recommended that the Office of Management and Budget assist the various federal agencies in "preparing sound estimates of the minimum manpower requirements of all types to accomplish authorized programs and functions," and then be able to justify those requirements to congressional committees and subcommittees during the course of the budgetary process. As with many such accounting office recommendations on ways to curb governmental waste, this one, too, landed with a thud.

A number of agency officials have expressed concern over the years about the unfavorable impact of personnel ceilings on their operations. Comments by William P. Davis, deputy assistant secretary for administration of the Department of Transportation in 1977, suggest that the true rationale for contracting-out is to put over a snow job on the public. Davis said that the most effective management of manpower resources "is probably not best achieved through the use of personnel ceilings," and he added, "We believe there are particular instances where personnel ceilings are necessary, especially from a public relations standpoint in the eyes of the general public."

The General Accounting Office has come up with dozens of examples over the years of how personnel ceilings drive up the costs of government services because agencies are forced to contract-out or pay overtime to in-house employees in order to compensate for the lack of sufficient in-house workers. For example, the General Service Administration's San Francisco office had to award four custodial contracts, totaling $1,171,000, because of personnel ceilings. GSA cost studies indicated in-house workers could have done the jobs for $153,000 less. In another case, the San Francisco office of the Department of Housing and Urban Development reported that personnel ceilings forced it to contract-out 46 percent of its housing appraisals for mortgage insurance—at a cost approximately 60 percent higher than that when using in-house staff.

Other studies came to similar conclusions. For example, a June 1976 report on personnel ceilings by the House Committee on Appropriations was especially critical of the practice. The report concluded, among other things: "It is clear that personnel ceilings greatly undermine the objective of maximum efficiency and economy in the expenditure of federal funds. The committee strongly believes that dollar levels and prudent management, rather than artificially contrived personnel ceilings, should govern the level of permanent positions allocated to the agency. The committee expects that . . . [the Office of Management and Budget] and the various departments will recognize the wastefulness and futility of artificially low ceilings." Needless to say, that suggestion too has gone generally unheeded. As of this writing, under the Reagan administration, personnel ceilings and reductions in force (RIFs) are being cited as ways of cutting governmental costs. Reagan had planned to cut 75,000 federal jobs by 1984, and another 75,000 by 1987, but made public no plan to prevent increases in the use of federal contractors to make up for the decrease in in-house employees.

Sometimes, federal agencies use contracting to evade personnel ceilings—even though they have in-house personnel who could do the work as an added duty. For instance, in 1980 the Office of Education had a $17,416 contract for "management" of an education conference.

Work under the contract consisted of "making travel arrangements for consultants to attend conferences . . . providing audiovisual equipment . . . scheduling meeting rooms and . . . arranging for publication of various publications." Clearly, the Office of Education had people in-house who were capable of performing such tasks.

At the Department of Labor in 1980, a $78,330 contract was issued for a personnel classification survey. To obtain this hefty sum, the contractor performed "routine 'desk audits' of the agency staff positions," government investigators later reported. Incredibly enough, agency officials initially contended they had no one in-house with the training to do such desk-to-desk work! Eventually, the agency changed its tune and acknowledged that its staff was capable of performing such routine chores, but by then the contract money was spent.

The Department of Labor has regularly contracted for work that should be performed in-house. In early 1979, the department completed a study of consulting contracts it had in effect and determined that 17 contracts, valued at $1.26 million, could have been performed by existing agency personnel. Thus, the money spent on the contracts was wasted. One year later, General Accounting Office investigators found that the Labor Department had taken no action to reduce or eliminate these apparently unnecessary contracts. GAO's review determined there was "little evidence that in-house capability was adequately considered" in the awarding of contracts. "In fact," the report stated, "in several files reviewed we found no evidence that in-house capability was even considered." The GAO concluded that the use of contracting without considering in-house capabilities was not only a misuse of resources but also made it questionable "whether the consulting service was even necessary."

Most Americans are probably unaware of the systematic abuses involved in government contracting, such as described by Carl Black. Nor are most people likely aware of the deception involved in the somewhat esoteric subject of personnel ceilings. Many people, though, are familiar with frivolous or unnecessary contracts that are often exposed in the press or publicized through Wisconsin Democratic Senator William Proxmire's periodic "Golden Fleece" awards for particularly questionable uses of taxpayers' money.

Some of these types of contracts sound as if they were written as a spoof on government. They range from the absurd to the outrageous. For example, the Department of Agriculture awarded a $46,000 contract to a consultant for a report on how long it takes to cook "popular breakfast-menu items." The Department of Transportation contracted with George Washington University for a $141,000 study on why people ride buses. In the same vein, the Department of the Interior hired a contractor to work on improving the department's image. Among the recommendations: have the interior secretary get his picture in the newspapers more often.

Then there was the Department of Transportation's venture into science fiction, a $225,000 contract with the Stanford Research Institute to "forecast transportation needs in the year 2025 under such hypothetical conditions as guerrilla warfare, the establishment of a dictatorship or major climatic changes." The study produced such findings as, "Hitchhikers will be ubiquitous" in the event of severe climatic changes; and, in the event of widespread guerrilla activities, "Cities would need more transit police," "Damage insurance rates would rise astronomically," and "Automobile use in affected areas would become risky."

If these various frivolous cases were isolated instances, one could hardly indict the entire contracting system. But based on readings of hundreds of hours of hearings, and many hundred federal reports, books, newspaper, and magazine articles, and after interviewing dozens of people in and out of government, it becomes clear that the contracting abuses discussed in this book are systematic, ingrained, and not likely to change unless Congress decides to enact tough legislation imposing limitations on the number, uses for, and money spent on contractors. The scores of examples listed in this book represent only a tiny fraction of the abuses that turned up in the research process.

Yet, despite the clear evidence of systematic contracting abuses throughout the federal government, the Office of Management and Budget, which has responsibility for issuing contracting guidelines, has generally failed to bring about a cleanup by the individual agencies. In hearing after hearing before Congress over the last two decades, representatives of the budget office have regularly testified that, while there are a few contract abuses, some new procedure or modification of an existing regulation will correct the problems. And then things continue as before, until the next set of hearings at which OMB again announces new procedures that are going to correct the problems once and for all. For more than 20 years, the budget agency has taken the position that it is the individual department's responsibility to see that OMB's contracting guidelines are followed.

The Office of Management and Budget's failure to enforce its own regulations was starkly shown in a joint hearing by Senate and House subcommittees on April 29, 1981, in testimony by Fred Dietrich, associate administrator in OMB's Office of Federal Procurement Policy. Representative Geraldine A. Ferraro, D-New York, asked Dietrich whether anyone had "ever been prosecuted for violating, or has a contract ever been canceled for violating" provisions of Circular A-76, which contains the major OMB guidelines on government contracting for commercial and industrial services and products. Dietrich, himself a former consultant, answered: "Not that we know of. Not that I know of personally. If we find one, we will put that in the record." (The record shows that no such submission was forthcoming.)

Ferraro pressed on. "How long has that circular [A-76] been in existence?" she asked. "Since 1966," Dietrich responded. "And you never found a violation of any of the restrictions in that regulation?" asked Ferraro. "Not to our knowledge," said Dietrich. "Nineteen sixty-six to nineteen eighty-one and there has never been any sort of violation, or no contract has ever been canceled for violating the circular; is that correct?" asked Ferraro. Dietrich answered, "That is right."

Ferraro, who chaired the Human Resources Subcommittee of the House Post Office and Civil Service Committee, also wanted to know what procedures OMB used to oversee the various agencies' use of contractors. Dietrich responded that when the agencies submit their proposed budgets to OMB, they are asked "to identify, as best they can, an estimate of the use of consulting services, studies, and analyses, and so forth. . . . We certainly do not have these as line items in the budget." Ferraro asked why contracts couldn't be put into the budget as line items, that is, listed by individual proposed contracts, rather than included anonymously in the budget under an agency's various programs. Dietrich rebuffed Ferraro's suggestion, saying: "It is feasible to do that, but it is hard for them to judge if that really does change the accomplishment of the mission. That is what you have the management for. That is what the executive branch is here for." An obviously frustrated Ferraro wondered why the federal budget could show the cost of the federal employee bureaucracy, yet not contain the list of contracts an agency proposes to undertake in the next fiscal year.

The absence of meaningful budgetary controls and of budget office and agency monitoring naturally lead to a number of types of contract abuses, which wastes money and lessens government accountability. According to a number of congressional and General Accounting Office investigations, one of the most wasteful aspects of federal contracting is the rush by many agencies in the last quarter of the fiscal year, particularly in the last month, to spend all of their budgeted funds. This "September Surge," so named because September is the last month of the federal government's fiscal year, is a turf-protecting device by agency managers to insure that their budgets in a future fiscal year don't get reduced because they produced a surplus in a previous year. Also, as the General Accounting Office has pointed out, agency managers are concerned about unspent funds because their "performance is evaluated at least in part on spending ability." Thus, when agencies have been underspending going into the last quarter and need to spend money in a hurry to use up their budgeted funds, one quick resort is to award contracts and grants without seeking competitive bids. Because of the general haste with which these contracts are issued, the result is often contracts that are unnecessary or overpriced, or both, and have a potential for costly modifications at a later date.

Some of the most flagrant examples of excessive yearend spending were in the old Department of Health, Education and Welfare (HEW), which was divided in May 1980 into the Department of Health and Human Services and the Department of Education. In fiscal year 1978, HEW obligated $169 million for consulting services; of this, $110.7 million—or 66 percent—was obligated in the fourth quarter. Similarly, in fiscal year 1979, HEW obligated $88.5 million for consulting services in the fourth quarter out of total annual consultant expenditures of $134.9 million—again, 66 percent. An agency with a balanced procurement program, of course, would incur around 25 percent of its obligations in any one quarter. Yet, at HEW the trend was to spend virtually nothing in the first quarter for consulting services (3 percent in fiscal year 1978 and 6 percent in fiscal year 1979), to spend moderate amounts in the second and third quarters (31 percent in 1978 and 28 percent in 1979), and then finish with a spending spree.

Examples of questionable, even absurd, last-quarter HEW contracts abound. One day before the end of the 1978 fiscal year, the Office of Education awarded a $36,828 noncompetitive contract for "guidelines to review vocational training programs." The agency justified the rushed, sole-source contract on the ground that it needed the guidelines by the next day! Needless to say, the contractor didn't deliver on time, and the contract was extended for 11 months. The need to obligate funds by the end of the fiscal year, rather than an urgent need for vocational training program review guidelines, was obviously the controlling factor in the awarding of this contract.

Another typical HEW effort was the awarding by the Office of the Secretary, three weeks before the end of fiscal year 1979, of a $15,904 contract to evaluate elementary and secondary education—a subject the agency's Office of Education had certainly dealt with at great length both in-house and through contractors in the past, hardly requiring another study. Also, given the comparatively low dollar amount of the contract, the agency could scarcely have been expecting an in-depth look at the issue. HEW's proposal evaluators were themselves skeptical of the contract, saying that it duplicated past efforts. Nevertheless, the contract was awarded. As General Accounting Office investigators discovered later, "The contract was negotiated over the telephone, and the contractor's proposed price was accepted with no documentation or cost analysis."

Of course, many of the contracts awarded in the closing quarter of a fiscal year are valid. The danger is that because of the pressure on the agency to spend its money as the clock runs out, it may award contracts to whomever may be in line (Carl Black's reference to "the firstest with the mostest"). The result is that low-priority projects often get funded while higher-priority programs remain sitting on the shelf because the agency isn't ready to proceed. Also, because of the rushed nature of such contracts, an agency is often not sure what it is getting into because it lacks contractor cost and technical data on which to base a reasoned decision.

Another clear example of the problems with last-minute contracting awards occurred at the Office of Education on the final day of the 1979 fiscal year. Acting Education Commissioner Dr. Mary Berry on that day signed 17 sole-source contracts over the objections of contracting personnel in the agency's Grants and Procurement Management Division (GPMD). General Accounting Office investigators were told later by Education Office officials that "procurement actions were turned into sole-source procurements and 'pushed' through the system at yearend." The accounting office independently reviewed seven of the contracts and found four of them "questionable."

In one of the contracts, to a state university to fund the state teachers' professional development program, the Office of Education's contract negotiator said he could not recommend signing the contract. Among the negotiator's objections to the contract was "the inability to ascertain the reasonableness of the cost proposal." The office's project officer also questioned the contract, on the ground that the proposal contained "insufficient technical and cost data and because the proposal was extremely vague." Nonetheless, as the GAO later reported, the acting commissioner signed in order to keep a promise to carry out former Commissioner Dr. Ernest Boyer's commitment to fund the $423,000 proposal.

Also on the final day of fiscal year 1979, the Office of Education awarded a $123,006 contract "to analyze the effects of post-secondary education on one's attitude to the self." Program officials later acknowledged that the project had been considered of marginal value, but the contract was awarded "when another project fell through and funds became available."

In the final month of fiscal year 1981, the Department of Education awarded 326 contracts, worth more than $76 million, and 2,051 grants valued at $131 million. This spending binge prompted Senator Max Baucus, D-Montana, to comment, "Contrary to what is being preached by the current administration, Education Department officials apparently believe the cardinal sin of the bureaucracy is returning money to the Treasury at the end of the year."

In the 1970s, the Department of Health, Education and Welfare's consultant budget had gone up so much and had produced so little of value that Congress acted to set a $194 million ceiling on the agency's consulting contracts for fiscal year 1979 and $170 million for fiscal 1980. The action came after an investigation of HEW's use of consultants by the Health, Education and Welfare Subcommittee of the Senate Appropriations Committee. In a May 1977 report, the subcommittee stated that it was "concerned over what it considers to be undue reliance upon the work of outside consultants in HEW." Further, the report came up with the remarkable finding that "The committee is unaware of any instance where a consultant's recommendation has produced a significant program improvement."

In its investigation, the subcommittee stated that many of the contracts duplicated "previous contracts performed for the same purpose" while others duplicated "contracts being let simultaneously within other parts of the department and the federal government." The report further expressed concern that "the expertise developed through the performance of such contracts cannot be retained within the federal government but must be repurchased at considerable cost each time such knowledge is again required."

HEW was certainly not the only offender in yearend spending abuses. The Department of Housing and Urban Development (HUD) spent 75 percent of its fiscal year 1978 contracting funds in the last quarter and 61 percent of its fiscal 1979 funds in the last quarter. Figures for the Environmental Protection Agency (EPA) were 48 and 47 percent for 1978 and 1979, respectively; for the Interior Department, 40 and 34 percent; for the State Department, 34 and 60 percent; for the Commerce Department, 33 and 37 percent.

At HUD, many of the contracts entered into in the last month of fiscal years 1978 and 1979 still hadn't been implemented one to two years later. At least four of these contracts came under a Small Business Administration (SBA) program designed to assist disadvantaged business owners in competing more effectively in the open market. Under the program, a federal agency enters into a prime contract with SBA to obtain goods and services from disadvantaged firms.

SBA then requests the agency, in this case HUD, to negotiate subcontracts with the firms. Presumably, before granting the prime contract, HUD already has firms in mind for such subcontracts. Yet for the four prime contracts awarded by HUD to SBA in the final month of fiscal years 1978 and 1979, subcontracts had still not been awarded to disadvantaged businesses more than two years later, in some cases.

One contract, awarded by HUD to SBA in the final three days of fiscal 1978, was for administration of HUD's Technical Clearing House. Almost two years later, HUD had yet to locate a firm able to do the work and had awarded no subcontract. The inescapable conclusion is that HUD had no subcontractors in mind at the time it awarded the prime contract, and that it made the award solely for the purpose of obligating surplus funds before the end of the fiscal year.

In the Commerce Department on the final day of fiscal year 1979, a noncompetitive $146,320 contract was awarded to "organize data" that had been collected under a project several years earlier. The contract came in response to an unsolicited proposal and was awarded to a company whose officers had worked on the project in the past. Again, the main reason for awarding the contract appeared not to be a need for the data, but rather a desire to spend all funds before the end of the fiscal year.

The Environmental Protection Agency, which significantly improved its yearend contract spending in the late 1970s, nevertheless continued to make many questionable awards during the "September Surge." Two days before the end of fiscal year 1978, for instance, EPA awarded a noncompetitive $161,000 contract, for which there were clearly other interested bidders, to "upgrade the audiovisual system and refurbish the auditorium" at Research Triangle Park, North Carolina. The facility was not owned by the government, but was leased from a private owner. The contract thus was questionable not only because of its noncompetitive nature, but also because some EPA officials, including the contracting officer, felt such a major upgrading project was inappropriate in a leased facility. Another contractor, who had been interested in doing the work but was given no opportunity to bid on it, filed a bid protest. Although it was decided in his favor by the Comptroller General, it was a Pyhrric victory for the unsuccessful contractor. The contract was allowed to stand because the project was virtually completed by the time the protest was decided. In commenting later on the contract, Comptroller General Elmer B. Staats observed, "The award of noncompetitive contracts, when competition is obtainable, is generally more costly." Such regular statements of principles, however, apparently have little effect on the practice of government contracting.

At the Small Business Administration, last-quarter spending has been a serious problem in recent years. For example, in the closing weeks of the 1979 fiscal year, officials in SBA's Office of Advocacy discovered that they would have a surplus at the year's end. As Dolores F. McElroy, an SBA procurement officer, stated in a memo, the SBA office "had approximately $3 million in unspent funds . . . which the agency would lose if contracts were not able to be awarded prior to the end of [the] fiscal year." An in-house task force formed to deal with the surplus proceeded to dole out more than 50 noncompetitive contracts, totaling $3 million, before the fiscal year closed. Many of the contracts went to firms backed by congressional pressure. William Mauk, SBA's deputy administrator until January 1981, himself suggested and approved many of the contracts, according to agency documents. Mauk acknowledged that by awarding so many sole-source contracts in such a short time, "good decisions could not be made in spending all that money. But given the political pressure from particular senators and congressmen, we did go ahead. I hope the money was well spent."

Some of the noncompetitive contracts went to former SBA officials. Robert Berney, SBA's former chief for advocacy, received a $39,969 contract a few weeks after he left his federal post, despite warnings from an SBA attorney before the contract was awarded. The lawyer, John P. Connors, stated in an internal memorandum that "there appears to be some duplication of work . . . it seems that Dr. Berney may only be memorializing the research he conducted during his tenure at SBA." Berney told a reporter that "in a way, it is duplicative. It's not new research, it's a continuation of some of the same topics I studied when I was chief economist. But it's a unique product that maxmimizes the return of my being in Washington for two years."

A Senate Small Business Committee investigation looked into numerous other SBA contracts, including the awarding of contracts to favored firms, the drawing up of contracts after the contractor has already completed the work, and allowing the contractor to bill the government for various luxuries or items seemingly unrelated to the contract.

In April 1981 hearings, committee members sharply criticized the SBA's Mauk for not challenging some of the items charged to the agency by Practical Concepts, Inc., a consulting firm in the Washington, D.C., area. The questionable items billed to the government included rental of a Jaguar and an oil painting, YMCA memberships for two company executives, private school tuition for children of the firm's officials, office liquor, and the use of a tennis court and pool built at the home of the company's president. The firm had defended the charges as being justified. Some committee members said that Mauk had been warned of PCI's questionable spending in early 1980 but had paid no attention. Instead, over the next nine months, Mauk authorized modifications to increase the contract from $70,000 to $250,000. After Mauk told the committee that it was "not unique" for auditors to question expense claims, Senator Don Nickles, R-Oklahoma, stated: "I am appalled at your indifference. Do you think liquor, pools, tennis courts, paintings, and Jaguars are legitimate expenses?"

On the military side of the ledger, the Pentagon provides scores of examples of wasteful, unnecessary yearend spending. For example, 19 days before the end of fiscal year 1978, officers at Fort Riley, Kansas, purchased 80 color television sets for a total of $32,264. Nine months later, "50 sets remained crated in the warehouse," the Army Audit Agency reported. On the last working day of fiscal 1978, the army awarded $187,000 in construction contracts "at a base that was scheduled to be closed." Nine days before the end of the same fiscal year, army officials awarded a $35,196 noncompetitive contract for 29 electric cookers. At least four of the cookers were never installed. An Army Audit Agency review found the purchase "not in the best interests of the government." Similar military contracting abuses will be discussed in chapter four.

Moving to another type of problem, among the most disturbing federal contracting abuses are the contractors' conflicts of interest, or potential conflicts, which put them in a position of making recommendations or influencing policy so that they will receive additional contracts—or their company or industry will otherwise benefit—at a later date. In a related type of abuse, the consultant assigned to work on policy areas will be in a position to make recommendations that will help his private sector business clients.

In the Department of Energy, potential conflicts of interest on contracts, rather than sending up warning signals, seem to be regarded as a plus by the agency. As shall be discussed in more detail in chapter five, major contracting and consulting firms such as TRW, Booz-Allen & Hamilton, Planning Research Corporation (PRC), and Price Waterhouse have held millions of dollars worth of Energy Department contracts while at the same time working for major utilities and oil companies—some of them even working for various Organization of Petroleum Exporting Countries (OPEC) oil companies. Yet according to recent congressional investigations, no questions were raised by the Energy Department about the appropriateness of having such contractors, with their wide-ranging private energy connections, involved in key policymaking work at the energy agency. When queried during congressional hearings in 1979–81, about these potential conflicts of interest, various Energy Department officials contended that although their agency had tough conflict-of-interest provisions, no firm would be disqualified merely for having private energy interests or clients. As Robert Paquin, an aide to Senator Patrick Leahy, D-Vermont, who investigated contracting abuses, commented in an interview, "For contractors, it seems that conflicts of interest are a recommendation for them to get the contract," rather than a deterrent.

In fact, under numerous contracts with the Energy Department, various contractors have failed to list, on disclosure forms filed with the agency, all of their ties with energy companies. Incomplete disclosure appears to constitute a loophole in regulations issued in recent years by the Office of Management and Budget's Office of Federal Procurement Policy covering organizational conflicts of interest. The regulations leave it up to the contractors to disclose whether any of their top officials, or potential subcontractors or consultants, would have a conflict of interest regarding the contracts. Many contractors apparently decided that having private energy clients in no way conflicted with the Energy Department contracts they were seeking. Given the energy agency officials' attitudes expressed in various congressional hearings, full disclosure by the prospective contractor would probably not have been construed as a conflict by agency officials and would not have blocked awarding of the contract.

The Office of Federal Procurement Policy had issued its organizational conflict-of-interest regulations in response to a controversy over a contract to study coal transportation that was held by the Bechtel Corporation, the giant engineering and construction management enterprise. Bechtel made an unsolicited proposal to get the contract. The result was a $418,000 noncompetitive contract from the Interior Department's Office of Coal Research (which later became part of the Energy Research and Development Administration). Under the contract, Bechtel was to formulate a computer model as part of a study to compare the economics of transporting coal from Wyoming to Arkansas, either by rail or by a coal slurry pipeline, which a consortium of energy companies called Energy Transportation Systems, Inc. (ETSI), hoped to build. As luck would have it, Bechtel just happened to own 40 percent of the slurry-building company, a situation that could certainly have cast doubt on Bechtel's objectivity in the matter. Yet Energy Research and Development Administration officials were later to maintain that there was no conflict of interest involved, because the agency's regulations then applied only to competitive contractors, not to sole-source contractors.

It is difficult to think of any more clearcut conflict of interest than a situation in which one company is in a position to make recommendations that will benefit its affiliated company. Yet Bechtel's vice chairman, Jerome W. Komes, took the position that there was no conflict at all. As Komes told a Senate Interior subcommittee, "We cannot believe that Congress takes the simplistic view that any financial interest in an area of technology automatically excludes a company from even a remotely related government effort."

Former Senator James Abourezk, D-South Dakota, whose subcommittee investigated the Bechtel contract, didn't see the Bechtel-Energy Transportation Systems relationship as remote. "It is apparent," Abourezk said, "that even if the government did not understand the relationship between the government study and the ETSI pipeline, Bechtel did." As evidence of this, Abourezk noted that as the study was winding down, "Bechtel personnel working on the . . . contract demonstrated their interest in informing ETSI personnel of the nature of the . . . study by specifically inviting the ETSI personnel to a briefing on it. Indeed, this relationship was apparently evident to Bechtel from the beginning. It was Bechtel—not the government— which proposed that the government award such a contract to study coal transportation. . . . That proposal was submitted to the Interior Department one day after ETSI was incorporated. Bechtel even managed to be awarded the contract on a sole-source basis."

By 1982 the still-unbuilt slurry pipeline project was continuing to stir up controversy. Indian organizations, ranchers, and landowners were concerned about the potential damage to their lands and water resources from the project. Especially controversial was the state of South Dakota's $1.4 billion agreement in 1981 to sell Missouri River water to the energy consortium for the slurry pipeline, even though the state was suffering from its worst drought since the 1930s. Also of concern was legislation, pending in Congress in the summer of 1982, to give developers of coal slurry pipelines the right of eminent domain to order the sale of property needed for pipeline rights-of-way. A House committee had approved the measure, but it had passed neither house of Congress by August 1982.

Lost in the controversy over Bechtel's possible conflict of interest was the question of why the government needed to hire a contractor to make a decision on such a fundamental policy matter as coal transportation. Had the study been performed in-house, there would have been no question of any organizational conflict of interest, and no concern that findings were tainted because of the contractor's affiliated interest. Although the Bechtel case did spur the Office of Federal Procurement Policy to issue new regulations on organizational conflicts of interest, such reforms—as usual—failed to halt the abuses. Contractors with close ties to energy companies and utilities continued to receive major energy contracts. As contracting critic Daniel Guttman wrote to the Office of Management and Budget at the time the new regulations were proposed, the revised rules "perpetuate the double standard by which individuals employed by the government, including members of the Civil Service, are held to the highest standard while private contractors are permitted to hide their private interests and activities."

Government contractors are involved in potential conflict-of-interest situations when they help write agency regulations, while at the same time working for private interests that would be affected by those regulations. For example, Arthur D. Little, Inc., the prominent management and technology consulting firm, helped set workplace asbestos safety standards for the National Institute of Occupational Safety and Health (NIOSH). The same firm, according to writer Paul Brodeur, was also involved in an effort that would be directly affected by the asbestos standards—namely, a project to help relocate a "major producer of asbestos brake linings, clutch facings and gaskets." As Brodeur concluded, "By involving Arthur D. Little, Inc., in the standard setting process, the Department of Labor was attempting to counter the recommendations of . . . NIOSH . . . of the Secretary of Labor's advisory committee on the asbestos standard, and of the members of the independent medical and scientific community who testified at the public hearings. It was also becoming clear how deeply the medical-industrial complex had succeeded in penetrating the workings of the government in matters relating to the prevention of industrial disease."

Potential conflicts of interest can also be readily seen in the contracts many federal agencies regularly hand out to special interest "client" organizations that lobby with, or whose members are regulated by, those same agencies. In addition to posing the conflict issue, many of these contracts are also of dubious value or are for work that more properly should be performed by in-house employees. The Department of Housing and Urban Development, for example, in recent years has awarded contracts to such "client" groups as the National League of Cities, the U.S. Conference of Mayors, the National Association of Counties, the Portland Cement Association, the National Fire Protection Association, the International Association of Assessing Officers, the Council of State Governments, the National Association of Homebuilders Research Foundation, the American Society of Public Administrators, and the International City Managers Association.

Some of the contracts awarded to these organizations included one for $92,000 to the National Association of Home Builders to "develop a profile of the home builders through a survey of builder members" of the NAHB, as well as of builders who are not NAHB members. A $38,476 contract was awarded to the National Association of Housing and Redevelopment Officials to permit a staff member to travel through a number of European countries and "prepare a report on current European experience in neighborhood preservation and housing development." The National Center for Housing Management received a $285,000 contract "to examine the real estate brokerage and salespersons' licensing mechanisms and the employment practices of major interstate real estate corporations." The Urban Institute received $149,800 to "prepare a book for the general public on the quality of life in metropolitan areas." Some of the work done under these contracts is, arguably, meritorious, but even in those cases there is the question of why the government, rather than the private associations themselves, should be funding efforts that benefit the organizations more than they do the public.

Conflicts, or potential conflicts, of interest run throughout the federal contracting system. An April 1980 study by the General Accounting Office cited possible conflicts of interest in 101 of 150 contracts reviewed at six federal agencies. At the Environmental Protection Agency, 51 of the 71 contracts reviewed contained possible conflicts. Part of one EPA contract, to study air pollution equipment, was awarded to a trade association whose member companies manufactured 88 percent of all such equipment. A March 1982 GAO study found that of 217 management support services contracts reviewed, 39 percent had potential conflict-of-interest problems. The same study also concluded that 92 percent of the contracts studied were partly or completely for basic managerial functions and should have been performed by EPA's in-house personnel.

Washington Post reporters Jonathan Neumann and Ted Gup, in a mid-1980 series of prize-winning articles, similarly found that federal agencies often turned to industries they were supposed to be regulating for studies and recommendations on how to do the regulating. Wrote Neumann and Gup: ". . . [T]he fact that the government awarded a research contract to a corporation that had a vested interest in the results is not at all uncommon. Every year, the government turns to industry members to help it decide how they should be regulated and, if so, to what extent."

One of the four major contracts *The Post* focused on was a $669,000 Environmental Protection Agency contract to Arthur D. Little, the consulting firm mentioned earlier in this chapter. The contract discussed in *The Post* called for Little, among other things, to determine the impact of regulating arsenic emissions from an Asarco plant in Tacoma, Washington. The problem was that "Little's copper expert, an outspoken critic of regulation, had recently completed a similar study funded by Asarco in response to proposed federal health and safety regulations." Not surprisingly, in both the Asarco report and the EPA study, Little recommended against regulation, contending that federal controls "would force the plant to shut down because of economic hardship." Asarco later cited the Little study for the EPA as justification for its opposition to any federal or state controls for its Washington plant.

To its credit, Little did not hide the fact that it had done the report for Asarco. "The conflict of interest was obvious," said EPA economist Robert L. Coughlin. Officials of Little themselves expressed concern to EPA before the contract was awarded that, as Ravindra Nadkarni of the consulting firm put it, "a conflict could be perceived. We wanted to make sure that if they chose us for the study, the issue was fully aired before anything was signed. We did not want to do the study if the EPA felt it was a conflict of interest." Despite the warning signals, EPA awarded the contract to Little. Said Alan Basala, the EPA research office project officer, "A.D. Little was our only alternative. We couldn't afford to go out and hire someone who would be wholly objective but naïve." By giving the work to Little under an existing research contract, Basala said, EPA did not have to go through a lengthy procurement process.

The Arthur D. Little type of contract, referred to by some agencies as "consulting," by others as "management support services" or "research," has produced a number of revealing investigations by various federal units. The investigators have focused on this type of contract because these are the ones in which private firms have the most direct input into the management, decision making, and policy making of federal agencies. In various investigations, one of the problems for investigators has been the lack of common definitions for such activities as consulting, support services, and research and development.

Indicative of this lack of common definitions were the results of the most wide-ranging survey of federal agencies' use of contractors that has been undertaken by a congressional committee in recent years. In 1976 and 1977, the Reports, Management and Accounting Subcommittee of the Senate Governmental Affairs Committee sent a questionnaire to 178 federal agencies to determine what they defined as consultants and contractors, and how many they had. The subcommittee's survey, published in August 1977, showed that agencies used varying definitions of the term "consultant" and often omitted from their totals contracts that clearly should have been included. Some agencies provided little, or useless, information; others stonewalled the survey; while others were reasonably cooperative. In all, 90 of the agencies responded. From these responses, the committee determined that there was "no standard, government-wide definition" as to what a consultant is. The committee found those agencies that did respond "reported in such a way that it was not possible to achieve a meaningful tally of the number of contractor-consultant arrangements" for fiscal year 1976, the period covered by the survey.

The inadequate nature of the agencies' responses prompted the subcommittee to conclude, regarding consultants, that "no one has been able to say with certainty how many there are, who they are, or how much we spend on their services. Nor have we had answers to other basic questions, which both Congress and the executive branch should have in order to provide informed oversight of and policy direction for consultants and contractors."

Still, the subcommittee did obtain some solid information that indicated just how deeply consultants had dug themselves into the federal bureaucracy. The Energy Research and Development Administration (ERDA), for example, had hired consultants at such a pace they put in 13 times as many work-years as ERDA's regular employees. Thirty-six percent of the agency's budget was consumed by consultants' costs, and more than 90 percent of its budget by contractors of various types. Other agencies were also found to have substantial numbers of consultant personnel, but none to the extent of ERDA. Of the relatively few agencies providing data on this score, the Council on Environmental Quality said that contractor employees made up 41 percent of the agency's combined civil service-contractor work force; the Nuclear Regulatory Commission, 26.2 percent; and the Small Business Administration, 18.9 percent.

Many of the agencies reporting to Congress listed only consulting arrangements they had with individual consultants, which fall under civil service regulations, rather than those with firms, which are covered by procurement regulations. The basic difference between the two types of consultants is that a firm is paid at a much higher rate, with its employees often billed out at more than $500 per day apiece, compared to individual consultants' top of about $200.

The subcommittee members weren't the only high-ranking government officials who couldn't get a complete story from the federal agencies regarding contractors. President Jimmy Carter also received misleading data on the extent of contracting out in the executive branch. In May 1977, Carter asked 89 federal agencies to determine how many consultants they were using, how much they were paid, and what they did, with an eye toward eliminating those arrangements under which consultants were being used "excessively, unnecessarily, and improperly." Carter did not define what he meant by a "consulting arrangement," thereby giving the agencies a loophole that many of them rushed right through. The 64 agencies responding used 20 different definitions of the term and said they were using 33,926 consulting arrangements at a cost of $1.8 billion. This was a gross understatement of consultants' actual involvement in government, as later studies indicated that consulting activities—individuals, firms, management support services, research—totaled many times that amount when the broader definition was used. John J. McGonagle, Jr., vice president of Helicon Group, Ltd., a management consulting firm, estimated the figure at $33 billion in 1981.

To clarify the situation, the Office of Management and Budget, in Circular A-120 issued on April 14, 1980, set down new regulations and a definition of consulting activities as "those services of a purely advisory nature relating to the governmental functions of agency administration and management and agency program management. . . . These services are normally provided by persons and/or organizations who are generally considered to have knowledge and special abilities that are not generally available within the agency." Individual agencies have their own definitions along the same lines.

In the nation's capital, consultants are regularly subjected to barbed comments, much as used-car salesmen might be in other parts of the country. Collectively, they are often referred to as the "Beltway Bandits," because many of them have their offices close to the Capital Beltway that encircles Washington, D.C. Representative Ronald Mottl, D-Ohio, has said that "the consulting game in Washington reminds me of a hungry and ever-growing flock of vultures preying on a bloated carcass." Admiral Hyman G. Rickover, former director of the navy's nuclear propulsion program, has stated, in his inimitable fashion, "If all the consultants were drowned today, I do not think the body politic would be harmed very much." Robert Townsend, author of the popular book *Up the Organization,* said that "Consultants are people who borrow your watch and tell you what time it is, and then walk off with your watch."

In the same vein, Gregg Easterbrook, in a perceptive and humorous set of articles in *The Washington Monthly* magazine, offered a number of tongue-in-cheek suggestions to would-be consultants to the government. "Save your dumbest ideas for the last month in the fiscal year . . . when agencies are desperate to dump money so they don't lose it on the next budget." Also, "Never, ever, ever offer any conclusions. . . . Conclusions imply that there is no need for additional study, which implies you right out of a job. . . . Whatever else you do, at all times, under all conditions, recommend further study." As to the value of consultants' work, Easterbrook wrote: "Swirling circularities . . . 'solutions' so vague as not to offend the comatose . . . calls for further study . . . this is consulting talk, all right. . . . They scurry about at all levels of government, jabbering in arcane dialects, mumbling half-heard benedictions. Their hollow language is fast becoming the city's only means of communication." The government consultant today, wrote Easterbrook, "dispenses numbing generalities, and would rather be bitten by a snake than give a definite answer about anything."

While much of the acid criticism of government consultants is on target, it should be remembered that it takes two sides to play this game. Often, government consultants are merely cashing in on a policy adopted by federal agency managers who want to pass the buck on important work. Then, if the consultant does good work, the agency managers can claim credit for their wise use of nongovernment personnel; if the consultant does poor work, the agency managers can blame the consultant. Thus, from the standpoint of weak managers, it makes sense to turn over major work to nongovernment personnel who are not directly under their control. And when consultants are hired to do key agency work, they are then in a position to control or influence governmental policies and operations.

This is especially true of those consultants who prepare congressionally mandated reports on various federal programs. During fiscal years 1977, 1978, and 1979, six agencies—the Environmental Protection Agency (EPA), the Department of Transportation, the Department of Housing and Urban Development (HUD), the National Aeronautics and Space Administration, the Nuclear Regulatory Commission, and the Federal Communications Commission—submitted 82 mandated reports to Congress. In 35 of these, consultants were used to prepare the reports, yet there was no disclosure to Congress of this fact in 13 of the reports, and inadequate disclosure in 13 others. Of slightly more than $25 million spent to prepare these reports, consultants received almost $16.6 million—or two-thirds of the funds. In three reports, two from EPA and one from HUD, the agencies even went so far as to state that the views contained in the reports were not necessarily those of the agency! This constituted the ultimate in buck-passing, since these reports were mandated by law or by instruction from congressional committees to be the *agency's* own view of how well its programs were functioning.

The reports were to be used by Congress so it could determine whether to expand, eliminate, or revise certain governmental programs. Yet Congress was often unaware that the reports it was receiving were not always the agency's view, but rather the view of private firms with possible financial interests in the reports' conclusions and recommendations. In 13 of 19 EPA reports, and 4 of 5 HUD reports, consultants were found to have contributed significantly; that is, consultants gathered the basic material that was to go into the reports and then, either on their own or jointly with agency staff, prepared the report itself.

Legislation to require agencies to disclose consultants' roles in preparing reports and studies has regularly been introduced in Congress in recent years, but has gone nowhere. In late 1980, the General Accounting Office recommended that the Office of Management and Budget issue regulations requiring agencies "to fully disclose [to Congress] consulting services used in reports required by law or at the request of Congressional committees or subcommittees."

As with so many other types of contracts, the work on the congressionally mandated reports by consultants was not a one-shot undertaking. At the Department of Housing and Urban Development, for example, consultants worked on the report for the Community Development Block Grant Program in 1977 and then received a followup contract for the same work on the program's 1978 report. Likewise at HUD, consultants worked on the reports for the Urban Homesteading Demonstration Program in 1977, 1978, and 1979, and on the reports covering the president's National Urban Policy in 1978 and 1980. This continuing involvement of consultants in these vital programs meant that private interests were helping shape the congressional perception of the programs. In the Urban Homesteading report, it seemed that the agency itself had only a vague connection to what went into the review. In the three-year period 1977 through 1979, $2.1 million was paid to consultants for preparation of the reports, while just $27,000 was spent in-house, indicating that most of the work was done by the contractors. To concerned members of Congress, such disparities clearly raised the question of just who is advising the legislators on federal programs.

Besides performing such important studies, contractors also undertake many other duties that turn out to be useless and a waste of money. For example, in 1977 the Defense Department spent $65.3 million for 374 consultant studies on human resources research. The General Accounting Office subsequently determined from interviews with the intended users of the reports that 38 percent were not used at all. The GAO found that the reports were not used because the intended users were "not aware that the reports existed," or they questioned the results, "or by the time the study was delivered, the problem under study no longer existed."

The Washington Post reported in its mid-1980 series on contracting abuses that "Tens of millions of dollars in studies and research sit unexamined in warehouses, agency files and cardboard boxes." Roy Higdon, a contract monitoring officer for the Environmental Protection Agency, commented that the public gets "maybe 10 percent of their money's worth" on the studies the government contracts for. William Stevenson, a contracting officer at the Energy Department, said: "We're so busy trying to shovel the money out the door, we don't have time to see what happens to it after it leaves. All the money could be stolen and I wouldn't know it. . . . The place is a madhouse."

Many consultants themselves, as Carl Black's testimony indicates, recognize that there are abuses in the government contracting system. In this regard, an employee of a major management consulting firm, bluntly but anonymously (for obvious reasons) told a reporter about one of the main functions of consultants in the governmental process: "Consultants are entirely client-oriented. They are not oriented toward solving the problem, but toward pleasing the client. When a political executive retains a consultant, he can be pretty sure they're not going to do anything to upset him—and if they do upset him, they can change it. The work that we do is helping the executive maintain and consolidate his position, and not help solve the problem."

As for the special expertise consultants are deemed to possess, the same consulting firm employee stated: "There is a problem when the consultant is assumed to be more objective than a civil servant or academic, or more knowledgeable than a political hack. We are not more objective; we have our own biases. We become eligible for contracts because we are the right social people, we have the right values, and we're trustworthy, just as other kinds of people who wear different clothes and have different values receive their contracts from the clubhouse."

In fact, so plugged in to the government are many consulting firms that their annual reports read like brochures for some federal agency. For example, one annual report by Booz-Allen & Hamilton noted its work for the government had included contracts requiring the company to "perform a nationwide market survey of the current use of and needs for postal services among businesses and institutions"; to determine "how and why resources are allocated to drug abuse programs, and then to set up a pilot program in one state"; to help "a U.S. government agency achieve overall improvements of its accounting operations, including budgeting"; to establish "accountability for state use of federal funds"; and to advise on "the international trade impact of pollution abatement." In addition, the annual report noted, "Several government agencies used our services to help them determine the extent to which the public is misinformed regarding health-care remedies." As one executive of a small consulting firm observed, "When you read a brochure for Booz-Allen & Hamilton, it reminds you of a lost government looking for a country."

Frank J. Popper, a self-employed consultant in Bethesda, Maryland, sees the nature of the relationship between the government and its contractors as being responsible for many of the federal contracting abuses. Said Popper: "The basic difficulty is that the federal consulting market contains incentives unlikely to induce good work. Most consulting firms are small, thinly capitalized, often evanescent businesses scrambling to survive in a buyer's market. In any one field, there are many consulting firms and few federal agencies to hire them. In such a situation, the firms inevitably tend to exaggerate their abilities and to promise more than they can deliver."

On the government side, Popper also sees much to blame. "With few exceptions," he said, "federal agencies rarely assign their best people to manage consulting contracts. The contract officers often know little about the subject matter of their projects. They tend to issue vague specifications that provoke vague or unfeasible proposals from consultants, who simply cannot tell what the contract officer has in mind."

As a project progresses, Popper said, most federal agencies lack mechanisms for reviews that would "allow timely adjustment in the consultants' work." Also, he said, most agencies "lack specific devices to abort projects where the consultant performs inadequately, events outrun the project, or the concept behind the project turns out to be misguided for reasons that are nobody's fault." To illustrate, Popper cited his own experience in 1973 as a member "of a large team examining the environmental and economic impacts of second-home developments in rural areas." The project was worthwhile at the time it was conceived, "But by 1974, the oil embargo and the recession had nearly destroyed the market for distant leisure homes. In 1976 our study was published anyway, and almost no one noticed."

Popper said that most consulting firms write many proposals for which they do not get contracts. To absorb the costs of writing unsuccessful proposals and of otherwise trying to obtain new business, he said, firms "have to overbid on projects. . . . They also have to provide for unpredictable periods when many employees have no paying work." Thus, said Popper, "the prized employee is not the one who conceives, carries out, or supervises publicly useful projects," but rather "it is the one who gets new business—work whose actual performance is often left to others. Another valued employee is the one who routinizes the work by selling what is essentially the same product to a whole series of agencies."

Because of the "turbulence of the firms' market," employee morale suffers and turnover is high, Popper said. "Staffers are hired and dismissed with great alacrity as projects come and go and specialties bloom and fade. Almost no one has time, inclination, or reason to acquire deep expertise in their fields."

To correct some of these abuses, Popper recommended that agencies, when in doubt, should use in-house personnel, rather than consultants. Such an approach may prove to be cheaper and may give the project's results some long-term influence within the agency. Popper also suggested that systems be devised to kill projects that are not working out; that contract officers' roles be upgraded, with their advancement tied to the success of the projects they manage; that financial incentives be put into contracts so that high-quality work by the consultant or the agency would be rewarded, while poor performances by either party would result in penalties.

Despite the widespread and varied criticisms of consulting and management support services contracts, industry representatives contend that the criticisms are unjustified. Earle C. Williams, president of the National Council of Professional Services Firms, has commented that blame for useless consulting studies should be placed on the federal bureaucrats who authorized such studies. "Consultants have become the whipping boys because it's easier to cut them off," said Williams. In a similar vein, Edward C. Leeson, director of the National Council of Technical Services Industries, which lobbies for increased government contracting-out of services, has said, "We're not trying to steal from the government. We're being tarred with a big brush. The criticism is unfair because the abuses are isolated."

Interviews with officials of three small consulting firms, however, produced a picture more like that discussed by Carl Black and Frank Popper than that described by Williams and Leeson. Consulting firms, said one official, regularly mislead the government agencies for which they are working, or from which they are seeking work. For example, she said, when consultants make proposals, "they provide lists of recognized, qualified personnel who they say would be available to work on the particular project." Often, though, the firm making the proposal "knows full well that these people will not actually be available for this particular study because they are working on other projects. The actual performance of many of the contracts falls back on less experienced consulting firm employees, with some occasional input from senior personnel." Thus, the government doesn't get the level of "expertise" it may have anticipated. Another official said that, in many instances, the federal agency obtaining such a study isn't entirely misled; many contracting officials, he contended, are aware of the shortcuts that the consulting firm is taking, because it's understood by people in government and on the outside that this is how the consulting game has come to be played in Washington. A third company official said that, after receiving a contract (preferably on an unsolicited proposal), the trick then is to ingratiate yourself with federal contracting officials or to write recommendations calling for followup studies, in order to try to win additional work "to keep your firm in business."

More often than not, recipients of consulting and management support service contracts will have no particular expertise in the areas covered by the contract, but instead employ generalists who are fast learners and gradually become able to speak knowledgeably about the subject matter. Also, firms have been given consulting contracts to deal with issues in which they had no previous interest—until they discovered there was money to be made off them. A prime example of this was the use of high-powered consulting companies and major corporations, which had previously shown no special interest in the plight of the poor, to run federal anti-poverty programs. Many of the anti-poverty programs originated by the Johnson administration had some favorable impact on the lives of poor people, but had an even more favorable impact on the balance sheets of many corporations. For example, Westinghouse, International Telephone and Telegraph, and Litton Industries were given lucrative contracts to run federal Job Corps programs. It was not that the programs did not help many poor people, but rather that so much more might have been done if so much money had not been handed over to contractors.

Just how favorable the anti-poverty war had been to private firms was emphasized in an investigation by *United Press International* reporter Donald Lambro. It is discouraging to note that Lambro found much of the $22 billion spent on anti-poverty programs from 1964–78 went not to the poor, but to corporations, consultants, academic researchers, and other "experts." Focusing on the Community Services Administration, the successor to the Office of Economic Opportunity's Community Action Agency, Lambro found, among other things,

- millions of dollars were spent on studies, surveys, research reports, data retrieval systems, and other materials, much of which ended up on government shelves;
- overhead costs in some cases swallowed up 50 percent or more of grants and contracts;
- CSA had no figures on how much of the money it spent actually reached the poor;
- as with other federal agencies, CSA had awarded many consulting contracts and grants as fiscal years were nearing a close. "We have to have all of our money out by the end of the fiscal year or else we must return the balance to the treasury," a CSA official was quoted as saying. "Congress doesn't like it when you have money left over at the end of the year."

Of some $9 million spent by the CSA in fiscal year 1978 on energy-related, anti-poverty consulting contracts, most went to private firms or organizations. A look at some of these contracts indicates that the projects were either unnecessary or could quite capably be handled by in-house government employees. For example, Lambro found contracts for $366,000 to the Urban Institute to analyze the CSA home winterization program; for $45,000 to study fraud by energy companies; for $72,380 for a film on energy conservation; for $700,000 to a Massachusetts firm for studies to promote utility rate structure reform; and for $40,000 for an "energy conservation and motivation study." While some of these may be worthy projects, the fact is that for every cent spent on studies and analyses there was that much less money that actually went into the pockets of the poor.

As we have just seen, while some federal contracts go to firms for subjects in which they have had no previous interest, other contracts go to help subsidize firms on matters in which they have a strong interest. Contracts of the latter type, especially in the area of research and development (R&D), have proved to be a windfall for private firms, think tanks, universities, and nonprofit organizations, while also having the effect of reducing the federal government's corps of competent managers and technical personnel. Although space had its heyday (and continued to get a significant portion of the money spent annually by the government for R&D), defense has always been the biggest recipient of federal R&D dollars. Annually, defense gets about half of the federal R&D dollars, while space and energy together receive about one-fourth.

Before World War II, the greater part of the federal government's relatively small R&D budget went to federally operated laboratories. After that war, federal R&D funds overall, and the private sector's share of those funds, increased dramatically. R&D funds created and had subsidized the nuclear energy industry to the tune of $40 billion by the early 1980s and had also helped keep alive the electronics and aerospace industries.

Of the federal R&D funds, well over half go to private profit-making companies, while the remainder is spent by state and local governments, nonprofit groups, universities, and colleges, and by in-house government installations. The greater federal subsidization of private R&D has lessened the government's capacity to do such work in-house and, at the same time, has reduced the expertise federal agencies need to keep tabs on what private firms are doing with the federal funds. R&D authority Daniel S. Greenberg noted this over-sight problem regarding the National Bureau of Standards. Greenberg wrote that the bureau, "once an elite institute of federal scientific service, has been so deprived of funds in recent years that an outside reviewing committee . . . judged it to be on the verge of decay."

As with other types of contracts, R&D awards are subject to a number of abuses that raise questions about the cost-effectiveness, efficiency, and desirability of their being performed by outside inter-ests rather than in-house. In this respect, a 1977 report by the General Accounting Office contained a far-reaching analysis and indictment of federal R&D contracting practices. The study looked at 220 R&D contracts awarded to private, profit-making firms by the Maritime Administration, the Environmental Protection Agency, and four units of the Department of Transportation (Federal Aviation Ad-ministration, National Highway Traffic Safety Administration, Fed-eral Railroad Administration, and Office of the Secretary of Transpor-tation). In fiscal year 1975, the six agencies together awarded almost $500 million in R&D contracts, with 39 percent of that spent in-house, 38 percent ($183.7 million) awarded to profit-making compa-nies, and the remainder given to educational institutions, state and local governments, nonprofit groups, and others.

One of the major abuses uncovered by the accounting office study was the wastefully high number of contracts that were awarded in the final month of the fiscal year. Of the 220 contracts in the study, 144 (or 65 percent) were awarded in the fiscal year's final month. One agency, the Maritime Administration, made 11 of its 26 awards for the year in the final two days of the fiscal year. This large number of contract awards in the fiscal year's closing weeks "suggests improper planning and implies that funds are obligated to prevent the authority from lapsing or to avoid reductions in future appropriations," the GAO reported, in an all-too-familiar refrain.

Perhaps the greatest unnecessary cost to taxpayers, the accounting office suggested, was in modifications that, by extension, meant tens of millions of dollars added government-wide to research and devel-opment contracts with private firms. Of the contracts studied, 62 percent of them had modifications increasing their costs and adding to the time allowed for their completion. Those contracts with dollar modifications increased in cost by an average of 72 percent each; those with time modifications added an average of nine months to the completion time. The Federal Railroad Administration was a particular offender, granting dollar and time increases in all eight R&D contracts it awarded, producing an average cost increase of 111 percent and an average time increase of 17 months.

Although noting that some contract modifications are justified, the General Accounting Office pointed out that a large number of modifications is a sign of poor planning or possible favoritism to certain contractors. Also, the excessive modification of contracts results in less cost competition, since modifications are tantamount to sole-source contracts. When completion dates for contracts are extended because of modifications, this may mean that the contractor will end up providing outdated information and conclusions to the government. Also, because federal agencies have to provide extra funds for unanticipated modifications, other planned projects may have to be deferred or eliminated because there will not be enough agency money to go around.

The accounting office also indicated that it was difficult to determine how many of the R&D projects were actually useful, because most of them had not been completed at the time of its investigation. Of the contracts reviewed, 88 percent were incomplete. Of these, 35 percent were running past deadlines, 47 percent had had their deadlines extended, and the rest were justifiably incomplete because the contract was for more than one year. But even had more studies been completed, the accounting office questioned whether the results would be put to any good use—or whether, instead, the reports would end up unused on a shelf somewhere. The reason for the accounting office's doubt was its finding that four of the agencies studied "did not have formal systematic procedures for evaluating the usefulness of contracted R&D end products," raising the possibility the reports might never be used.

Senator Charles H. Percy, R-Illinois, who had requested the accounting office study, commented the report also indicated "that reported federal research and development expenditures are greatly understated." Percy had especially strong words for the way the government and R&D contractors deal with each other, saying, "The extensive pattern of contract modifications implies cozy relationships between agencies and contractors and certainly prevents others from bidding on the modified awards."

While many of the contracts discussed thus far have involved improprieties of one type or another, few have been as egregious as those entered into by the General Services Administration (GSA). The GSA, often referred to as the government's "landlord," oversees the construction, leasing, and maintenance of buildings occupied by federal agencies. It also provides supplies and equipment for government agencies. Throughout the last decade, GSA has been involved in one major scandal after another.

Prominent among these, in the late 1970s and early 1980s, was a nationwide investigation that produced indictments of more than 200 government employees and contractors on charges related to the filing of false claims and the payment of kickbacks on GSA contracts. The criminal cases detailed tens of millions of dollars in overcharges fraudulently billed to the government. One former building manager for GSA's State Department field office received a six-year prison term after pleading guilty to receiving kickbacks that, prosecutors said, exceeded $614,000. One of the accused contractors was charged with performing $200,000 worth of work under a GSA contract, yet billing the government for $581,000.

For years before that round of scandals broke, the General Accounting Office had warned in report after report about possible corruption in GSA contracting. One Hyattsville, Maryland, painting contractor, as early as 1976 told the Federal Bureau of Investigation, the GSA, House Public Works Committee investigators, and others that many contractors were being paid for work never done and, in return, were making payoffs to GSA officials. The contractor said he had paid off GSA officials with trips, money, prostitutes, and free painting jobs on their homes in order to get federal contracts. Finally, in 1978, federal investigations got underway, pushed along by a series of articles on GSA corruption by Ronald Kessler, of *The Washington Post*. According to Kessler's articles, many GSA contractors were routinely being paid for work actually done by government employees, or for such things as applying two coats of paint when only one was actually used, or for painting (or allegedly painting) the same wall seven times in five years. Companies that did not exist were paid for work never done. In return for these unjustified contract payments, the contractors were paying off many GSA officials.

Prior to *The Post*'s disclosures in early 1978, many federal employees and government union officials stated in interviews that there were dozens of instances in which they felt GSA contractors had fleeced the government on repair and maintenance contracts. The American Federation of Government Employees (AFL-CIO), the nation's largest federal workers' union, had compiled in late 1977 long lists of abuses and forwarded the lists to a number of members of Congress.

Among the abuses revealed were ones that showed shoddy work by contractors that in some cases required later correction by federal employees (or by other contractors) at government, rather than at the initial contractor's, expense.

In the Baltimore area alone, contractors' abuses were extensive. For example, at the Customs House there, a contractor was hired to install a heating system in the engine room basement. The job was done improperly, causing water to condense on, and ruin, the ceiling. A second contractor was called in to plaster and paint the ceiling at added cost. In another room at the Customs House, a plumbing contractor was hired to fix a floor drain. In the process, the contractor broke one of the walls. Federal employees had to go back and finish the work, and the contractor was not assessed for the damage.

Also at the Customs House, a company was awarded a contract to remove and replace window air-conditioners, even though GSA had plenty of in-house personnel to do the work. As evidence of this, GSA painters were called in on 12 work days to paint all windows and sills from which the air-conditioners were removed. Then, after the air-conditioners were put back in their original positions by contract workers, GSA employees had to go back and make sure the air-conditioners worked and, in some cases, repair those that weren't functioning properly.

GSA also contracted at a cost of about $22,000 to bird-proof the entire exterior of the Customs House. The contractor broke several electrical systems while doing the work, and GSA electricians had to spend three weeks repairing electrical wires that were broken or improperly connected to transformers by the contractor. On another contract, at the Curtis Bay Coast Guard Yard, in Baltimore, a contractor renovated the firehouse. After the contractor supposedly completed the work, GSA employees had to touch up and repaint walls and doors on five occasions, at no cost to the contractor.

At the Appraisers Store Building at the Baltimore Customs House, two GSA employees spent 64 hours plastering stairwells in preparation for work by a painting contractor, even though this work was supposed to be performed by the contractor. Again, the work was done at government, rather than contractor, expense. At the Federal Depot at Middle River, in Baltimore, a contractor was hired to complete a new computer room. After the contractor left, federal employees had to replace tiles in the ceiling that had been improperly installed by the contractor. The federal employees' time was charged to building maintenance, rather than to the contractor.

In some instances, contractors were unnecessarily being hired to do work already being performed by in-house GSA employees. For example, at the Baltimore Appraisers Store, a contractor was hired to install lowered fire sprinkler heads on the seventh floor. Yet GSA employees did exactly the same work on the eighth floor and obviously could have been called upon to do the work on the floor below. At the Federal Depot in Middle River, a contractor was hired to repair 12 roof fans that had been maintained by GSA employees for more than a decade. GSA justified using a contractor, rather than in-house workers, on the ground that an emergency existed. Yet before any work could begin, a GSA supervisor from the electrical shop at the Federal Office Building in Baltimore had to be sent to Middle River to show the contractor what to do. The list of similar questionable arrangements went on and on.

The same types of overcharges, charges for work never done, noncompetitive contracts, and other abuses have been found extensively in recent years in painting, repair, and maintenance contracts in the military—perhaps to an even greater degree than at GSA.

Despite the widespread allegations by government employee unions and by Congress's watchdog agency, the General Accounting Office, it wasn't until 1978 that a congressional committee decided to look into GSA. One reason for Congress's reluctance to investigate GSA corruption, according to journalist Don Lambro, was that "members of Congress are unconcerned about what goes on in the agency so long as their states and districts get government office buildings, lucrative long-term leases, and big multi-million dollar purchasing contracts."

Certainly, congressional and high Executive Branch political pressure on GSA in the awarding of contracts has been a way of life in Washington. Arthur F. Sampson, GSA administrator during the Nixon administration, publicly acknowledged in 1974 that probably 40 percent of the architect and engineering contracts he had personally awarded were given for political reasons. As Sampson matter-of-factly explained: "A Congressman or a Senator has the right to make a recommendation for his constituents. To me, that's part of the democratic system. . . . If I've got three firms and they're all equal and the Vice President has made a recommendation, I'd go with the Vice President or with Senator [Joseph] Montoya or with Senator [Hugh] Scott of Pennsylvania." Montoya, a New Mexico Democrat, at the time headed the Appropriations Subcommittee that handled GSA's budget; Scott was the Republican minority leader who, under the Nixon administration, was given control over top GSA patronage jobs, including Sampson's.

Sampson made his disclosures of political influence on the contracting process on June 10, 1974, as he was announcing changes in the way GSA would award future architect and engineering contracts. Previously, Sampson had sole authority to choose these contractors. But from then on, he said, career civil servants would handle "most" of the responsibility for the awards. Under the revised procedure, GSA evaluation panels would select three firms they felt to be most qualified for a job, rating them in order of preference. If Sampson were to award the contract to other than the top-rated firm, he would have to state his reasons in writing; his written statement would be a public record, subject to scrutiny by any interested party.

But even with the change in policy, Sampson said he expected political influence would still be part of the contracting procedure—in fact, he said he would continue to welcome contract recommendations from politicians. Sampson said he saw nothing wrong with a member of Congress trying to influence the awarding of a contract and was concerned not with eliminating political influence as such, but rather with eliminating "improper" influence. As Sampson put it, in explaining the new policy: "This is necessary to minimize opportunities for improper influence, and by that I mean the perception as well as the fact. Ranking gets away from the mystery of the darkroom —the idea that somebody can call me up and say, 'Hey, pick the third firm on the list.' "

GSA figured in an earlier, more-publicized contracting scandal involving Spiro T. Agnew, who resigned the vice presidency in 1974 after pleading guilty to a tax charge that grew out of a federal bribery investigation of Agnew. The Justice Department, in conjunction with Agnew's negotiated plea, released a summary of its evidence against him. The prosecutors' statement alleged that Agnew had received bribes from Maryland-based architects and engineers to influence the awarding of state, local, and federal contracts. (Agnew previously had been governor of Maryland and county executive of Baltimore County.) Two Baltimore engineers, according to the statement of evidence, admitted to making cash payments to Agnew after he had become vice president. The Justice Department said one engineering company official, Lester Matz, told investigators that a firm in which he held a financial interest received a GSA contract after he made a $2,500 payment to Agnew through an intermediary in April 1971.

Although the government did not assert that Agnew directly influenced the awarding of the GSA contract to Matz's firm, there was nonetheless, as *The Wall Street Journal* put it, a "belief among many architects and engineers that it's necessary to make political contributions" in order to obtain government work. In the Maryland contracting scandal that snared Agnew and other high-ranking local politicians and business people in the early 1970s, "political contributions" was a euphemism for bribes. Even after Agnew resigned the vice presidency, other allegations surfaced. A federal grand jury in Maryland in 1975 heard allegations by a Montgomery County, Md., architect that he had obtained six contracts from the GSA after making payments to a close associate of Agnew. The probe produced no indictments, but it managed to cast another cloud over GSA's contracting practices.

Government contracts are not just small change to private sector architects and engineers. Through the federal contracting process, architects and engineers are an integral part of the hidden bureaucracy. Federal, state, and local government contracts are estimated to account for 40 to 45 percent of all architects' income nationwide, and 29 percent of all consulting engineers' income. A mid-1977 report of the General Accounting Office noted that "The federal government is the largest single client of the architect and engineer. Federal expenditures for A/E work have totaled about $300 million a year, of which about two-thirds is for preparing plans and specifications used in federal building construction. Other services include site surveys, field investigations, construction inspections, shop drawing reviews and feasibility studies."

This particular study dealt with the GSA and the Defense Department, which are two of the largest agencies that contract with architects and engineers for designing and constructing federal buildings. Architect and engineering contracts totaling $63.4 million were awarded, on construction projects of about $2.4 billion for fiscal year 1975, by GSA and Defense's primary design and construction units, the Naval Facilities Engineering Command (NAVFAC), and the Army Corps of Engineers. The study determined that much money was wasted because of design deficiencies by the contractors, resulting in change orders producing cost overruns. The GAO could put no overall dollar figure on the waste involved in unnecessary change orders, but suggested that it could run into the tens of millions of dollars.

An earlier General Accounting Office study, in mid-1976, found that there was inadequate competition among private firms for the architect and engineering contracts. The GAO suggested that this lack of competition resulted in the government paying too much for these services. The accounting office said that some modified form of competitive negotiations (rather than outright competitive bidding) was needed to insure that the government was getting the most for its money. The accounting office noted that this would be a radical departure from past practice, stating: "The architect and engineering societies long have endorsed a procedure . . . [under which] fee or price is not discussed prior to selecting a firm with whom to negotiate a contract. The societies oppose the consideration of fees in the selection process. They fear that this would result in price competition and deterioration of the quality of services rendered."

In addition to the federal government and Maryland, several other states, including New Jersey, Louisiana, and Pennsylvania, all had scandals in the 1970s involving architect and engineering contracts. Leaders in the two professions have acknowledged that the system of payments in exchange for contracts has been widespread.

"It's a universal evil, a blinding scar on my profession," said Charles Colbert, a New Orleans architect and former dean of the Columbia School of Architecture. "The architect and engineer dealing in public works provide the front money for the aspiring politician." William Slayton, executive director of the American Institute of Architects, voiced similar views. "It stinks; the whole business of financing campaigns stinks," he said. "The architect is put into a box he can't get out of. He's a cow to be milked." Donald Buzzell, executive director of the American Consulting Engineers Council, said the pressure on some engineers to contribute is so great that "some firms have to hire former legislators and public officials who have influence so they don't have to give as much."

In addition to the GSA scandals already described, the agency has regularly been in hot water over the years for its federal building construction and leasing programs. Although GSA has some buildings constructed for government ownership, it relies more heavily on leasing facilities from private owners. Nationwide, the GSA spends close to a billion dollars annually on leases for space in privately owned buildings. Under terms of the leases, the GSA has also spent more than $40 million annually improving the buildings. Often, GSA has permitted building owners themselves to contract for the repairs and bill the government for the work. Seldom do the building owners seek competitive bids, so the government is usually paying a premium price for these repairs and alterations. One San Francisco businessman even had the nerve to bill GSA $131,814 for art work for his building, adding another $11,000 "commission" fee for his services in buying the art!

GSA has also enriched building owners by leasing space, then having it sit vacant for years with no federal agency occupying it. For example, a Rockville, Maryland, building leased by GSA for the Bureau of Alcohol, Tobacco and Firearms sat vacant for two years while the GSA spent more than $2 million remodeling it to accommodate a laboratory. Thus, the building owner in a two-year period received more than $400,000 in rent from a tenant who never occupied the building, plus receiving a free $2 million remodeling job.

Similarly, the GSA paid more than $600,000 in rent on a building in Martinsburg, West Virginia, that remained unoccupied for about 18 months. The building was to house an office of the Internal Revenue Service. The IRS was getting ready to move in when, as *The Washington Star* reported, "they discovered that the lease did not include such amenities as electricity, heat or running water." In Queens, New York, a GSA-leased office building remained vacant for close to two years at a cost of almost $500,000. Likewise, a building leased by GSA in Washington, D.C., remained vacant for two and a half years at a cost of $700,000 in rent.

Congressional critics of GSA's leasing program argue that the federal government could save millions of dollars annually by constructing its own buildings, rather than leasing private facilities. The problem is that many members of Congress use the GSA leasing program, just as they use other federal public works projects, as patronage plums for their own districts. What is especially appealing to these members of Congress is that the true cost of the GSA leasing program, unlike public works projects such as roads and dams, can be somewhat hidden in the federal budget. This is so, *The Washington Star* noted, because, "When Congress approves a new building, the entire cost of capital construction must be listed in the budget during the first year. But when GSA signs a long-term lease, Congress lists only the rent payments for the first year in the budget—even though the government is committed to pay the rent for the next 20 years." Also, any GSA construction, lease, or repair job over $500,000 "can be authorized with just a stamp of approval from the House and Senate public works committees." Thus, while both houses must later approve the financing for the projects, the projects themselves "never have to face a floor vote in either chamber."

This procedure, coupled with old-fashioned horse-trading involving other public works projects, means it is reasonably easy for an influential member of Congress to push through a boondoggle federal building project. For example, in the closing days of the lame-duck Congress in late 1980, the House and Senate approved funds for a federal courthouse and office building in Redding, California. Just who would occupy the building was a big question. GSA officials themselves told Congress they knew of no plans for a federal judge to sit permanently in Redding, which meant there would be a courthouse with no full-time court. The Department of Agriculture, which GSA had listed as the other proposed major tenant for the building, said it already had enough space to meet its needs. The House Public Works Committee's lameduck chairman, Representative Harold T. Johnson, D-California, whose district included Redding, had requested the building some months before his election defeat; GSA officials were quick to agree to the request from the man whose committee oversees their activities. Senator Alan K. Simpson, R-Wyoming, who tried unsuccessfully to block the project, suggested that in the future, "In these types of projects . . . if a member of either body is retiring, then I propose that we give him or her a solid gold $50,000 watch—carefully engraved, 'Paid for by the taxpayers'—and that will be eminently less painful" than paying the cost of an unneeded building.

The negative effect of using contractors, of personnel ceilings, and of federal employee layoffs on minorities, women, veterans, the handicapped, and other groups that have traditionally been discriminated against in private job markets must be mentioned. Over the last few decades, it has become government policy to set the highest standards by hiring, at decent wages, persons who have been systematically discriminated against in the private sector. When federal jobs are contracted out, or layoffs or personnel ceilings are imposed, the groups that have been the major victims of private-sector discrimination are hurt the most. As Herbert H. Denton wrote in *The Washington Post* in early 1982, recession-sparked layoffs at the federal, state, and local levels of government had hit minorities and women the hardest. At the federal level, he wrote, "blacks and women in the upper grade ranks and those in administrative jobs have been most affected. Women managers are being laid off at a rate more than twice the average, minority group members at a rate 3½ times that of all administrators." The Reagan administration, he wrote, "has taken no action to mitigate the effects of layoffs on women and minorities in the federal government." Denton was writing solely about layoffs, but the effects he describes would be the same when personnel ceilings are imposed and jobs are contracted out.

Carl Clewlow, deputy assistant Secretary of Defense in the Ford administration, put this issue in perspective some years ago when he noted in congressional testimony that decisions to contract-out government services "impact directly on such important areas as labor relations, wage policy, equal employment, and other federal government policies, such as those designed to promote employment of special groups, e.g., veterans, handicapped—including mentally retarded—disadvantaged minorities, etc." Yet, he said, in most decisions to contract-out, it is considered to be "irrelevant" by the contracting agency "that substantial numbers of minorities, disabled veterans, handicapped and mentally retarded, and Vietnam-era veterans, many of whom are long-term civil service employees, will lose their jobs." This, he said, was despite the fact that "nearly one-third of the employees whose jobs will be eliminated [by contracting-out services formerly performed in-house] are in those categories, many as a result of federal government efforts to bring them into productive employment in the federal service."

When contractors do hire displaced federal employees, it is usually at lower wages and benefits than they received as government workers. Clewlow said that contractors, by paying lower wages and providing fewer benefits, particularly in blue-collar jobs, are able to hold down their costs and show that they can perform certain government services at less cost than can in-house employees. In contracting-out, Clewlow said, cost should not always be the bottom line; there must also be serious consideration of what contracting does to the jobs and wages of persons from traditionally disadvantaged groups. Too often, contracting-out clashes with the government's stated goals of affirmative action and providing decent wages and benefits.

As with individual employees, minority businesses, too, have received relatively few benefits from government contracting policy, despite federal programs with stated goals of giving minority firms a fair share of prime contracts and subcontracts. One federal study showed that for a three-year period in the mid-1970s, minority businesses received less than 1.4 percent of all defense subcontracts awarded by prime contractors in each of those three years. This occurred even though Defense Department regulations require recipients of prime contracts over $500,000 to make a determined effort to subcontract some work to minority companies. Undercutting such an effort, the study showed, was the Pentagon's action allowing 39 of its top 100 prime contractors to be excluded from the minority business enterprises program. Thus, fourteen oil companies, three automobile manufacturers, and assorted other major corporations were not obligated to give subcontracts to minority firms.

When some members of Congress and some newspapers raised questions about poor treatment of minority businesses by the Pentagon, a reluctant Defense Department in mid-1977 released figures to show specifically what certain major contractors had done to assist minority enterprises. It wasn't much. The report showed that various corporate giants provided to minority companies subcontracts totaling a mere fraction of 1 percent of their prime defense contracts. For example, Boeing had received more than $1 billion in defense contracts for fiscal year 1976 yet provided subcontracts totaling just $554,000 to minority firms. For Litton Systems, Inc., the figures were $960.9 million and $487,000; for AM General Corp., $122.3 million and $4,000.

Another government program designed to help minority businesses has had an even more shocking record of abuses. A July 1977 Senate subcommittee investigation showed just how unscrupulous some white business people could be in undermining a well-intended program. The particular program, created by the Small Business Administration (SBA) in 1968, was designed to help minority citizens set up businesses and then guarantee them a certain amount of government work through noncompetitive federal contracts. These firms thus would gain the experience and expertise to compete later on more equal footing with established companies.

Instead, as Senator Lawton Chiles, D-Florida, chairman of the Subcommittee on Federal Spending Practices and Open Government, observed, the program became "a disaster which has cost the taxpayers $1.5 billion," without providing much help to minority businesses.

Throughout the country, Chiles said, the program was a "sham" under which white business people "would name a minority citizen to be president or vice president of their firm and contend that he owns 51 percent of the stock." Chiles called the program "a national disgrace" used "to further benefit persons who are not disadvantaged now and never were disadvantaged in the first place."

The subcommittee's investigation turned up a number of shocking examples. In one case, a broken-down cannery plant, worth no more than $20,000, qualified as a minority business and received some $200,000 in federal contracts. The minority "officers" had been set up as fronts for white business people. The minority "officers" received $2.35 an hour for picking tomatoes and had no control over the operations of the company.

In another case, investigators found that few, if any, contracts were awarded in SBA's southern Region IV to minority firms that did not have a white business "sponsor." One group of white-run companies in Dunn, North Carolina, established "a series of black-front companies to obtain $16 million in government contracts. The white sponsors, in turn, extracted more than $4 million of this amount for 'management fees' and other services." The SBA, according to Chiles, attempted to correct the situation but "characteristically made it worse. By forcing the sponsors to divest themselves of their 49 percent interest in the fronts, the wealthy sponsors earned almost a 3,000 percent return on their invested capital."

Investigators also found cases in which a white businessman who was in no way socially or economically disadvantaged had been given $29 million in government contracts, and another in which a Kinston, North Carolina, millionaire businessman's firm was awarded contracts. Another front company had as its secretary-treasurer a 73-year-old black farm worker who could neither read nor write. In one particularly despicable case, a black man who was set up as the president of a Virginia company controlled by whites testified that, although he was nominally the firm's president, "I did not have an office nor even toilet facilities at the plant site. The other [white] company officers did have both offices and facilities. New transportation, using company funds, was purchased for the white employees, but the blacks, including myself, had to do whatever they could to get to and from work. . . . I asked to see the company records several times, including the checkbook for items bought by the company, but I was told that this was none of my business, so I never saw the records."

In addition to the abuses in programs designed to help minority contractors, there is the additional problem of race and sex discrimination in employment by companies holding government contracts. Overall, the federal government has shown itself to be reluctant to go after companies with poor records in hiring and promoting minorities and women. When Labor Secretary Raymond Marshall in late 1977 barred a Rockford, Illinois, machine company from further federal contracts because of alleged employment discrimination against minorities and women, this marked only the 13th company so debarred since the issuance of a 1965 presidential order prohibiting government contractors and subcontractors from employment discrimination based on race, color, religion, sex, or national origin. For minority contractors, and minority workers on federally funded projects, the promise of equal opportunity seems tragically unfulfilled.

3 · Ever Since Washington

Two centuries ago, in the dark days of the American Revolution, George Washington visited Philadelphia and was appalled to see, as one writer put it, that "those who had prospered on wartime contracts now rolled about Philadelphia in gaudy coaches," while the Continental Army "survived on half rations, slim supplies, and often no pay." During that visit in 1778, Washington remarked that "Speculation, peculation, and an insatiable thirst for riches seem to have got the better of every other consideration and almost of every order of men."

War profiteering at government expense was the order of the day. There were alegations that Dr. William Shippen, head of the government's medical department, had profited from the sale of hospital supplies, and that Thomas Mifflin, as quartermaster-general of the army, and his successor, Nathanael Greene, "had used government wagons to haul goods later sold on the open market."

The biggest scandal, though, centered around what came to be called the Deane Affair, named after Silas Deane, who was sent by Congress to Paris in 1776 to obtain war materials: clothing, arms, ammunition, and field pieces. Deane was directed unofficially by the French government to deal with Caron de Beaumarchais, whom the government had placed at the head of "a dummy organization through which war goods could be funneled to America without involving the crown." The venture was secretly subsidized by French and Spanish contributions, and many of the materials were to be given quietly by the French King as gifts to the struggling colonists.

De Beaumarchais, famed as a playwright *(The Marriage of Figaro* and *The Barber of Seville),* knew nothing about business, but he learned fast. Muskets that had been "discarded by the French Army and given to Beaumarchais for nothing were passed along" to the American Army "at half their original price." De Beaumarchais sold gunpowder at a 500 percent markup of its actual price, even though it was supposed to be a gift to the Americans. Deane sent letters accompanying de Beaumarchais's vouchers and bills, saying that the billings were legitimate and should be paid by Congress. A suspicious Congress summoned Deane home and began an investigation in August 1778. Thomas Paine, relying on classified documents that he was sworn to keep secret, went public with allegations "that the stores which Silas Deane and Beaumarchais pretended they had purchased were a present from the Court of France, and came out of the king's arsenals." For this early act of whistleblowing, Paine, threatened with censure, was allowed to resign his post as secretary for foreign affairs to the Congress. The Deane investigation ended inconclusively, largely because Deane had conveniently left all pertinent documents in France. He was allowed to return to Europe in mid-1780 "without receiving censure or praise from Congress."

The profiteering on government contracts, in addition to the conspicuous consumption and high living engaged in by the profiteers, and contrasted with the plight of those who were sacrificing to win the war, prompted John Adams to warn that "a civil war in America" was a distinct possibility. Adams, Richard Henry Lee, of Virginia, and Henry Laurens, of South Carolina, all felt the Deane Affair, in the words of historian Gordon Wood, symbolized all the "avaricious and ambitious men" who "sought to reverse the Revolution and to establish an aristocratic and mercantile society that would allow full play to private interests."

More than two centuries have elapsed since the nation's first procurement system, the Commissary General, was established by the Second Continental Congress in 1775. The system had as its goal, much as does the system today, to "maximize competition, obtain fair prices, and assure accountability of public officials for public transactions." Yet the system was a failure on most counts. Despite two hundred years of experience to draw on, the government today continues to have a procurement system that falls far short of those original objectives.

Over the years, the federal contracting system has evolved into a mish-mash of statutes, regulations, directives, and circulars that provide for no uniformity and are often ignored. The two major statutes that cover federal contracting, and give authority to government agencies to issue their own regulations governing contracting, are the Armed Forces Procurement Act of 1947 (which applies to the procurement activities of the Defense Department and the National Aeronautics and Space Administration) and the Federal Property and Administrative Services Act of 1949, as amended (which applies to procurement by civilian agencies).

These two basic statutes are supported (some would say, dragged down) by more than 4,000 other legislative provisions covering some aspect of contracting. There are also a number of circulars affecting contracting that have been issued by the Office of Management and Budget over the years, the primary one being Circular A-76, which sets guidelines for contracting for commercial and industrial goods and services. (Such services cover a variety of blue-collar and white-collar jobs, ranging from maintenance work to photography to managerial functions.) On top of this, close to 500 federal officials regularly issue procurement regulations of some kind, and there were in the early 1980s almost 900 different sets of contracting regulations covering almost 65,000 pages—and these were being revised or added to at the rate of 21,000 pages a year.

To understand how the system of government-by-contract evolved from its simple beginnings in the Revolutionary War, it is useful to review briefly some additional history. From the late 1700s until the early 1900s, a number of laws and regulations covering procurement were promulgated. These generally fostered the goal of maximizing competition and accountability through formal advertising for bids. These early procurement activities were mainly for goods rather than services.

During World War I, the government stepped up its contracting activity, relying heavily on the private sector to help mobilize the necessary resources to fight the war. Competitive standards were relaxed during the war, but then restored in the postwar years.

As it did during the Revolutionary War, disclosure of wartime profiteering provoked investigations, which resulted in a number of post–World War I laws designed to curb excessive profits and to halt influence peddling in contract awards. On another issue, Congress noted in hearings in 1932 that many government-created industrial and commercial activities, established to help carry out the war effort, were still in existence. A special House committee recommended that many of these activities be eliminated, but government agencies didn't follow the advice and even expanded some facilities and created new ones prior to World War II.

During the Great Depression, efforts were made to use government procurement for socio-economic goals. Various federal laws were passed to set minimum wages on federal construction project contracts (Davis-Bacon Act); to upgrade wages and working conditions on federal supply contracts (Walsh-Healey Act); and to bar salary kickbacks on federal construction contracts (Copeland Act). Congress in 1938 also ordered the government to purchase products from workshops for the blind; in 1971, this was expanded to require purchases of products from other handicapped persons as well. Similar efforts were made after World War II when a number of laws and regulations were enacted to promote additional socio-economic goals in connection with federal contracts. These included the barring of employment discrimination by contractors against minorities and women; programs to help minority enterprises obtain government contracts; and an extension of labor standards laws of the 1930s to cover employees of government service contractors in the areas of wages, hours, fringe benefits, and health and safety conditions.

World War II marked a turning point in federal policy regarding the use of private firms to do the government's work. Government alone was clearly not equipped to deal with the massive problems posed by fighting full-scale wars simultaneously in Europe and Asia, so total mobilization of resources in both the public and private sectors was needed. The private and scientific sectors were called upon by the government for everything from manufacturing and construction to such top-secret enterprises as the Manhattan Project, under which the atomic bomb was developed. Federal employment reached 3.6 million during the war (compared to 2.85 million in 1982) while several times that many people performed government work for private employers involved in the war effort.

In the wartime atmosphere, citizens became accustomed to the notion of private enterprise being deeply involved in government functions, so there was no public concern expressed when this liaison was continued after the war. As former Civil Service Commission Chairman John W. Macy, Jr., noted, "The success of this public-private partnership was carried over in pursuing new national goals in the postwar and cold-war periods."

Within just a few years after the war had ended, the greater use of private contractors made it increasingly difficult to tell where private enterprise left off and the government began in the conduct of federal programs and services. In Macy's words, "The dividing line between public and private employment" became "vague and wavering."

With a new dependence on federal contracts, large segments of American business after World War II began shifting away from customers in the private sector and toward those in the public sector. In the decade and a half following World War II, this shift came mainly in the atomic energy and space R&D fields and in weapons and space technology production. While receiving much less publicity, private firms during those years gained greater influence in the government by obtaining consulting and management contracts. Large corporations, as well as smaller companies, were becoming so dependent on government contracts that, as contracting critic H.L. Neiburg put it almost two decades ago, "Instead of a free enterprise system, we are moving toward a government-subsidized private-profit system."

After World War II, Congress had again investigated government commercial and industrial activities created specifically for the war effort but remaining in existence. Various congressional committees concluded that many of these activities were nonessential and unfairly competitive with private businesses. Responding to the congressional initiatives, the Defense Department in September 1952 issued a directive calling for elimination of its commercial and industrial facilities in cases where the products could be obtained from the private sector or from some other government facility.

In 1953, Congress established the Commission on the Organization of the Executive Branch, the purpose of which was to "eliminate nonessential services, functions and activities which were competitive with private enterprise." Two years later, the commission issued a number of reports recommending elimination of or reductions in government activities deemed to be in competition with private businesses. It specifically recommended that private contractors be allowed to take over such government activities.

President Eisenhower, in his January 21, 1954, budget address, signaled the new trend in government by saying, "This new budget marks the beginning of a movement to shift . . . to private enterprise federal activities which can be more appropriately and more efficiently carried on in that way." The "contract state," as Nieburg has dubbed it, was on its way.

Eisenhower, who by the end of his two terms in office was issuing warnings of the growing influence of the military-industrial complex over the American way of life, at the outset of his presidency in 1953 was the leading cheerleader for a policy of turning over to private contractors as much government business as possible. Contracting-out had many appealing political angles: It was a form of patronage and handouts to the Eisenhower administration's legions of business supporters, while at the same time an effective device to limit the number of civil service employees and thereby create the illusion that a conservative, money-conscious administration was halting the trend toward "big government." As former Civil Service Commission Chairman Macy explained the sleight-of-hand used by Eisenhower and succeeding administrations: "Counting the number of federal employees had become a favorite political game. The management success of any administration was frequently measured in terms of its ability to keep the count stable or declining. Monthly strength reports were dispatched to Capitol Hill, where each new [civil service] increase inspired press releases, describing the wastefulness of a bloated government."

The politicians' response to what was perceived as a growing federal bureaucracy was, in Macy's words, "to exercise even greater control over the agencies' manpower expansion" through the use of employee ceilings and rigid clearance processes for creation of new jobs, in addition to using the already existing budgetary controls over federal employment.

Such concern over a growing bureaucracy could be viewed as an exercise in sensible, fiscally sound government, except for one major factor: federal government programs—primarily in, first, atomic energy and defense and, later, in space and related fields—were expanding at a pace far exceeding the work capacity of the civil service bureaucracy. This was certainly no secret to the president or the Congress, which, after all, had proposed and approved the very programs that were increasing the federal budget and necessitating additional personnel to perform the government's work. With limitations imposed on increased civil service personnel, contracting-out in most instances afforded the only means of getting certain government work done. As Macy stated, "with mounting workloads and staffing limitations, administrators turned to the contracting-out device as a means for accomplishing the work. Since the counting of contract personnel was far more difficult, the increased manpower could be applied to the agency's mission without committing the political sin of raising the level of federal employment."

Of course, the level of federal employment actually was rising if all persons doing federal work were counted. Whether they are called civil service employees, or contract employees, the taxpayers still have to pick up the tab. But beginning with President Eisenhower, presidents as well as Congress have for the last three decades winked at the rapidly expanding contractor bureaucracy while leveling their most scathing attacks against the civil service bureaucracy.

Following up on the president's 1954 budget message, the Eisenhower administration officially promulgated its pro-business contracting philosophy on January 15, 1955. On that date, the Bureau of the Budget (BOB) issued Bulletin 55-4, which stated that henceforth it would be the policy of the government to purchase goods and services from the private sector. There were to be some exceptions to this policy: for example, in instances in which it was clearly more costly to rely on the private sector, or in which it was not deemed to be in the public interest to contract-out, activities would be kept in-house for performance by civil service employees.

In the next six years, under Eisenhower, BOB's 1955 directive was expanded: in 1957 (BOB Bulletin 57-7) and in 1960 (BOB Bulletin 60-2). In an effort to give private business even more government work, the latter document called upon federal agencies to examine all of their activities not previously reviewed to see if these could be contracted-out. There was no similar call by Eisenhower or any succeeding president to examine contracted-out programs to see how well they were working out.

In the early years of the Eisenhower administration, the government was clearly involved in some activities that placed it it in competition with segments of the private sector. Many of these activities made little sense from either an economic or good-government standpoint. In the area of military support, for example, the government had paint-manufacturing and coffee-roasting facilities. Few people would argue that the government should be producing paint or roasting coffee, so enterprises such as these were turned over under contract to private concerns. In such cases, Macy noted, "the use of private sources was clearly supported by cost comparisons as well as by policy considerations."

But private firms were not content to obtain contracts only in manufacturing areas where the government was, or appeared to be, in direct competition with them. Instead, beginning in the Eisenhower years, private companies moved in on functions and services that, by virtue of their sensitive government nature, should be restricted to federal workers. Such activities included preparing departmental budgets, reorganizing agencies, recommending managers and other personnel for agencies, formulating and implementing agencies' policies, operating missile test ranges, and providing unqualified, underpaid rent-a-cops to guard installations handling classified data or operations.

Following up after World War II on the precedent established by the Manhattan Project, which relied primarily on contractors from universities and industry for development and production of the atomic bomb, the newly formed Atomic Energy Commission decided to continue to rely chiefly on contractors for its programs, rather than turning them over to government employees. While the government had for many years used private contractors for architectural and engineering services and for construction activities in its public works programs, it had never before its atomic energy program so heavily entrusted its research and development efforts to private firms in peacetime. So, it marked a tradition-breaking decision when the AEC after the war decided to continue the operations of the Brookhaven, Los Alamos, and Argonne laboratories, which had been established during the war through contracts with universities.

When the Soviet Union's Sputnik burst upon the scene in the Cold War atmosphere of the late 1950s, the Eisenhower administration determined that a massive program was needed to overhaul the Soviets' lead in space. The magnitude of the effort begun under President Eisenhower (and then expanded under President Kennedy, who set the goal of putting a man on the moon by the end of the 1960s) placed enormous strains on the government's highly specialized and technical personnel. The newly formed National Aeronautics and Space Administration (NASA) used technical personnel from university laboratories and industrial plants in order to make up for the lack of qualified government personnel and to meet the demands of the ambitious space program. Since then, the bulk of NASA's work has been performed under contract.

NASA's and the AEC's use of contractors had a "debilitating effect on the large federal counterpart establishment," according to John Macy. Eventually, it was to lead to a situation in which the government lacked the in-house capacity to do much of the technical work itself and, perhaps even more significantly, lacked the capacity to monitor effectively the work of outside contractors. This lack of in-house capacity to monitor contractors has become especially serious in the energy and defense areas.

By the end of Eisenhower's terms, evidence was mounting that government contracting was rife with waste and conflicts of interest amounting to a giveaway of government accountability and decision-making authority to private interests. For example, a 1957 study by the New York City Bar Association on conflicts of interest in federal policymaking and procurement concluded that existing laws were ineffective in controlling conflicts of interest in government contracts.

By the time John F. Kennedy succeeded Eisenhower, there had been a number of publicized cases in which companies with government research and consulting contracts had made recommendations that resulted in those same companies receiving additional contracts to develop weapons systems or to manage military programs. These obvious conflicts of interest caused Kennedy to appoint a special high-level committee, including Cabinet members and the heads of NASA and the AEC, to study government contracting, particularly in the R&D field. The committee was headed by David E. Bell, the director of the Bureau of the Budget, and the committee's subsequent report came to be known as the Bell Report.

The Bell Report sounded warnings that the government was losing the capability to evaluate the performance of private contractors and was thereby turning over key government functions to those contractors. In a letter to President Kennedy accompanying its final report, the Bell committee warned, concerning research and development contracts, that the "management and control of such programs must be firmly in the hands of fulltime government officials clearly responsible to the President and Congress. With programs of the size and complexity now common, this requires that the government have on its staff exceptionally strong and able executives, scientists and engineers, fully qualified specialists, to make policy decisions concerning the types of work to be undertaken, and to evaluate the results." Yet, despite this need, there had been in recent years "a serious trend toward eroding the competence of the government's research and development establishments," in large measure because of "the keen competition for scarce talent which has come from government contractors."

The Bell Report also cautioned that U.S. businesses were coming more and more to depend on government contracts to keep themselves financially strong. The report suggested that these companies were, in effect, government agencies and had little to do with any traditional notion of "free enterprise." This had created a situation in which industries relied "almost entirely on government sales for their business," contrary to "the open competitive market of traditional economic theory." It also caused contractors to seek mainly government work, "which will give them both the know-how and the preferred position to seek later follow-on contracts." The panel asked: "Should a corporation created to provide services to government and receiving 100 percent of its financial support from government be considered a 'public' or a 'private' agency? In what sense is a business corporation doing nearly 100 percent of its business with the government engaged in 'free enterprise?'"

The Bell Report, as persuasive as it was in pointing to the dangers of putting control over government programs in the hands of private contractors, failed to stem the contracting-out tide during Kennedy's brief three years in office. Then, under President Lyndon B. Johnson, contractors got a big shot in the arm when the Bureau of the Budget (later, the Office of Management and Budget) on March 3, 1966, issued Circular A-76, which provided guidelines for accelerating the pace of contracting for government industrial and commercial goods and services. A-76 was revised again on August 30, 1967, and then again by the Carter administration on March 29, 1979. This circular has been the basic contracting guideline through the Nixon, Ford, Carter, and Reagan administrations.

Under the Nixon and Ford administrations, contracting-out attained new heights. As with their predecessors, those two presidents brandished the shibboleth: private enterprise can do it better and cheaper; the government should not be in competition with the private sector. But as with their predecessors, neither Ford nor Nixon undertook any study to see how contracting-out was working in practice. Was it saving money overall? Were there functions that were inherently governmental in nature and should not be, or should not have been, contracted out? Was the decision-making and policymaking power that rightfully belonged in the government being turned over to private businesses? Were government contracts undermining competition in the private sector by subsidizing certain businesses at the expense of others? Was contracting-out harming the integrity of the Civil Service?

In their failure to ask these kinds of questions, Nixon and Ford carried to an extreme the policy first laid down under Eisenhower. Tied to an upsurge in contracting-out in the later years of the Nixon administration was the selection in 1973 of Roy Ash to run the Office of Management and Budget (OMB), the agency designated to oversee federal contracting policy. Ash was the former chief executive officer of Litton Industries, Inc., a major government contractor. He also played a key role in the establishment of a leading contracting-out lobbying group, the National Council on Technical and Service Industries.

Then-Rep. Jerome R. Waldie, D-California, singled out Litton and Ash for criticism in an early 1974 statement on budget office proposals to contract-out operational support services at military bases, as well as some functions of the Social Security Administration and the Veterans Administration. Waldie noted that Litton "is the company that has millions of dollars worth of government contracts, but always seems to be in court demanding more money after enormous cost overruns" and that Ash "has long been of the opinion that it would be best if government work now performed by hundreds of thousands of career civil servants, were turned over to private contractors on a cost-plus basis." Waldie said such a view "is quite understandable if you are the head of a company which stands to be a major beneficiary of any increased contracting out; but it is totally irresponsible, and smacks of conflict of interest, when that individual is put into a position to directly implement his philosophy . . . with little, if any accountability."

Under Ford, the unquestioning reliance on public firms reached a peak in mid-1976 when he ordered each federal agency to identify five types of activities that were being performed in-house and to move to contract them out wholesale. Coming as it did during a tough election campaign, Ford's order was widely interpreted by government employees' unions and Democratic members of Congress as a blatant political appeal to business.

The effort to proceed with such wholesale contracting-out was dubbed "Operation Barnacle Remover" by the Ford administration. In a July 24, 1976, memo to Budget Director James T. Lynn and Cabinet officers, President Ford had given the operation its name, saying, ". . . just as it is more exciting to build a new boat than to scrape away the barnacles year after year, there is a tendency to give higher priority to a new dramatic policy initiative than to consider the programs we already have to see how they can be improved—to scrape away the 'barnacles' that build up over time around almost any program or agency."

Within three months, the Ford administration took another step designed to make it easier to justify agency decisions to contract-out still more government services. Hugh E. Witt, administrator of the budget office's Office of Federal Procurement Policy, announced that the government would compute employees' retirement costs using the figure of 24.7 percent of a federal employee's base pay, instead of 7 percent, which had been used for years. This new figure would be used to determine in-house costs for performing government services. A number of members of Congress attacked the increase as an election-year plum for the private sector.

The change in figures had a dramatic effect, making at least 75,000 federal jobs more expensive—on paper, at least—than if the same jobs were performed by contract workers. In fact, as was revealed a few months later, the Ford administration had drawn up a confidential list calling for massive contracting-out of additional blue-collar and other services at scores of military bases and other federal installations. The list included trash collection and disposal, custodial work, aircraft and motor vehicle maintenance, computer services, laundry, clothes alteration, audiovisual services, guard services, typesetting and editing, translating, mess-hall services, radioactive waste disposal, appraisals and surveying, and dozens of other jobs. The Agriculture Department even proposed contracting-out some of its legal work and the processing of food stamps.

After President Carter took office, the immediate pressures for full-scale contracting-out lessened somewhat. The new administration decided to take a look at the issue as part of Carter's over-all program for reorganization of the government. Within five months of taking office, the Carter administration halted President Ford's order to increase the use of contracting-out and temporarily reduced the 24.7 percent retirement figure to 14.1 percent. However, it was later raised to 26 percent. President Carter also reaffirmed his support of personnel ceilings as a valid means of holding down federal employment and government costs.

On May 12, 1977, Carter seemed to take a step away from indiscriminate contracting when he ordered a crackdown on instances in which consulting and expert services from outside the government were "being used excessively, unnecessarily and improperly." Carter told agency heads that his areas of concern included the use of consultants to perform work of a policymaking or managerial nature that should be retained directly by agency officials; repeated appointments or contract extensions; use of consultants to provide both studies and analyses that are nonessential or have no useful impact on agency operations; use of consultant arrangements as a device to bypass or undermine personnel ceilings, pay limitations, or competitive employment procedures; "revolving door" abuses whereby former government employees may be improperly favored for individual or contracted consulting arrangements; inter-agency duplication of consultant efforts; conflicts of interest between consultants' advice and their other outside financial interests and affiliations.

Late in the summer of 1977, President Carter signed legislation that imposed a moratorium on new contracting-out in the Defense Department until March 15, 1978. The legislation came about after severe congressional criticism of defense contracting practices, particularly from the House Appropriations Committee and its chairman, Rep. George H. Mahon, D-Texas. Mahon charged that contracting-out for commercial and industrial services in the Defense Department had wasted taxpayers' money and harmed the civil service system, among other effects.

The Office of Management and Budget took yet another step in the contracting area in early 1978 when it announced that, after years of planning, it would establish within the year a central government system to keep track of federal contracts. This new Federal Procurement Data System would provide some information on the number and kinds of federal contracts, but would have several shortcomings. For example, it excluded contracts under $10,000, thereby ignoring a conservatively estimated $12 billion in contracts annually. It still would not be able to provide the number of contract employees and the number of hours worked by contract employees. It was not designed to identify contractor conflicts of interest, or unnecessary contracts, or duplicative studies, among other things. And because of widely varying definitions used by individual agencies, it would not be able to tell accurately how many contracts there are of certain types. But, at least, it bore the promise of giving the government more information than it had ever had on the number and dollar amounts of most contracts—and, in the process, some indication that contracting-out has been among the major causes of increased federal spending in recent years. In April 1982, the General Accounting Office, the watchdog agency for Congress, reported that the system still was deficient, primarily because some agencies were submitting late, incomplete, and inaccurate information.

The Reagan administration, following through on recommendations made in 1973 by a special bipartisan Commission on Government Procurement, in October 1981 issued a proposal calling for creation of a generally uniform federal procurement system. The final plan, submitted in February 1982, would amend existing statutes to try to put defense and civilian procurement under similar standards for the first time. The system, proposed by the Office of Management and Budget's Office of Federal Procurement Policy, was still awaiting congressional action by late 1982. The proposal, which budget office officials hoped would bring some order to the confusing contracting system, is discussed in greater detail in chapter six.

Also, following up on an effort begun in the Carter administration, the Office of Management and Budget in late 1981 issued a draft (by then already a year overdue) of a "model control system" for agencies to use to monitor the awarding and implementing of consulting contracts. The draft proposal appeared to be generally a good one, but it suffered from the same shortcoming as all of the budget office's circulars, directive, guidelines, etc.: the lack of any mechanism to see to it that the agency managers actually use the system.

In the 30 years since the old Bureau of the Budget first issued its contracting guidelines, the government's policy has been strongly pro-business in its decisions on whether to use contracts or in-house employees. The March 29, 1979, version of Circular A-76, issued by the Carter administration, states: "In a democratic free enterprise system, the Government should not compete with its citizens. The private enterprise system, characterized by individual freedom and initiative, is the primary source of national economic strength. In recognition of this principle, it has been and continues to be the general policy of the Government to rely on competitive private enterprise to supply the products and services it needs." The circular also states that "certain functions are inherently governmental in nature, being so intimately related to the public interest as to mandate performance by federal employees."

The circular goes on to define "governmental functions" as including "investigations, prosecutions and other judicial functions . . . ; management of government programs requiring value judgments, as in directing the national defense; management and direction of the Armed Services; conduct of foreign relations; selection of program priorities; direction of federal employees; regulation of the use of space, oceans, navigable rivers and other natural resources; direction of intelligence and counter-intelligence operations . . . ; regulation of industry and commerce, including food and drugs. . . . Monetary transactions and entitlements, as in government benefit programs; tax collection and revenue disbursements by the government; control of the public treasury, accounts and money supply; and the administration of public trusts."

The circular further states that contracting cannot be used to replace the "in-house core capabilities in the area of research, development and testing, needed for technical analysis and evaluation and technology base management and maintenance."

As will be shown in this book, A-76 is systematically violated, particularly regarding the prohibitions on management of government programs, selection of program priorities, direction of federal employees, and the replacement of the "in-house core" with contractor employees.

The other key points of A-76 are also regularly ignored by contracting agencies: namely, restrictions on entering into "contracts which establish a situation tantamount to an employer-employee relationship between the government and individual contract personnel" and on contracting-out to get around personnel ceilings and salary limitations imposed on the federal work force.

Although most government officials regularly roll their eyes heavenward and swear they never contract-out to avoid agency personnel ceilings, occasionally one of them is bold enough to speak the truth. Admiral Alfred J. Whittle, Jr., Chief of Naval Materials, was one such man. In an April 1979 speech, Whittle acknowledged that the navy was "going to have to contract out more . . . simply because of the personnel ceilings which are placed upon us each year. We would prefer to have ships overhauled in naval shipyards because we get a better job; we would prefer to have our aircraft overhauled at naval air rework facilities. The law says we will not contract-out solely to meet civilian personnel constraints, and yet it's inevitable that that happens when we don't have enough people to do it in-house."

Whittle's statements reflect clearly the shellgame that administrations engage in when they ballyhoo their efforts to hold the line on federal employment. As former Rep. Herbert E. Harris II, D-Virginia, noted, the situation is "ludicrous and senseless," especially when applied to military readiness. "We know that contracting-out can be more expensive than in-house performance," Harris said, and "we know that our defense posture can suffer as a result. Yet both Congress and the presidents continue to reduce personnel ceilings and thus require increased contracting." It makes no sense to "save" money by cutting federal employees, then oftentimes taking those savings plus something extra to pay contractors to replace federal employees.

Another recently issued Office of Management and Budget Circular, A-120, is also important to any discussion of government contracting. A-120, issued by the Carter administration on April 14, 1980, applies to the use of certain narrowly defined consulting services, but does not include similar activities that come under the categories of R&D and management support services. A-120 covers only "those services of a purely advisory nature relating to the governmental functions of agency administration and management and agency program management." The circular provides for "rigorous cost comparisons" between in-house and private-sector performance of a service and calls for competitive awards of contracts "to insure that costs are reasonable."

A-120 also specifically bars contracts "of a policy/decision-making or managerial nature which is the direct responsibility of agency officials" and provides that consultants be retained "only on an intermittent or temporary basis" and that repeat or long-term arrangements be entered into only "under extraordinary circumstances."

Critics of federal contracting practices expected A-120 to be no more effective in the long run than past government directives in curbing overpriced, unnecessary, noncompetitive, and long-term contract arrangements. The problem, they say, is Office of Management and Budget issues directives that look good on paper but are not rigidly enforced either by the procurement policy office or the contracting agencies. In 1980, for example, the procurement policy office, even though it has responsibility for contracting regulations governmentwide, had only 45 employees. Karen Hastie Williams, then the office's administrator, testified before a joint Senate-House subcommittee hearing that "we cannot do the monitoring ourselves" of contracts because of the lack of personnel. Instead, she said, her office tries to "set in place agency controls" that will permit individual agencies to monitor their own contracting activities. Howard Messner, assistant director of management improvement and evaluation at the Office of Management and Budget, testified at the same hearing that OMB tried to control contracting through the budgetary process, but itself exercised no oversight of agency contracting. Echoing Williams, Messner said OMB instead relied on "control systems and management systems" to correct contracting abuses. Rep. Benjamin A. Gilman, R-New York, commented that this reliance on the contracting agencies for oversight was "to my mind . . . like telling the fox to take care of the chickens."

Most of the restrictions on contracting in Circular A-76 and other circulars have been repeatedly ignored by agencies determined to contract-out more of their functions. This can especially be seen in the area of cost comparisons, where figures are often slanted to support contracting-out. Contracting costs often are based on a program of less work than that performed by government workers. Thus, by doing less work with fewer people, contracting costs are sure to be cheaper initially. And in a difficult situation, from the standpoint of government workers or anyone trying to investigate a specific contract proposal, cost comparisons are often publicly disclosed only after a contract is awarded. Thus, government workers usually cannot prove, before a contract is awarded, that it would be more economical to do a job in-house. Some agencies, in some cases, in recent years have given federal employees a chance to reorganize their work in order to show that they can do particular jobs more cheaply than can contractors, but generally such consideration is not given.

Circular A-76 does not have the force of law, but rather embodies the government's contracting philosophy, which is to let private enterprise do it whenever possible. In the absence of anything else, A-76 has become the major instrument of accomplishing contracting-out through its inherent bias against keeping many federal services in-house. A-76 also states that its guidelines can in no way usurp civil service regulations. Yet the Civil Service Commission (reorganized January 1, 1979, as the Office of Personnel Management) had repeatedly refused to review the validity of most contracting-out cases—even when there is evidence that A-76 guidelines or civil service regulations are being violated. This leaves federal employees with no administrative remedy, and they must turn to the courts to challenge such actions. There, too, judges have frequently ruled that government unions lacked standing to challenge those cases of contracting-out in which no federal employees' jobs were lost. Also, court challenges of any sort are costly, so many questionable contracting-out cases go uncontested. Thus, when a federal employee loses his or her job because of contracting-out rather than through a reduction in force (RIF), the Civil Service Commission—and later the Office of Personnel Management—generally have washed their hands of the affair.

The Civil Service Commission's reluctance to involve itself in contracting-out disputes is ironic in light of the fact that its then-chief counsel, L.M. Pellerzi, issued guidelines in 1967 to be used by agencies to determine the legality of proposed contracting-out efforts. Known as the Pellerzi standards, the guidelines include six elements that, if substantially present, should prohibit contracting-out:

- performance on government site;
- principal tools and equipment furnished by the government;
- services applied directly to an integral effort of agencies or organizational support in furtherance of assigned function or mission;
- comparable services, meeting comparable needs, performed in the same or similar agencies using civil service personnel;

- need for the service to last beyond one year; and
- requirement by virtue of the inherent nature of the service, or the manner in which it is provided, of government direction or supervision of contractor employees in order to protect adequately the government's interest, to retain control of the function involved, or to retain full personal responsibility for the function supported in a duly authorized federal officer or employee.

A 1968 supplement to the Pellerzi standards further noted that "The touchstone of legality under the personnel laws is whether the contract creates what is tantamount to an employer-employee relationship between the government and the employee of the contractor." If these standards were strictly applied, a sizable percentage of the contracting cases discussed in this book would be in violation of them.

For the last 20 years, the General Accounting Office and various congressional committees have periodically examined one or another facet of contracting-out, including violations of the Pellerzi standards. Generally these accounting office and congressional investigations have found much to criticize about federal contracting policy. Typical of the earlier probes were hearings focusing on contracting abuses, which occurred in May 1968 before a House Special Studies Subcommittee. The panel uncovered a number of examples, especially in the defense and space areas, of private contractors performing vital functions of government that clearly should have been performed by civil service employees.

Among the witnesses who pointed out such examples was Comptroler General Elmer B. Staats. Included in the functions being performed by contractor personnel, which he said should be handled by civil servants, were the operation of such major defense systems as the Distant Early Warning (DEW) Line, the Ballistic Missile Early Warning System (BMEWS), both the eastern and western missile test range facilities of the air force, as well as the National Aeronautics and Space Administration tracking and data acquisition network and certain computer operations at the Apollo Mission Control Center. Twelve years later, Staats' General Accounting Office was again reporting that the Pentagon and other agencies were continuing to contract-out basic functions of government that should have been performed in-house. Nothing had changed in the interim—other than an increase in the number of questionable contracts.

During the last twenty years, the General Accounting Office has also issued more than thirty reports critical of contracts for consulting services alone. Variations of the same problems—excessive costs, lack of competition, conflicts of interest, disproportionate numbers of contracts awarded at the end of the fiscal year, unnecessary contracts, loss of agency control, etc.—kept recurring during the two decades. Various reforms have been instituted by the Office of Management and Budget to deal with specific abuses, but still the problems continue.

By early 1982, the budget office was proposing revisions to its regulations that it contended, as it had in the past when it announced other reforms, would reduce contracting abuses. The proposals would expand the definition of government functions to limit further the types of activities that can be contracted out; would require review of all contracts every twelve months to determine whether contracting was still appropriate; would bar most awards of sole-source contracts on unsolicited proposals; and would increase the types of contracts that would be included under existing regulations covering consultants. Certainly, the proposed changes appeared to be an improvement over past regulations; however, they suffer from the same defects as previous rules: the contracting agencies would have responsibility for policing themselves to see that the regulations are enforced, and the rules would not have the force of law. Critics of contracting policies expressed skepticism that the proposed changes would make much of a dent in the abuses.

Senator David Pryor, D-Arkansas, sees the need for tough legislation, rigidly enforced, to end the abuses. Pryor said that the Office of Management and Budget's regulations "are to a large degree meaningless . . . a band-aid approach that doesn't even temporarily slow down the abuses." Unless Congress takes legislative action to end the abuses, Pryor said, "we could well find a General Accounting Office report in the year 2000 saying that the problems found in 1980 still exist, just as the problems of 1960 exist today."

In 1980 Pryor and then-Representative Harris sponsored similar bills aimed at curbing some of the worst consulting, research, and management support services contracting abuses—lack of competition for contracts, conflicts of interest, and the absence of information on contracts in agency budgets. Another measure proposed by Harris would also have required agencies, before contracting for services, to determine whether a job could be done more economically in-house. If the work could be done at less cost in-house, but the agency lacked the personnel to do it, then the agency could have its personnel ceiling increased; if it proved to be cheaper to contract-out an existing function, then the agency's personnel ceiling would be lowered.

Both bills encountered stiff opposition from business and contractors' organizations, as well as from the Office of Management and Budget, but the Harris bill on personnel ceilings came in for the most vitriolic attacks. The United States Chamber of Commerce called the measure "an insidious bill . . . [that] could be devastating to every contractor who relies on the federal government for much or all of his livelihood." A Chamber lawyer contended that, by introducing the bill, Harris was "responding to the appeals of the American Federation of Government Employees, his biggest political ally," which represents thousands of federal workers in Harris's Northern Virginia congressional district. The attorney, Mark Schultze, said that the measure, with its provision for sliding personnel scales instead of fixed levels, provided "an irresistible temptation for agency managers to increase their personnel slots." Harris, who said his bill would cause federal employment to increase in some cases but decline in others, responded that he found it "incredible that those who have preached economy in government now say they don't want to interrupt the gravy train for this group of contractors. They only want economy for someone else."

Contractors critical of the legislation, standing the English language on its head, also labeled the proposed measure "a step toward socialism" and a "death blow to the private enterprise system in America." Somehow, a system in which contractors felt entitled to earn—in the Chamber's words—"much or all of" their livelihoods from the government had become synonymous with "private enterprise." On the other hand, efforts to bring competition and fiscal accountability into the federal contracting system constituted, under the contractors' curious logic, a clear manifestation of "socialism."

The contractors, in letters to their members and even in some unusual testimony before Harris's Subcommittee on Human Resources, stated that their main objective in the 1980 elections was to unseat Harris. In a letter sent to prospective organization members by George Monroe, president of the National Council of Professional Services Firms, on March 21, 1980, the group stated: "For some time, Congressman Herbert Harris of Virginia's Eighth District has been conducting a campaign which ultimately will destroy the professional services industry. The National Council of Professional Services Firms (NCPSF) has been opposing Harris and others like him for over 11 years. Our success will only be limited by our resources. Don't you think it is time to join the battle?"

This blunt admission that the contracting industry's fortunes were intimately tied up with regular contract payments from the government prompted Harris to quiz industry representatives during an August 1980 hearing of the Human Resources Subcommittee. Asked Harris: "Do you feel if you knock off Harris, this sort of investigation will come to an end? Is that the notion?"

Robert Erikson, president of Cerberonics, Inc., a consulting firm member of NCPSF, answered: "Yes, sir, I believe if there is another gentleman occupying that seat for the Eighth Congressional District, that appropriate mechanism which is in place in the government will handle the kinds of abuses that you have brought to attention." Erikson's firm, incidentally, did 95 percent of its total business with the government in the year prior to his testimony.

Dr. George Daoust, chairman of the legislative committee of the contracting industry's umbrella organization, the Committee on Contracting Out, defended the letter that called for Harris's defeat. He stated at the same hearing that he felt it was valid to state, as had the letter, that the Harris bill, if passed, would "ultimately destroy the professional services industry." Daoust said that the proposed legislation, "if it were enacted as currently written, would cause an end to professional services to the U.S. government and a fourfold expansion in civil service within a matter of a year. It is my firm belief and that of many others that your bill would end contracting by the federal government."

Public interest organizations, unattached to either labor or contractor groups, saw the Pryor-Harris legislation as a necessary, even modest, step to correct recurring abuses. Nancy Drabble, of Congress Watch, an organization affiliated with consumer advocate Ralph Nader's Public Citizen, testified that federal agencies too often were "delegating out large chunks of their work to private interests; there are numerous conflict-of-interest problems, and the value of products that consultants submit is very questionable. . . . I think taxpayers do expect that government officials should be the ones who analyze questions of policy and then make the decisions."

Edwin Rothschild, director of Energy Action, another public interest group, testified that the existing contracting system was "subversive of good government and costly to the public." The system also "turns on its head the standards of intellectual craftsmanship and integrity . . . rewards mere regurgitation rather than difficult research . . . assumes most expert knowledge resides outside rather than inside the government . . . abuses civil servants and encourages their cynicism and surrenders public authority to private corporations."

Rothschild made an especially telling point regarding the built-in conflict between business, with its profit motive and obligation to itself and its stockholders, and the government with its obligation to represent and perform services for all citizens. Said Rothschild: "Chief Justice John Marshall recognized long ago that the federal government, which is supposed to operate on behalf of all the people, becomes seriously compromised when private corporations do the govenrment's work. Marshall warned that a corporation should not share in the civil government of the country for precisely this reason. Although he, himself, was a landowner and a merchant, Marshall recognized that there had to be a clear line drawn between the public and the private sectors. He knew all too well that the goals of private corporations diverged from the goals of government. This view is not outdated."

Unfortunately, the business lobbyists and the Office of Management and Budget, rather than the public interest organizations, carried the most clout. The Harris-Pryor legislation never came up for a floor vote, and business and contracting organizations pumped in more than $100,000 to Harris's opponent in the 1980 congressional election. Harris lost to Republican Stan Parris by just 1,094 votes. Several members of Congress and committee staff people interviewed for this book believed that the business support for Parris was the decisive factor in such a close contest. Representative Patricia Schroeder, D-Colorado, said that Harris's defeat had weakened congressional support for any contracting reforms along the lines of the Harris-Pryor legislation. By early 1982, the Harris-Pryor measure had not been reintroduced in the House, and one unhappy House staffer told me, "Everybody is afraid that what happened to Harris will happen to them, if they push it." Pryor said he intended to continue to work for contracting reform, but doubted he could get anywhere with it unless the Reagan administration decided to support some legislation, which in mid-1982 seemed an unlikely event.

For his part, Harris said he had jokingly suggested that he had been Parris's "number one fund raiser" because of his contracting legislation. While he says contractor opposition did help defeat him in 1980, he believes the failure of the legislation was due more to opposition by the Office of Management and Budget than to that of the contractors. The budget office, he said, is basically pro-contracting and sees any legislation as a threat to its authority. And Congress, he said, is usually unwilling to pass any measure to which the budget office strongly objects, as it did to the Harris-Pryor legislation. With the legislative status quo maintained, federal agencies—particularly the Defense Department and the Energy Department—were free to continue to turn over major functions to private contractors.

4 · Pentagon Contracting: The Open Money Sack

Representative G. William Whitehurst, a conservative Republican from Virginia's Second Congressional District and a navy veteran of World War II, recalled the time in the late 1970s when he went to a navy shipyard and had occasion to visit the men's room.

"I never saw anything sloppier," Whitehurst said in an early 1982 interview. "There was water on the floor, no toilet paper or paper towels, dirty basins, a real mess. It was a disgrace, not like the navy I knew. I went to the commander and asked him who is the captain of the head. He told me they didn't have one, that instead the men's room was contracted out and that it was hard to get that type of contract canceled for nonperformance."

To someone such as Whitehurst, who is a member of the House Armed Services Committee, contracts for cleaning military latrines are pretty small change compared to, say, programs for major weapons systems. But, his restroom story makes the larger point that many congressional conservatives and liberals were making by the early 1980s in response to President Reagan's call in 1981 for $1.6 trillion in defense spending over a five-year period: the Pentagon often doesn't get its money's worth in the acquisition of goods and services. Various critics contended also that the Pentagon purchases items and services it doesn't need; that some of its weapons systems are too sophisticated to be understood or used properly by the average military person, or may be obsolete by the time they are actually produced; that its inter-service rivalries result in unnecessary and duplicative weapons systems and military equipment; that its contracting practices give some favored contractors and consultants too great a voice in defense policy matters; and that it is losing in-house expertise and running up costs by contracting increasingly for policy, technical, and managerial services.

No less an authority than David A. Stockman, President Reagan's budget director, had in an unguarded moment in late 1981 characterized defense spending as wracked with "blatant inefficiency, poor deployment of manpower, and contracting idiocy." To Stockman, the Pentagon was a "kind of swamp of $10 to $20 to $30 billion worth of waste that can be ferreted out if you really push hard."

To the contrary, said William A. Long, deputy assistant secretary of Defense for acquisition management, "my overall view is that the Department of Defense has the finest procurement system in the world." Long, an attorney for defense contractors before he assumed his Pentagon post in September 1981, said in spring 1982 interviews that Defense has some 12 million contract actions each year and "the overwhelming majority go very well, without a hitch." Any large institution will have some waste and abuses, he said, but the Pentagon, compared with other large public and private entities, does not have serious problems along those lines. Likewise, Defense Secretary Caspar W. Weinberger said Stockman was dead wrong in his allegation of waste at the Pentagon.

Studies by congressional committees and the General Accounting Office, internal audits by the Pentagon and the military services, investigations by think-tanks and journalists, and interviews with government officials produce stories that are closer to Stockman's observation than to Long's or Weinberger's views of the Pentagon. Defense contracting, according to these other reports, is characterized by a lack of competition, which results in overpriced contracts; by huge cost overruns on weapons systems; by useless and duplicative studies and consulting arrangements; by contractor conflicts of interest, including a "revolving-door" situation in which former Pentagon civilian and military officials go to work for private firms and help win lucrative contracts for their new employers; and by the granting to contractors of too great a voice in the decision-making process on weapons and military planning.

As the biggest contracting agency in the federal government, with awards running well over $100 billion by the early 1980s and likely to be double that by the end of the decade, the Defense Department merits particularly close scrutiny from Congress and others concerned with federal spending and accountability.

In the single area of noncompetitive (often referred to as sole-source) contracts, the Pentagon spends many billions of dollars more than it has to each year. In fiscal year 1981, the Defense Department awarded $105.2 billion worth of prime contracts; only 7.6 percent of the money was awarded competitively. In the previous year, there had been competition on only 7.3 percent of the contract dollars, while in some years during the 1970s the percentage fell even lower. Using the Office of Federal Procurement Policy's late 1981 estimate that there is a potential saving of one of every four procurement dollars converted from noncompetitive to competitive awards, this would mean potential waste on this item alone of more than $16 billion on the Pentagon's prime contracts during fiscal year 1981.

Jacques S. Gansler, a former deputy assistant secretary of Defense, makes the point that even when the Defense Department does use competition for contracts on major weapons programs, it is usually too limited or is the wrong type of competition. The traditional Pentagon policy, he said, is to have competition for the initial weapon system production award, but from then on the firm with that winning bid produces the weapon throughout the life of the program on a sole-source basis.

This "winner-take-all" or "you bet your company" system of bidding is "a principal cause of the inefficiencies, overruns, and other problems that exist in defense programs today," Gansler contended in April 1982. The reason for this, he said, is that "Each firm is required to bid unrealistically low ['buy-in'], since the whole issue is winning. Only large, multibillion-dollar firms can afford to play this game. History has shown that such an 'auction' leads inevitably to future program 'cost growths.' The winner—once he is the only supplier—begins to encourage technical or program changes (usually thousands of these changes occur annually on a large military procurement), thus allowing him to price these changes on a noncompetitive basis and thereby to recover his 'buy-in' losses. It's called the 'get well' program—for obvious reasons."

Gansler recommended that the Defense Department try to create real competition by having more than one firm produce a particular weapon. When such dual or multiple sourcing had been tried in the past on fighting ships, missile systems, and electronics equipment, costs had been reduced by an average of 30 percent "and the reliability of the systems significantly improved." Nevertheless, the Pentagon for the most part plods along with the costlier, more inefficient sole-source production contracts.

As an example, Gansler said that "after an extremely successful dual-source development of the cruise missile, the government awarded sole-source contracts to Boeing to build the air-launched version (for the air force), and to General Dynamics to build the ground-launched version (for the army), and the ship-launched version (for the navy)." This, despite independent studies indicating the potential for hundreds of millions or even billions of dollars of net savings if both firms had been awarded contracts to compete to produce all three varieties of the missile.

The lack of competition on Pentagon contracts extends from the higher-priced production contracts, to R&D, to consulting studies and management support services, to overhaul and maintenance, to procurement of the thousands of items the military services need to function on a day-to-day basis.

For example, in the purchase of such a basic item as meat for troops, the Pentagon has not been getting the best bargain for its money because of a lack of competition in awarding contracts. A 1978 Senate subcommittee study found that from a potential base of 2,500 meatpackers only two or three firms were usually the sole suppliers of beef items, with the result that the Pentagon often paid more than it had to. In 1975 there were 25 firms supplying about 98 percent of the beef products to the Pentagon; by fiscal year 1980, only 13 firms were providing 96 percent of the beef items, which meant that the limited competition had declined even further.

Of 256 Pentagon management support contracts studied by the General Accounting Office in an early 1981 report, 211—or 82 percent—were awarded noncompetitively. These sole-source contracts were valued at $156.7 million, or 89 percent of a total of $175.4 million for all the contracts reviewed. Although Pentagon definitions are a bit slippery, the accounting office considered management support services generally to include contracts for studies and analyses, management of programs and installations, and various consulting services. In defending the lack of competitive awards, Defense officials cited deadline pressures, or the contractor's "unique experience," or "in-depth knowledge of operations." About half of these noncompetitive contracts went to firms that made unsolicited proposals (the companies initiated the proposals, rather than responding to a government request for assistance). And, as a clear illustration of the advantages of the "revolving door," half went to firms having former Pentagon civilians and military personnel on their payrolls. The latter contracts raised questions as to the degree of influence used by former high-level Pentagon officials in securing contracts with the Defense Department, as well as to the extent the former government employees were undertaking functions similar to those they performed while on the federal payroll.

One such sole-source contract, which navy officials later admitted could have been awarded competitively, went to Hughes Aircraft Company for studies and analyses relating to the MK-23 target acquisition system. Navy officials initially justified the award on the ground that Hughes had manufactured the MK-23 and was, therefore, the only company capable of handling the studies and analyses. The contract ballooned from $49,277 to $362,623, and navy officials estimated in 1981 that another $300,000 would be needed to complete the work. The General Accounting Office reported that the navy need not have contracted at all, because it had the in-house capability to perform the work itself.

Another significant example of the lack of competitive awards came in late 1981 when, despite congressional and General Accounting Office criticism, the army said it intended to go ahead and award a sole-source, $22-million contract for construction equipment to the Caterpillar Tractor Company. The items, including bulldozer tractors, scoop loaders, scrapers, road graders, and water distributors, were needed by the XVIII Airborne Corps, which constitutes the army's major rapid deployment force.

The army claimed that only one firm—Caterpillar—could supply the needed products and the contract was, therefore, justified. The General Accounting Office disputed this, saying that Caterpillar could actually provide five of the six items needed, as could John Deere & Company and International Harvester Company. The GAO said there was no need to buy all of the items from one company, and that money could be saved by buying the items individually from various companies. In addition, the congressional watchdog agency said no harm would be done to the rapid deployment force concept by buying the equipment from more than one supplier. Despite the criticism, the army said it was too late to go back and award the contract competitively because the delay would harm the XVIII Corps's mission.

Sole-source contracting, though a major problem in Pentagon spending, is a relatively low-profile item compared with the well-publicized issue of cost overruns on weapons systems. Overruns have been particularly excessive in shipbuilding by private contractors for the navy.

By the late 1970s, major shipbuilding overrun claims by contractors against the navy totaled $2.7 billion. Chief among these were almost $1.1 billion in claims by the Ingalls Shipbuilding Division of Litton Systems, Inc., $843 million in claims by the Electric Boat Division of General Dynamics Corporation, and $742 million in claims by Newport News Shipbuilding and Dry Dock Company, a unit of Tenneco, Inc. These claims were assailed by Admiral Hyman Rickover, then-director of the navy's nuclear propulsion program and long a critic of defense contractors, as being without merit. Rickover asserted that the common practice was for a shipbuilder to "estimate how much he wants and then assign people to make up a claim to yield that amount."

In June 1976 testimony before a subcommittee of Congress's Joint Economic Committee that was examining $1.9 billion in claims by eleven companies on seventy ships, Rickover attacked a Defense Department plan to invoke extraordinary legal powers to settle those claims for between $500 million and $700 million. Rickover warned,

"If contractors believe they can evade their contractual obligations by submitting inflated claims, refusing to honor contracts, complaining to higher authority and the like, then all defense contractors will be encouraged to follow this approach in the future." The plan to settle the claims, advanced in the name of national defense, prompted Senator William Proxmire, D-Wisconsin, to charge collusion between the Pentagon and the shipbuilders "to manufacture a crisis designed to cover up cost overruns and possible false claims that could cost the taxpayers hundreds of million of dollars."

Lending substance to Rickover's and Proxmire's charges was the testimony at the same hearings by William C. Cardwell, a former employee of Newport News Shipbuilding, which had $742 million in claims pending. Cardwell, who had been dismissed from his job in early 1976, testified that he had helped draw up deliberately inaccurate construction schedules for nuclear attack submarines his company was building for the navy. He said the company kept two sets of schedules for the shipbuilding program. One schedule, submitted to the navy, promised that the company would build one submarine in two and a half years, even though the company "knew we couldn't keep up with that pace" because "we didn't have enough skilled labor to do it." The other schedule, kept for internal use only, contained a slower, more realistic plan.

"We knew when we were going to deliver the ship and it wasn't what the master construction schedule that went to the Navy showed," Cardwell said. A company spokesman denied there were two sets of books, but acknowledged that the published construction schedules didn't always reflect the actual building progress. However, he said the navy was always aware of any deviations.

The navy settled the major claims on terms that weren't all too favorable to United States taxpayers. On the Electric Boat claims, the Navy Claims Settlement Board determined that the navy was to blame for $125 million of the overruns, while the contractor was responsible for the other $718 million. Nevertheless, the navy, saying it would be more expensive to drag out the claims disputes in the courts than to settle, sought and won congressional approval to pay Electric Boat $484 million. In the Ingalls case, the navy again went beyond what the Claims Settlement Board had ruled was justified; the board said the navy was responsible for $312 million of the $1.1 billion in overruns, but the navy obtained congressional authority to pay $447 million. Newport News Shipbuilding's $742 million claim was settled by the navy for $189 million.

The shipbuilding cases also produced several federal criminal investigations, one of which resulted in a 1977 indictment of Litton on charges of defrauding the government of $37 million. In 1978 the case was transferred from United States District Court in Alexandria, Virginia, where the indictment had originated, to Mississippi. By the summer of 1982, no trial had been held. Still pending in 1982 was an investigation into Newport News Shipbuilding for its multimillion-dollar claims. Also in early 1982, the Justice Department announced it had dropped its investigation of Electric Boat regarding its overrun claims.

Admiral Rickover, in a letter written to Attorney General William French Smith in January 1982 and made public five months later, charged that the Justice Department was attempting to scuttle the Litton case and the Newport News investigation. The letter, written just before Rickover's retirement, contended that the Newport News probe had been all but dropped by Elsie L. Munsell, who had just assumed office as United States Attorney in Alexandria. Rickover said Munsell had abolished the special unit conducting the investigation and had reassigned to other duties two of the senior fraud prosecutors.

Rickover said that, before Munsell took office, prosecutors had recommended an indictment be returned against Newport News, but that no such action had been forthcoming. "Although the Newport News investigation has not been dropped officially," Rickover wrote Smith, "I can think of no better way to scuttle a complex investigation of this sort than to abolish the unit handling the investigation, split up the investigation team, and impose additional responsibilities upon those familiar with the case." In urging Smith to renew vigorously the Newport News investigation, Rickover termed the shipbuilders' claims as possibly "the most massive raid on the federal treasury in the history of the United States." The admiral further accused the Justice Department of making no effort to bring the Litton case to trial since it was transferred to Mississippi in 1978.

While neither the Litton nor Newport News companies had any

comment on Rickover's charges, Munsell responded that both matters were "open cases to which we are devoting appropriate time and energy. They're not as dead in the water as the admiral might think." A Justice Department official said that the Newport News case "continues to be the subject of investigation and close review" and that in the Litton case the department was committed to devoting to it the necessary resources to move it "expeditiously to a fair and just conclusion." A federal judge dismissed the Litton case in December 1982. The government could appeal.

Contractors' claims against the government provoked Navy Secretary John F. Lehman, Jr., in late 1981 to accuse two of them, Electric Boat Company and McDonnell Douglas Corporation, of attempting to "rip off" the government through the filing of "preposterous" contract claims. In the navy's long-running battle with Electric Boat over shipbuilding claims, Lehman contended that the company was trying through the claims procedure to gain payment for problems "caused by their own faulty performance." Lehman charged that McDonnell Douglas was attempting to get the navy to reimburse it for the cost of an F-18 plane that crashed after a British air show in 1980, even though the plane was on a nonmilitary marketing trip. He said the company was "tempted to construct a case to rip off the navy" for the cost of the plane because a navy passenger was aboard. The company issued a statement saying it was not liable for the loss. Lehman said that the navy, under his direction, would bring countersuits against contractors who try to "take advantage of the inherent disadvantage that the taxpayer suffers in the area of corporate litigation."

Given the history of overruns on major weapons systems, critics of the massive military buildup laid out by President Reagan in 1981 expressed concern that the outlays would unduly enrich contractors and produce sizable cost overruns. The prospective huge defense budgets would also possibly add to mounting federal budget deficits and thereby weaken economic conditions generally, according to the critics. So costly have weapons systems become that, the *New York Times* whimsically speculated, "if present trends continue, sometime fairly early in the next century it could take the entire military budget to purchase one combat aircraft and, not long after that, the entire gross national product."

In this light, the General Accounting Office warned in late 1981 that based on past miscalculations concerning rates of inflation and contractors' production costs, the army could anticipate sharply rising costs in fourteen major new weapons systems. The GAO cited, as an indication of things to come, the experience with the only three of the systems that had already reached the production stage: the Blackhawk helicopter, the Stinger missile, and the M-1 tank. From 1978 to 1981, the Blackhawk's unit production cost more than doubled from $2.8 million to $6.2 million; the Stinger's unit cost had almost doubled, from $36,900 to $70,600, while the M-1's unit cost had gone up more than 80 percent—from $1.4 million to $2.6 million. Similar increases could be anticipated for the other eleven programs—the Fighting Vehicle System, AH-64 advanced attack helicopter, Hellfire missile, Multiple Launch Rocket System, Copperhead artillery projectile, Pershing II ballistic missile, Patriot missile, Roland missile, Division Air Defense Gun, CH-47D Chinook helicopter, and the Standoff Target Acquisition System.

The General Accounting Office was concerned that the escalating costs would prohibit the army from buying the weapons at economical rates, but that in addition to the high production costs there would be substantial operation and support costs to ensure that the weapons would be at a high level of combat readiness over the next ten to twenty years after their production. The anticipated cost escalations again raised the question, the GAO said, of whether the army and other military branches "could financially afford all the programs under development." The ink was hardly dry on that GAO report when, in early 1982, news leaks from the Pentagon disclosed that top Defense officials believed another $750 billion (on top of the $1.6 trillion sought by the Reagan administration) would be needed to carry out a strong defense program over the next five years.

In its original fiscal year 1982–86 spending plan, before the Reagan administration announced its five-year goals, the army was confronted with what is called the procurement "bow wave"—basically, all of the systems it wanted were competing with one another for funds for those years, with the result that original procurement schedules could not be met, and stretched-out schedules had to be devised. The Reagan administration's spending proposals called for an additional $16 billion to put these programs back on their original schedules. The General Accounting Office, however, remained skeptical as to "whether even those increases would be enough to offset the increasing costs of the major weapons systems."

The extent of cost escalations in military programs was further illuminated in an April 1982 General Accounting Office report that showed, as of September 30, 1981, that 147 major defense projects had increased in cost by 82 percent (from $233.7 billion to $424.3 billion) over previous estimates. Major reasons for the increases were underestimations of the rate of inflation; changes in scope, quantity, engineering, and scheduling; inaccurate cost estimates; and funding delays. More than fifty programs were found to have increased in cost by more than 100 percent from their original estimates, and two by more than 1000 percent: the navy's AD-41 destroyer tender, 1057 percent (from $90.6 million to more than $1 billion) and the army's fighting vehicle systems, 1521 percent (from $726.4 million to almost $11.8 billion).

The reason major weapons systems and their contractors are such high-profile items is that on many of these projects the Pentagon is required to submit periodic reports on costs and scheduling to Congress. Consequently, it is cost overruns on these highly visible weapons systems that give Pentagon contracting a bad name, said Deputy Assistant Defense Secretary Long in spring 1982 interviews. While contending that most abuses in Pentagon contracting are the exceptions, rather than being systematic, Long recognized that there were persistent problems with escalating costs and a lack of competition on defense contracts.

Long said the Pentagon was making renewed efforts to correct these abuses by injecting an element of competition into most contracts. On major weapons systems acquisition, he said Defense would attempt to use a dual-source, or contractor-team, concept on some future production contracts with an eye toward saving money through the competitive process. At Long's instigation, the Pentagon in late 1981 also undertook a study to identify those types of contracts that could benefit from increased competition and those that could not.

Long said the Pentagon was also trying to inject more competition into their prime contractors' awarding of subcontracts. Too often, he said, prime contractors go to a single source for goods and services, even though many other sources are available; consequently, they do not always get the best price.

Despite Reagan administration talk of increasing competition in Pentagon contracting, the Defense Department did not look kindly on proposals by Congress for reforms along those lines. For example, a bill proposed in the House in 1982 would have cracked down on noncompetitive, sole-source contracts of more than $100,000 by making the sole-source process more public, and by making it harder for lower-level employees to award noncompetitive contracts. The measure would have required the head of each military department to approve the contract personally and to publish notice of such a contract in the *Commerce Business Daily* thirty days in advance of awarding it. The bill would also have required the secretary of Defense to prepare annual reports on all sole-source contracts of more than $100,000 that were entered into by each military department in the previous fiscal year.

Testifying before a House Armed Services subcommittee in May 1982, Long said the Defense Department "is strongly opposed to this bill, primarily because its provisions would add to the administrative workload, place an onerous burden on the department, and extend the already lengthy procurement lead times for those procurements that would be affected"—and thereby "adversely affect the carrying out of the defense mission." As had representatives of administrations preceding President Reagan, Long was restating the Pentagon policy of keeping Congress out of the contracting process and instead allowing the Defense Department to devise its own procedures for dealing or not dealing with contracting problems.

Asked in 1982 interviews if he could estimate the amount of waste in Defense Department contracts of all types, Long said, "I have difficulty with that concept of waste and abuse." He reemphasized his feeling that the Pentagon has the best procurement system in the world, public or private, and rejected any suggestion that contractors have too great a role in shaping defense programs and policies, or that their profits are too high. "I could give a damn about profits," he said. "If anything, profits are probably too low."

In acknowledging controversies over contract cost overruns, Long said that in the past some of these costs were "out of our control while some were within our control." Sometimes, he said, overruns occurred because the Pentagon had budgeted "too optimistically" or had inadequate estimates. The Reagan administration was attempting to "budget more realistically" by getting cost estimates independent of those provided by contractors and was trying to speed up the contract awarding process so as to minimize long delays, which produce cost escalations. A late-1981 report by the Defense Department Acquisition Improvement Task Force, chaired by Long, recognized the cost issue, cautiously reporting that "Despite some initial steps, controlling cost growth (both real and perceived) remains a major problem."

At the time of the interviews with Long, he had been in office less than eight months, after leaving the Los Angeles-based law firm of Latham & Watkins, which represents defense contractors, including the giant Hughes Aircraft. When interviewed, Long was not fully familiar with many of the problems that had been raised over the years concerning various types of Pentagon contracts. For example, he said he couldn't comment on whether there were continuing serious problems with consulting and management support contracts, which have been the frequent target of congressional and General Accounting Office investigations. He said that after additional study the Defense Department was planning to issue a new directive on management support services contracts. For his part, Defense Secretary Weinberger in July 1981 pledged tighter contracting policies, penalties against contractors for cost overruns and delays, and elimination eventually of contracts that guarantee companies too high a profit.

The basic Reagan administration policy for Pentagon contracting was set out in an April 30, 1981, memorandum to top Defense Department, army, navy, and air force officials from Deputy Defense Secretary Frank C. Carlucci. The memo called for the use of multi-year (instead of year-by-year) contracting on selected projects, more realistic budgeting, and limitations on technological changes in weapons to techniques already known, rather than pursuing more advanced, untested technology. It also established the concept of "controlled decentralization" under which lower-ranking program managers in the various military services would be responsible for carrying out particular weapons programs after the go-ahead has been given by higher authorities. The system, hailed by Defense Secretary Weinberger as a cost-cutting technique, was viewed with skepticism by some experts outside of government who felt it put more authority in the hands of those who have borne a major responsibility for escalating costs on past programs—namely, the military services themselves.

Laurence E. Lynn, Jr., professor of public policy at Harvard University, sharply criticized the Weinberger/Carlucci emphasis on decentralization in the acquisition process. Lynn in late 1981 noted that in the past much of the gold-plating of weapons costs occurred after the defense secretary had given the branch of service the go-ahead on a program; these increases occurred because of a lack of effective management from the top. The way to control costs, he said, "seems to call for more, not less, active management by the Office of the Secretary of Defense." Unlike General Motors, which can have decentralized divisions produce Chevrolets, Pontiacs, and Oldsmobiles, the defense procurement system is affected by military politics among the branches of service "and by members of Congress with military bases and contractors in their districts." The result of further decentralizing such a politics-laden system likely would be "the same expensive, poorly performing products . . . [and] weapons that reflect an unreasoning obsession with maintaining technical superiority over the Soviet Union, that are so complicated that they break down constantly, that are expensive nightmares to maintain, and the designs of which are based on ludicrous assumptions about how soldiers actually behave in combat."

The Pentagon under the Reagan administration was also attempting to ease the regulation of contractors. In early 1981, Carlucci testified before a congressional committee that certain programs designed to achieve socio-economic goals had overburdened defense contractors and thereby added to contract costs. Among the regulations that supposedly hampered the acquisition process, Carlucci specifically mentioned programs designed to guarantee some contracts to small and minority-owned businesses, as well as requirements that contractors comply with fair labor standards, equal employment opportunities, safety in manufacture, and environmental protection. Carlucci's criticism of these programs seemed in line with the Reagan administration's general policy throughout government of attempting to roll back programs that were designed to assist minorities and disadvantaged persons and to protect workers.

Long said the programs criticized by Carlucci, along with hundreds of other contracting regulations, "taken individually may be worthwhile," but their cumulative effect was burdensome on contractors and Pentagon contract administrators, and undoubtedly added to costs and inefficiencies within the defense contracting system.

In his April 30, 1981, memorandum, Carlucci had also emphasized that the relationship between the Pentagon and its contractors should not be adversarial. Rather, he said, industry and government "have a shared responsibility and must assume a new spirit of cooperation." In that spirit, Fred C. Ikle, undersecretary of Defense for Policy, later that summer disclosed new benefits for contractors: the Pentagon planned to spend $500 million annually over the next several years to build up industry's standby capability to move rapidly into wartime production. Ikle said the nation's defense contractors lacked the capability to spring into action quickly, thereby lessening the United States's chances of successfully waging a lengthy, conventional war.

One of Ikle's proposed solutions: financial incentives to contractors to build extra defense production capacity and to recruit additional workers for emergency service on production lines. As shall be seen, Ikle was merely following a Pentagon tradition of bending over backward to keep contractors happy and profitable.

By mid-1982, President Reagan's plan for the five-year, $1.6 trillion defense buildup had escaped largely unscathed through Congress, despite apparent growing public concern expressed in polls that military spending should be cut and that there should be no more reductions in social programs. Key to Reagan's defense buildup proposals were several controversial programs; the B-1 long-range bomber; the MX intercontinental ballistic missile; more powerful and more accurate missiles for the Trident submarine; and the most massive naval expansion in the nation's peacetime history, with a 1983–87 program calling for spending $71.7 billion for naval aircraft and $96.2 billion for shipbuilding, conversion, and recall of some mothballed battleships.

To the critics, the 100 B-1 bombers proposed by Reagan would be obsolete by the time they were produced and, at a cost of at least $260 million apiece, too expensive. Strategic Air Command studies determined that the B-1, or even more advanced versions thereof, could not be expected to penetrate Soviet defenses beyond the 1980s. As former top Defense Department official Robert Komer expressed it, "To push for a B-1 that will be obsolescent before the first production model takes off from the runway seems to me sort of dumb." Some critics said that the emphasis should instead be on developing the Stealth bomber, which they said would be able to fool Soviet radar, by the 1990s.

Likewise, critics of the MX missile have argued that, no matter whether it is based in 4,600 shelters scattered across most of Nevada and Utah (a Carter administration plan shelved by Reagan in 1981), or in hardened, existing silos (as Reagan proposed in 1981), or in a closely spaced "dense pack" system (as Reagan proposed in late 1982), or is flown from place to place, the MX is unnecessary, too costly, and would cause the arms race to escalate further.

The Reagan proposal for 100 MX missiles had a late 1981 price tag of $27 billion, a figure sure to rise rapidly as costs of major weapons systems traditionally have. *New York Times* columnist Tom Wicker argued in late 1981 that the MX was not needed at all because, among other things, the Minuteman III missile improvement program, coupled with development of the submarine-based Trident II missile by the late 1980s, would provide deterrent power and invulnerability superior to that of the MX. More seriously, the Soviet Union was likely to view the MX as "an American first-strike weapon"—which could lead the Soviets to respond with development of an anti-ballistic missile system and/or improvements in their own missile accuracy, thereby increasing the arms race and mutual suspicion and the likelihood that one side or the other would start a nuclear war.

Criticism of the MX has also come from some unexpected sources. Former Central Intelligence Agency Director Stansfield Turner in early 1981 termed the project "a serious mistake." He contended that "great vested and parochial interests in the military and in industry are intent upon going ahead with the project. But the United States cannot let such interests dictate the course of its security, and indeed, the security of the world." Retired Marine Corps Major General W.T.

Fairbourn, former strategic planner with the United States Joint Chiefs of Staff, observed in early 1981 that "To continue the development of a system that is already vulnerable, that cannot be fully deployed for ten years, that cannot accomplish its mission when deployed, that increases the attractiveness of the United States as a target . . . is in the author's judgment strategic lunacy."

On top of the MX, B-1, and other expensive systems, the Reagan administration and the Pentagon were also pushing controversial and costly plans for revitalizing U.S. chemical warfare capabilities and producing neutron warheads and such exotica as weapons for waging wars from outer space. Looking at the Reagan administration's overall defense program plans, Representative Les Aspin, D-Wisconsin, a longtime critic of wasteful Pentagon spending, quipped in early 1982 that the administration, "to paraphrase Will Rogers . . . has never seen a weapons system that it doesn't like. . . . We're just buying things without any relation to the threat."

'Buying things,' of course, is where the contractors come in. While greater defense spending may mean more military security as far as many government officials are concerned, to large and small defense contractors and subcontractors it is an opportunity for contracts for production of weapons, for research and development work, for sales of equipment and parts, for consulting and management support services, for studies and reports, for repairing and maintaining military weapons systems and equipment, for painting, repairing and constructing buildings, and for performing dozens of other blue-collar and white-collar jobs ranging from janitorial to food services. Even the most mundane items can mean big sales for contractors: each year, the Pentagon uses more than $6 million worth of cleaning rags.

The extent of the stakes involved in defense contracting can be seen by looking at the amounts of federal money received by some of the top Pentagon contractors. In fiscal year 1981, eighteen companies each received prime defense contracts totaling more than $1 billion. With the amounts of their contracts shown in billions of dollars, these were: McDonnell Douglas Corporation, $4.4; United Technologies Corporation, $3.8; General Dynamics Corporation, $3.4; General Electric Company, $3.0; Boeing Company, $2.7; Lockheed Corporation, $2.7; Hughes Aircraft Company, $2.6; Raytheon Company,

$1.8; Grumman Corporation, $1.7; Chrysler Corporation, $1.4; Litton Industries, Inc., $1.4; Martin Marietta Corporation, $1.3; Philbro (Philipp Brothers) Corporation, $1.2; Exxon Corporation, $1.2; Tenneco, Inc., $1.2; Rockwell International Corporation, $1.1; Westinghouse Electric Corporation, $1.1; FMC Corporation, $1.1. Sixteen of these were involved in major weapons systems contracts, while two —Philbro and Exxon—were primarily petroleum suppliers. Many of these companies also received sizable contracts from the $5 billion spent annually by the Energy Department for military purposes—i.e., nuclear weapons—and from the $1.5 billion spent annually by the National Aeronautics and Space Administration for military purposes.

The top one hundred contractors obtained two out of every three defense prime contract dollars (for contracts of more than $10,000) in fiscal year 1981, while the top ten took more than 28 percent of all prime contract dollars. The effects of obtaining new contracts can be dramatic for a corporation. For example, in early 1982 Rockwell received air force contracts totaling $2.2 billion for development of the B-1 bomber—an amount double its total from the Pentagon for fiscal year 1981.

In the category of Pentagon contracts for research, development, test, and evaluation, nine firms received more than $200 million in contracts in fiscal year 1981. These nine, which include many of the same companies that received the largest dollar amounts of prime contracts, are: Martin Marietta, $844.3 million; Boeing Company, $646.7; Rockwell, $605.9; Hughes, $546.3; General Electric, $471.2; General Dynamics Corporation, $345.4; TRW, Inc., $270.2; United Technologies, $230.8; and Boeing Aerospace Company, $200.7.

For the defense industry states, the stakes in the Reagan budget proposals were also high. In billions of dollars, the states that received the most from prime defense contracts of more than $10,000 in fiscal year 1981 (and stood to benefit the most from the Reagan proposals) were California, $16.7; Texas, $7.5; New York, $6.5; Massachusetts, $4.6; Connecticut, $4.5; Missouri, $4.4; Virginia, $3.6; Florida, $3.2; Louisiana, $3.0; and Washington State, $2.8. Idaho, with $40.8 million, was the lowest.

Like those states that have come to depend on defense dollars, many contractors have become so interwoven with the Pentagon that their companies would be on the verge of bankruptcy without defense contracts. In the decade of the 1970s, the eight largest defense contractors over-all gained more than 50 percent of their revenues from federal contracts, while hundreds of smaller defense contractors, subcontractors, think-tanks, and consultants earned sizable portions of their revenues—often between 90 and 100 percent—from defense and other government contracts. For example, Lockheed reported in April 1982 that sales to the government made up 82 percent of the company's total sales for the first quarter of 1982. The more modestly sized Evaluation Research Corporation, a technical and management consulting services firm based in Vienna, Virginia, obtained 83 percent of its $3.1 million in sales in 1978, and 92 percent of its $6.2 million in sales in 1979, from contracts and subcontracts with the Departments of Defense, Energy, and Health and Human Services.

This reliance by contractors on the government for their livelihood prompted economist John Kenneth Galbraith to observe in 1969 that major defense contractors are really public firms and should be nationalized. In his proposal, Galbraith suggested that any firm that did more than 75 percent of its business with the Pentagon over a five-year period be reconstituted as a public corporation with all stock in public hands. In support of Galbraith's proposal, Pentagon critic and author Richard F. Kaufman noted that defense contractors "do not possess the most important characteristics of private enterprise, for a very large part of their fixed capital and working capital is owned and supplied by the government; they engage in little or no competition with one another; their success or failure is not dependent upon the success of their operations. . . . On the other hand, the contractors participate in public policymaking; they define the missions and the needs for the armed services, make proposals for new weapons systems for which they help develop and then fill the specifications, and their top officials occupy positions of authority within the Pentagon." To Galbraith, "The defense contractors and the Department of Defense are, in fact, complementary bureaucracies." The contractors have the advantages of state socialism combined "with all the rewards and immunities of private enterprise."

Economist Murray Weidenbaum, before he became chairman of

the Council of Economic Advisers under President Reagan in 1981 until mid-1982, had made much the same point: "The close, continuing relationship between the Department of Defense and its major suppliers is resulting in convergence between the two, which is blurring and reducing much of the distinction between public and private activities in an important branch of the American economy."

These criticisms of defense contractors are variations of President Eisenhower's warning to the nation, in his farewell address at the close of his second term, of the growth of the "unwarranted influence" of the "military-industrial complex." "Only an alert and knowledgeable citizenry," the World War II hero warned, "can compel the proper meshing of the huge industrial and military machinery of defense with our peaceful methods and goals, so that security and liberty may prosper together." Eisenhower warned that the military-contractor alliance makes its influence felt "in every city, every statehouse, every office of the federal government."

British journalist Godfrey Hodgson has observed that various United States presidents and secretaries of defense "have sought to impose their authority" on defense contracting, but "they have rarely succeeded for long." Hodgson, writing in 1980, said it had become respectable to say that the military-industrial complex does not exist. "But it does exist," he said, "so long as hundreds of uniformed Pentagon liaison officers are at work stroking dozens of senators and congressmen who sit on the committees that authorize and appropriate tens of billions for weapons systems, and so long as the contracts to build those systems can make the fortunes of major corporations and mean ruin or prosperity for whole sections of the country."

Hodgson might have added that military contracts can also mean prosperity on the nation's campuses, as well as a further blurring of distinctions between the military and the rest of society. In the turbulent 1960s, many colleges and universities, under fire from anti-war organizations, ministers, alumni, and student and faculty activists, shamefacedly severed the most controversial of their contractual ties for research with the Defense Department. But in the latter part of the quieter decade that followed, military contracting activity on the campuses was on the upswing, increasing by a startling 70 percent between 1979 and 1982. Military contracting was becoming, in the words of Nuke Watch, an anti-nuclear project of The Progressive Foundation, "the fastest-growing and most reliable source of income on the nation's campuses." Military research at Princeton University was so extensive by the early 1980s that 160 staff members, including the president and the provost, held security clearances. University of Michigan researchers were hard at work on an army contract relating to "optics, lasers, electronic detection instruments, and a guidance system for the cruise missile." To the critics, the universities' reliance on military contracts not only threatens their academic freedom and independence to speak out on controversial issues such as defense spending and nuclear weaponry, but also makes them complicitious in the ever-more-dangerous arms race with the Soviet Union.

For the military establishment's contractors and subcontractors, the Reagan administration's defense buildup was a Godsend. For example, Rockwell International, the prime contractor for the B-1 bomber, estimated in late 1981 that the project could earn Rockwell $10 billion to $11 billion in sales. Rockwell also had a major share of the MX missile, being responsible for production of the on-board computer guidance system and stage-four rocket engine for the prototype missile.

Gordon Adams, of the Council on Economic Priorities, a think-tank that has done extensive research on major military contractors, in late 1981 credited Rockwell's lobbying on Capitol Hill and at the Pentagon with keeping alive the concept of the B-1 bomber program after it was killed by President Carter. Defense contractors typically work to resuscitate such major projects through relatively small research, development, testing, or evaluation contracts in the hopes of selling to a future administration something that is "not popular with a current administration." Bastian Hello, a Rockwell executive in charge of the B-1 program, said Rockwell kept the project alive, after the Carter administration decision to kill it, by means of contracts for R&D, and construction of the fourth test model B-1.

In support of their efforts to push a particular project, defense contractors regularly get subcontractors and other influential persons from areas that will benefit from contracts to help them lobby United States House of Representatives and Senate members whose constituents would likely gain from the project. Much of this lobbying has traditionally been charged off to the government as overhead on defense contracts, or written off as tax-deductible business expenses. With the unveiling of the Reagan administration's defense spending proposals, contractor lobbying seemed on the increase.

In late 1981 and early 1982, for example, officials of Hughes Helicopters, Inc., the prime contractor on the army's AH64 attack helicopter, mobilized a high-powered lobbying effort that included representatives of such major subcontractors on the helicopter project as Rockwell International, Litton Industries, General Electric, and Martin Marietta. Among those used by Hughes and the subcontractors to push the program were former Representative Jim Lloyd, D-California; Les Gilbert, a former army colonel; Charles H. Cromwell, a former member of the Senate Armed Services Committee staff, and Charles Botsford, a former air force officer. Heading what he preferred to call an informational, rather than a lobbying, effort was J.S. (Stan) Kimmitt, a former secretary of the U.S. Senate who had become vice president for government affairs at Hughes Helicopters.

Hughes and its subcontractors were concerned that members of Congress, looking for major items to cut from the Pentagon's budget, would target the AH64 because of rapidly escalating cost estimates for the helicopter. By early 1982, the projected cost for the helicopter program had gone from $6 billion for 536 helicopters, to $7 billion for 446 aircraft: a per-unit increase of 40 percent. Kimmitt told one reporter that Hughes and its subcontractors were especially concerned about the congressional committees (the budget, armed services, and appropriations committees) that hold life-and-death or budgetary power over weapons programs.

In budget-cutting situations, it's important for contractors and their lobbyists to be on good terms with committee members. To this end, Kimmitt had a role in arranging a three-day hunting trip to Montana in October 1981 for two members of the House Appropriations Committee. Coincidentally or not, the trip—for Representatives Silvio O. Conte, R-Massachusetts, and Bill Chappell, Jr., D-Florida —came at a time when the committee was about to mark up the Pentagon's money bill, which included the AH64. As Walter Pincus of *The Washington Post* later observed, there were signs at the time the trip was taken that the AH64's costs were escalating so rapidly there was the possibility the committee would delete from the fiscal year 1982 bill the $365 million for construction of the first fourteen production-model helicopters.

Kimmitt said he had not initiated the trip. Rather, he said, he had been "approached by a noncongressional person who said these members wanted to go elk hunting," and that he then got them an invitation to a cabin in Montana. He said he had an appointment to attend a Montana International Trade Commission meeting in the state at the same time, and so was invited to join Conte and Chappell.

Conte had a different version. He said Kimmitt not only had set up the trip, but had arranged for Conte to make a speech in Montana and thereby have the congressman's travel costs paid for by the sponsoring group. The outing, Kimmitt said, "had no connection with lobbying the AH64." Conte and Chappell both said that Kimmitt didn't even mention the helicopter during the visit. At the very least, though, as Pincus wrote, the trip was viewed "by some members of Congress and their staffs who work on defense matters as another sign that a congressional insider could develop access to members whose vote might be needed during committee deliberations."

In addition to the direct lobbying, political action committees formed by Hughes Helicopters and various subcontractors made many contributions to key members of Congress in 1981 and early 1982. For example, the Hughes Helicopters committee made contributions to five of the seven Democratic members of the House defense appropriations subcommittee during that period. Political action committees for Hughes and its subcontractors kicked in amounts ranging from $250 to $3,000 apiece for a fundraiser for Chappell alone for the 1982 campaign.

Despite the contractor's and subcontractors' courting of key members of Congress, the helicopter program came under attack in congressional hearings in early 1982, with Senator Barry Goldwater, R-Arizona, a traditional strong supporter of increased military spending, leading the criticism. Goldwater, chairman of the Tactical Warfare Subcommittee of the Senate Armed Services Committee, pointedly observed that, if the $1.2 billion already spent for research and development on the project were included, then the per-unit construction cost increase for the helicopter would be "an incredible 45 percent."

Goldwater's criticism prompted Army Undersecretary James R. Ambrose to state that the army would delay signing a production agreement with Hughes until some determination could be made "over the reasonableness of substantial portions of its proposed costs." Ambrose said it seemed to be "an institutional phenomenon" that major weapons programs "start with gross underestimates by both government and contractor," increase slightly in estimated costs during the early development period, "and then experience sharp increases toward the end of development and in the early production phases." The committee later cut $700 million from the $965 million the army was seeking for the helicopter for fiscal year 1983.

Boeing, in May 1982, also showed just how effective a contractor's congressional lobbying campaign can be. Skillfully using Washington State senators, Boeing subcontractors, bankers, and other influential parties in its lobbying effort, Boeing won Senate passage of an amendment to a military authorization bill to allow the Pentagon to buy fifty-five new and used Boeing 747 civilian jumbo jets and convert them to military cargo planes. The 747s would replace Lockheed's C-5, which had been plagued by design flaws and substantial cost overruns.

The Defense Department wasn't interested in the 747s, primarily because large items such as tanks and helicopters couldn't fit through its narrow doors. Boeing, in its Capitol Hill lobbying effort, countered that the Pentagon's existing supply of C-5s could handle the large cargo, thus allowing the use of the cheaper-to-fly 747s for smaller cargo—and at a substantial savings. Despite Pentagon opposition, the influential Democratic Senator Henry M. Jackson, one of the Senate's leading defense specialists and referred to by some as "the senator from Boeing" because of his support for that company's activities in his home state of Washington, argued that a $6 billion saving far outweighed "the convenience of airplanes with big doors."

Lockheed, for its part, countered with a massive public relations and private lobbying effort after the Senate passed the amendment favoring Boeing. The public effort included expensive, full-page newspaper advertisements touting the C-5 as the one aircraft "military experts" said could fill United States defense needs for outsized cargo capacity. Boeing responded with an advertising campaign emphasizing that the use of its 747s "can save taxpayers as much as $7.9 billion . . . guaranteed."

In its effort, Lockheed joined forces with the Defense Department for a full-scale lobbying program to try to persuade the House of Representatives to authorize spending $5.35 billion to buy fifty of the C-5s. Morton Mintz, of *The Washington Post,* reported in late June 1982 that a detailed computer printout originating with Lockheed showed that the company and the Pentagon "mapped out an elaborate plan to try to enlist at least 40 of Lockheed's subcontractors as well as various government officials—from high-ranking military officers to the president"—to contact more than 260 House members to try to win their support for the C-5 purchase. (Lockheed subsequently prevailed in the House vote in late July 1982, creating a standoff and leaving the issue to be resolved later by a conference committee of both houses.)

The Pentagon acknowledged its joint undertaking with Lockheed and said that the lobbying effort was being directed by Major General Guy L. Hecker, air force director of legislative liaison. Instead of being embarrassed at being caught in such a questionable enterprise, Air Force Lieutenant General Kelly H. Burke, who was responsible for the C-5 program, said, "I do not want to sound platitudinous, but all you're seeing is democracy in action. This is the way the system is supposed to work." And, Burke noted, "You're just wrong if you think this is a highly unusual happening. Anytime you get competing views, it's customary for government to work with those contractors whose views are congruent with the president's."

Disclosure of the Pentagon's role in the lobbying campaign prompted several members of Congress to call for a General Accounting Office investigation of the matter. In an October, 1982, report, the GAO said that Defense Department and air force officials had violated criminal and civil laws in connection with the lobbying campaign. The GAO asked the Justice Department to consider possible prosecution under a law barring government officials from spending public funds to assist outside lobbying of Congress. A Pentagon spokesman again denied that any government officials had done anything wrong in the matter.

After Senate passage of the amendment favorable to Boeing and while a House vote was pending, one Boeing aide, who asked not to be identified, told a reporter, "This isn't the first time we've ever told the Pentagon that we know better than they what they want." One need not argue the relative merits of either the C-5 or the 747 to see the Boeing and Lockheed lobbying campaigns as examples of corporations' economic interests overriding proper military planning. As Paul Taylor wrote in *The Washington Post* in regard to Boeing's lobbying, "Not least among its considerations is that Boeing's profits are tumbling, its civilian customers are recession-struck and there are plenty of 747s parked in hangars around the world, keeping Boeing from making new sales of 757s and 767s." Likewise, Lockheed was not going to stand idly by and watch more than $5 billion in potential sales to the Pentagon go down the drain.

Besides the 747 sales effort, Boeing also had a major interest in the B-1 program, which it anticipated in 1981 would provide the company with $2.2 billion in contract sales and create some 2,500 new jobs in Seattle, Washington, and Wichita, Kansas. For the B-1, Boeing would manufacture the devices that instruct the craft on how to get through enemy defenses and to launch its missiles; it also hoped to get the contract to build the hardened silos for the MX program, if the government decided to go with that option.

Other corporations anticipating lucrative contracts from the B-1 and MX programs were Lockheed, Martin Marietta, General Electric, Northrop, and TRW, among others. Billions of dollars and tens of thousands of jobs are at stake in these major programs, so it is no wonder that the major contractors and more than 100,000 subcontractors and their trade associations might feel strongly about pushing projects from which their firms might get a piece of the action. These more than 100,000 companies, large and small, located throughout the country, constitute a lobbying force that is hard for many members of Congress to resist. Not only is it politically risky to oppose a project that could mean jobs for your state or district, but such opposition would likely cut off the member of Congress from much-needed campaign funds from contractor political action committees.

Between 1976 and 1980, for example, political action committees set up by the eight leading defense contractors alone contributed more than $1.26 million to federal election campaigns throughout the country, with Grumman Corporation being the highest with almost $340,000.

Sometimes, contributions from persons or organizations with financial interests in Pentagon contracts can cause problems for politicians. Illustrative of this were published accounts in early 1982 alleging that many contributions to the 1978 campaign of Representative Frederick W. Richmond, D-New York, may have been improper because they may have come from persons involved in navy ship repair contracts and subcontracts. The *New York Times* reported that one of the contractor contributors credited Richmond with helping him obtain navy contracts exceeding $310 million since 1976. In Richmond's 1978 and 1980 campaigns, the contractor, his family, company executives, and subcontracting company officials were listed as contributing about $50,000. The contractor said he had obtained contributions for Richmond from subcontractors because "they got something out of it."

Later, the contractor amended this statement to say he had approached the subcontractors on a "personal" basis and as "friends," rather than in their business capacities. Campaign contributions by individuals are, of course, legal, but the law bars contributions to federal campaigns that come from corporate funds and prohibits contributions from anyone who does business with the government.

At the time of the disclosures, Richmond was under investigation by federal authorities on a number of matters, including navy contracting. He was subsequently indicted on several charges and pleaded guilty in August, 1982, to tax evasion and marijuana possession charges, as well as to a charge that he made an illegal $7,240 payoff to a navy employee in connection with getting government contracts for the former Brooklyn Navy Yard.

In addition to the lobbying and campaign contributions that create a more favorable climate for major military projects in Congress, defense contractors also exert leverage at the Pentagon through their memberships on various defense-related advisory committees influencing defense planning and policy issues. Thus, at an early stage, corporate members of those bodies can push for particular weapons systems that may be to their advantage later on and can learn what programs the government is planning to move ahead on.

The Defense Science Board, for example, is concerned with "policy matters in the area of long-range planning" and advises the secretary of Defense and deputy director for research and engineering on the scope and substance of the research, development, engineering, testing, and evaluation efforts that the Defense Department should undertake. By 1980, there were almost eight hundred members on various defense advisory panels: some from government agencies, some from research institutions, and others from contractors' companies.

Among contractors, Boeing had the most members on the advisory panels with 16 on 23 committees. Lockheed was next with 15 company officials on 20 panels. As Gordon Adams, of the Council on Economic Priorities, wrote, membership on these key committees provides contractors "with access to decisions about new weapons at the earliest possible stage, well before Congress or the general public are aware of them."

Ultimately, in the contractors' use of lobbying, campaign contributions, and inside influence, contracts and profits are the name of the game. The proposed increases in defense spending under the Reagan administration should, in the words of the *New York Times* in late 1981, "provide a torrent of profits for thousands of military contractors and subcontractors over the next six years." *Forbes,* in early 1982, ballyhooed "the coming defense boom."

Noting this anticipated situation, Donald J. Horan, director of the General Accounting Office's procurement, logistics, and readiness division, testified before a congressional subcommittee in June 1981 in support of legislation to limit profits on defense contracts. Horan noted that, in constant dollars, "budget projections for defense expenditures are about three times larger than during the Vietnam War buildup" and that defense sales for some contractors could be expected to double over the next two years. In such a climate, some profit-limiting measure was needed.

Until 1979 there had been in place a mechanism—the Renegotiation Board—for recovering at least some excessive defense contract profits. Then, bowing to defense contractor lobbyists, Congress refused to extend the board's life, cut off its funding, and caused it to go out of existence. The board could trace its origins to the Renegotiation Act of 1942, which authorized the government to renegotiate the price of any contract on which there were excessive profits. Despite many limitations in the act, the government did manage to recapture $11 billion in excess profits during World War II. The act was terminated in 1945.

A weaker version of the act was passed in 1948, and then, in 1951, a new law modeled on the World War II act went into effect. The 1951 law set up the Renegotiation Board as an independent civilian agency, but a number of amendments to the act in subsequent years substantially weakened the board's authority. Such amendments exempted many types of contracts from the act and exempted contractors who did less than $1 million in defense work during a given year. Also, the board's congressional opponents worked to reduce its budget so that it had to cut from a high of 742 employees in 1953 to about 200 by 1969. Nonetheless, the board was still potent enough to recapture $750 million in excess profits on contracts during the Korean War. Until its demise, the board regularly won back up to $33 million a year in excess profits.

Even after making the refunds to the government, many defense contractors came away with higher profits than they could have obtained in business with nongovernmental customers. A study released by the General Accounting Office in late 1975 showed that 94 percent of 245 contractors reviewed by the agency still had profit rates above the industry average even after making Renegotiation Board-ordered refunds of excessive profits. After the refunds, profit rates in almost one-half the contracts were still more than double the industry profit averages.

Because computing profits is a tricky business and can be done in various ways, some other studies are ambiguous on the question of whether contractors do better on Pentagon contracts than on nongovernment business. For instance, the General Accounting Office's Horan pointed to a 1976 Defense Department study containing ammunition for both supporters and critics of the level of defense contractors' profits. The study showed that profits on Pentagon contracts, measured as a percentage of sales, were lower than those generated in nongovernment operations; it also showed that when measured on the basis of return on investment, defense contract rates of profit were higher than for comparable nongovernment work by a margin of 13.5 percent to 10.7 percent.

Some critics contend that certain aspects of defense contracting make the contracts more profitable than is usually shown on paper. Admiral Rickover has argued that some companies make profits up to five times higher than they actually report because of accounting techniques and lax Pentagon contract management, allowing contractors to charge excessively high overhead amounts, which, unlike profits, are not taxable. Said Rickover, "It seems clear to me that contractors have a far greater incentive to increase these tax-free overhead costs than they have to cut costs and pay taxes on the profits."

Several Defense Department sources agreed that overhead costs allowed under defense contracts constitute a form of hidden profits. One contracting official noted that it was policy in his agency to approve overhead costs exceeding labor costs by a ratio of between 2.1 and 2.6 to 1. Thus, if labor costs on a contract were $100,000, then acceptable overhead costs could be as high as $210,000 to $260,000. When asked if that amount of overhead weren't excessively high, the official responded that it was in line with private businesses' cost of carrying out a contract. He said that in the early 1970s the permissible ratio had been 1.8 to 1, but that this had been raised primarily because of inflation. (Of course, inflation also affected labor costs, so the ratio should have remained somewhat constant.) Other accountants in private businesses and in government commented that the 2.1/2.6 to 1 ratio was excessive, even for a manufacturing enterprise, and was out of line for businesses that provide contract services—such as consulting or guard and food services.

Such generous overhead provisions have naturally produced a number of questionable items that have been charged to the Pentagon on contracts. Some of these items have included Aerojet/General charging the government $101,000 for the cost of leasing Disneyland for one day to entertain its Los Angeles employees; a Martin Marietta plant billing the Pentagon $1,800 for the cost of flying crabs from Baltimore to a Colorado plant for a party for some supervisory personnel; Hughes Aircraft billing the Defense Department $53,000 for a series of Christmas parties, farewell and retirement dinners, dances, and the like. As noted in an earlier chapter, there have been other examples in recent years of some Pentagon consultants charging to their government contracts the costs of such things as schooling for their children, membership in an athletic club, and building a private swimming pool at a company official's house. Contract mischarges are also common.

In this regard, Rockwell International was reportedly under investigation by a federal grand jury in mid-1981 on allegations, made by present and former Rockwell employees, that it had charged work done on an air force fixed-price satellite contract to its prime contract for the space shuttle. The space shuttle contract, with the National Aeronautics and Space Administration, provided for reimbursement for all costs plus a guaranteed profit, while the air force contract (for Navstar, a navigational satellite system) provided that the original bid would cover both costs and profit.

In early 1981, a Rockwell spokesman, Earl Blount, acknowledged that some work at one Rockwell facility had been mischarged, but that it had not been done with top management's knowledge. He said several employees had been disciplined and then returned to their jobs. Blount said an internal investigation disclosed there was $60,000 worth of work mischarged, while NASA investigators contended the mischarges ran to many millions of dollars.

Also under investigation were allegations that Rockwell officials awarded space shuttle subcontracts to firms in which they held financial interests; that decorating work at the businesses or homes of Rockwell executives was billed to the shuttle contract; and that excessive travel vouchers were charged to the same contract.

The criminal investigation of Rockwell was hampered by prosecutorial delays and inadequate company records and was finally dropped in favor of a civil suit. In November 1982 Rockwell, represented by Gibson, Dunn & Crutcher, the old law firm of Attorney General William French Smith, agreed to pay the government $500,000 in compensatory damages. Rockwell also agreed to spend another $1 million to devise a computerized timekeeping system that supposedly would prevent mischarges on future contracts. Ray Sena, one of the former employees who had made the mischarging allegations against Rockwell, charged that the government's handling of the case was a whitewash. Ironically, under its contract provisions, Rockwell was entitled to charge all of its legal expenses in the case as overhead on its space shuttle contract.

In addition to items such as questionable overhead charges, many Pentagon production contractors get other perfectly legal advantages that their counterparts doing nongovernment work lack—and such advantages can add to their hidden profits. These include the use of government-owned plants and government-provided equipment and materials. The extent of these subsidies is unknown because the government over the years has failed to keep accurate accounting of them. One economist, Robert J. Gordon, has estimated that the government had provided some $45 billion worth of plant and equipment for contractors' use between just 1940 and 1965. In late 1981, the President's Council on Integrity and Efficiency reported there was an estimated $52 billion worth of government materials in contractors' hands—a figure some congressional aides feel may be substantially understated.

Defense contracting critic Richard Kaufman has noted the advantages that Pentagon contractors enjoy. "Many defense contracts," he wrote, "are performed mostly with government-owned property in government-owned plants on government land with government machinery, tools, test equipment, and office furniture. Thus to a large extent the big contractors are able to operate on government fixed capital rather than risk their own."

Even when contractors pay minimal rents for the use of government property, these "can be charged back to the government as part of the costs of the contract and the contractor is reimbursed for the amounts paid." In addition, some contractors have also benefited by using the government property for their commercial, nongovernment ventures. Sometimes they have charged plant rehabilitation as overhead on defense contracts and then used the plant for private, nondefense work later on. For example, Chrysler Corporation, until 1981 a producer of army tanks, received reimbursement for overhead for rehabilitating an automobile plant. Although the government footed the bill for this work, Chrysler later used the plant for commercial purposes.

Because the government lacks specific data on the amount of materials it has provided to contractors, the potential for abuse of those materials is great. The General Accounting Office found in late 1980 that neither the air force nor the navy had any requirements for keeping accounting data on any materials they furnished under contracts. While the army had some accounting requirements for materials it supplied to contractors, the data it kept were found to be inaccurate and incomplete.

This lack of oversight produced such situations as a late 1980 discovery that four defense production contractors had in their possession $1.3 million more in government-furnished materials than they were authorized under their contracts. At about the same time, thirteen communications shelters worth $76,000 were found to have been stored at a contractor's plant for four years without the army knowing it. The shelters were in excess of the contractor's allotment under the contract, and army officials determined later that various army activities could have used the shelters during the period the contractor was holding them.

In another case, a $65,000 computer, which could have been used by the navy, was shipped to a navy contractor and then sat unused at the contractor's plant for three years. The computer was in excess of government-furnished materials called for in the contract. Likewise, the air force shipped eight items essential to telecommunications, and valued at $120,000, to a contractor—even though the items were not provided for in the contract and were not wanted or needed by the contractor. In another case, a former contractor on an air force overhaul and repair contract reported shipping $5,609,960 of government material to the new contractor; however, the new contractor reported receiving only $3,766,690 of material. The air force, of course, lacked any records to verify either amount, or any way to reconcile the $1,843,270 difference.

In the same vein, House of Representatives hearings on defense appropriations in 1979 and 1980 turned up information that contractors were authorized to order spare parts and other products directly from the Department of Defense supply system, no questions asked, just as would any military unit. Members of Congress were chagrined by the potential for abuse this afforded.

Periodically, allegations turn up that contractors have used materials furnished by the government for their nongovernment work, but then charged the government for the materials. For example, in 1976 the General Accounting Office contended that Pratt & Whitney Aircraft Division of United Technologies Corporation had improperly charged materials costs to the government. The agency alleged that up to $123,800 of material, partially paid for by Pentagon research and development funds, was used on Pratt & Whitney's commercial efforts. Pratt & Whitney officials countered that there was nothing improper in its use of the materials.

Again in 1977, the General Accounting Office reported that both Pratt & Whitney and General Electric Aircraft Engine Group, which between them accounted for about 80 percent of the annual military engine sales, had charged some production costs of commercial aircraft engines to their government R&D contracts. Both contractors denied they had done anything improper.

Despite the hundreds of allegations over the years by the General Accounting Office, and congressional and Pentagon investigators, of overcharges on defense contracts, criminal charges result in a very small percentage of such cases. (Government-wide, the General Accounting Office found that only 11.7 percent of the cases of suspected fraud are criminally prosecuted. Of those cases actually prosecuted, the government was successful 95 percent of the time. In some cases, the Pentagon has even awarded contracts to firms that had been indicted and had been barred by other agencies from holding contracts.) Even rarer are those instances in which, after criminality is proved, the government recovers large sums of money that were fraudulently obtained by contractors.

So, it was somewhat newsworthy when the government announced in 1978 that it had recovered $600,000 from an army contractor who had been convicted of submitting fraudulent bills on a contract for generator work at Fort Belvoir, Virginia. The company, General

Environments Corporation, of Springfield, Virginia, had been indicted on two counts of filing the false claims. The company was convicted and fined $20,000.

After the conviction, the government filed suit under the False Claims Act to try to recapture the money the contractor had obtained by fraud. In January 1978, General Environments and its parent firm, Howell Corporation, of Houston, agreed to settle the case and pay $600,000 to the government.

Assistant U.S. Attorney Theodore Greenberg, of Alexandria, Virginia, said that often when a firm is convicted of fraud on government contracts it is at or near bankruptcy. The government, therefore, is unable to recover money it feels is owed it because of the fraud, and the criminal conviction is usually the final step in such contract matters. The fact that money was actually recovered from a convicted contractor, Greenberg said, made the General Environments case particularly significant. Also, from the standpoint of the taxpayer who ultimately bears the cost when money is defrauded from the government and is not recovered, the case was especially good news.

In recent years, there have been numerous other cases of contract criminality. In one case, nine former employees of Grumman Aerospace Corporation and seven of its subcontractors on government work pleaded guilty to an elaborate kickback scheme involving millions of dollars worth of navy subcontracts. Federal prosecutors in Brooklyn said officials of firms that subcontracted with Grumman for some $15 million worth of work paid the Grumman employees between $400,000 and $500,000 in kickbacks. The subcontractors produced maintenance manuals, instruction books, and other technical printed materials for use with aircraft that Grumman developed under contracts with the navy. Prosecutors said the kickbacks in these and other cases they had investigated averaged 5 to 10 percent of the face value of a contract. The kickbacks were disguised as overhead items in the subcontracts, which again meant that the kickback funds ultimately came out of the public's pockets.

Another case of Pentagon contract corruption involved a navy officer who pleaded guilty to accepting a bribe in connection with the installation of a $250,000 computer on the aircraft carrier Kitty Hawk. He was sentenced to five years' probation and fined $5,600 in early 1978 by a federal judge in San Diego. A former president of a computer company pleaded guilty to giving the bribe.

Another instance of corruption came to light when three subcontractors admitted paying an estimated $125,000 in kickbacks between 1962 and 1975 to a Raytheon Company buyer in order to obtain or retain subcontracts on the Pentagon contracts. In February 1976, the Raytheon official pleaded guilty to one of the four kickback counts against him and went to prison for three months, with two more years on probation. The three subcontractors, in return for their testimony, were not prosecuted. Government investigators determined that the kickbacks were always made in cash and amounted to 2½ to 5 percent of the labor cost portions of the subcontracts. The subcontractors hid the payments in their accounting records by writing checks for cash or for additional salary payments and bonuses to officers.

Usually, contract bribery is not as clearcut. As syndicated columnist Jack Anderson has observed, "The way to many a defense contract has been greased by a mixture of booze, blondes, and barbecues." Noting past disclosures of possible conflicts of interest involving Pentagon and contractor officials, Anderson wrote: "The brass hats and the industrialists shoot together in duck blinds. They ski together on the Colorado slopes. They drink together and play poker together. And invariably, the tab is picked up by some smiling corporate executive."

Disclosures in 1975 and 1976 showed that Pentagon officials were, in fact, entertained by defense contractors—and at taxpayers' expense. The taxpayer has also had to foot the bill for defense contractors' expenses for lobbying and for salaries for high-powered, often big-name "consultants" who know the right political people to see in order to obtain or retain contracts, or to win overrun claims.

Typical of this taxpayer subsidization of contractor lobbying was an air force decision in mid-1976 to reimburse Northrop for $3,-982,000 of the more than $5.5 million in fees the giant corporation had paid fifty-three consultants on its Pentagon contracts from 1962 to 1974. In 1975, the Defense Contract Audit Agency had challenged all $5.5 million of the fees Northrop was trying to charge off to the Pentagon as overhead expenses on its contracts.

Reimbursements allowed by the air force included $155,000 of

$100,000 Northrop requested to pay Anna Chennault, a supporter and close friend of former President Nixon and widow of Lieutenant General Claire Chennault, who attained prominence in World War II with his Flying Tigers. Ms. Chennault was paid for her efforts, including parties, that helped to sell Northrop's F-5 fighter plane overseas. The air force also approved $496,000 of $512,000 sought by Northrop to pay Kermit Roosevelt, a former Central Intelligence Agency official and grandson of President Theodore Roosevelt. Roosevelt had been in Iran in the early 1950s to help set up the coup d'état that brought the shah to power. In addition, approval was granted for fees paid to two retired air force generals—Bernard A. Schriever, former chief of the Air Force Systems Command, and Winston P. Wilson, former head of the National Guard Bureau—and retired Air Force Colonel S.L. Towle. The air force approved $24,000 of the $115,000 paid to Wilson, the entire $36,000 paid to Schriever, and $69,000 of the $145,000 paid to Towle.

Northrop also asked for partial reimbursement for $564,000 in fees it paid to a Washington attorney. The lawyer and many of the other prominent persons Northrop hired as consultants, were selected not for their expertise in aircraft, but rather for their ability to exert influence, according to Northrop's critics. Then-Senator Frank Church, D-Idaho, chairman of the Senate Subcommittee on Multinational Corporations, remarked at the time that the attorney's importance to Northrop was that he "knew the right people, and that is really what the Northrop case is all about."

In a particular display of boldness, Northrop had also asked for repayment for $190,000 it paid to a man accused by federal investigators of laundering money used by Northrop to make illegal contributions to President Nixon's 1972 reelection campaign. According to a Securities and Exchange Commission complaint, the man posed as a French consultant but was actually a conduit for money sent by Northrop to France. The man would pass the laundered money to a Northrop vice president, who would "then expend it for political contributions and related expenses, a substantial portion of which was unlawful," the SEC alleged. The air force disallowed the entire claim. (Incidentally, Northrop and its president and chairman, Thomas V. Jones, pleaded guilty to charges of making $150,000 in contributions to the Nixon campaign, in violation of a federal law prohibiting contributions by federal contractors.)

Northrop was not alone in its taxpayer-supported spending to win contracts or to make overseas sales of its products. In a followup to published disclosures of vacations and weekend trips provided by contractors to Defense Department officials, the Congressional Joint Committee on Defense Production conducted a survey of the entertainment practices of forty-one of the nation's top defense contractors. In a 1977 report, the committee found widespread abuses of existing regulations pertaining to the acceptance of gifts and favors by Pentagon officials from contractors.

The committee reported that at least 30 of the 41 companies surveyed had made tickets to cultural and sporting events available to Pentagon officials; that 30 of the companies had sponsored almost 1,200 hospitality suites at trade and professional association conventions over a three-year period; that at least 35 acknowledged buying meals for government employees; that at least 16 sponsored sporting activities in which government officials engaged, ranging from golfing matches to extended out-of-town trips to fishing and hunting resorts. On the out-of-town trips, the contractors' "payments in some cases involved transportation, hunting licenses, ammunition, meals and lodging, hunting and guide fees and game preparation"—benefits that could amount to several hundred dollars for the individual government employee who was entertained.

In many instances, the committee said, it could not be determined whether the acceptance of various gifts or gratuities constituted violations of conflict-of-interest and ethical codes for federal employees. The panel nevertheless "found the provision of prohibited gratuities and favors to be common throughout industry and the acceptance of these prohibited benefits a common occurrence throughout the ranks of federal employees," including military officers. Many of those receiving gratuities were found to be in positions to influence the awarding of contracts or the payment of contract cost overruns.

After the acceptance of gifts and gratuities by Pentagon officials had become a matter of controversy, the report said, the Defense Department took steps to tighten up its ethics regulations. However, the committee was skeptical whether this action would stop such practices over the long run. It pointed out that "Congressional inquiries in 1959 and 1967 also led to an abatement, which nevertheless proved temporary through lack of consistent interest in preventing conflict-of-interest situations on the part of the Department of Defense."

The giving of gifts and gratuities seemed also to violate provisions of federal law that permit the government to cancel a defense contract if the contractor or his agent "offered or gave any gratuity, such as entertainment or a gift, to an officer, official or employee of the United States to obtain a contract or favorable treatment in the awarding, amending or making of determinations concerning the performance of a contract. . . ."

A federal contracting official may sincerely believe his acceptance of a meal or a weekend trip to a hunting lodge does nothing to undercut his objectivity when it comes to awarding or amending contracts, or approving cost escalations, or renewing the contract. But it is, of course, human nature to favor the person with whom you are familiar, or with whom you regularly have lunch or socialize. The essence of the skilled lobbyist is to build up these contacts. Even if the person with whom the lobbyist makes these contacts does not always perform the way the lobbyist wants, in the long run these relatively inexpensive gifts and gratuities can reap benefits for the lobbyist's clients.

Even if no harm were truly done to the contracting process through the contractors' lobbying and entertainment practices, it should be noted that the costs of these activities have been regularly passed on to the taxpaying public. A 1981 study by the public interest group, Common Cause, showed the Defense Contract Audit Agency had found that in 1974 and 1975 ten contractors' offices in Washington, D.C., were reimbursed more than $2 million by the government for lobbying, entertainment, and advertising expenses. The reimbursements included, among others, the following: $42,976 to Hughes Aircraft for a Washington, D.C., condominium; $7,350 to the General Dynamics Corporation for tie tacks and models of the F-111 and F-16 fighter planes; $8,516 to Raytheon for lodging and guides for goose-hunting trips in Maryland; $181,861 to Martin Marietta for developing "support" from members of Congress from thirty-five states in which the company has divisions; $12,032 to Lockheed for first-class air fares and travel expenses of company executives and their spouses who attended air shows in France and England; and $17,185 to Rockwell for one hundred prints of a film advocating the B-1 bomber.

Senator David Pryor, D-Arkansas, a leading critic of the contractors' practice of charging off questionable overhead items to the government, noted that even unsuccessful bidders on contracts are reimbursed for their lobbying expenses, thus inflating the costs of contracts even further. Noting that the government keeps no accurate records of how much contractors have been reimbursed for lobbying in recent years, Pryor said that by 1982 the figure for the Defense Department alone has to be far above the 1975 figure of $2 million-plus, because the number of contractors' offices in the Nation's Capital had increased from about one hundred to five hundred since 1972.

The issue of companies being reimbursed for lobbying expenses became a hot topic in late 1981 when Defense Secretary Weinberger, responding to criticisms from public interest groups and Senator Pryor, issued a new directive, which he contended would insure that Pentagon contractors do not get reimbursed for lobbying for their pet projects. While the directive appeared to rule out reimbursement for lobbying, it also contained a loophole permitting reimbursement if the lobbying were performed "after receipt of an invitation or request from a Congressional or Executive Branch source."

"In other words," commented Gordon Adams, of the Council on Economic Priorities, "if a contractor succeeds in getting the Defense Department to ask him to lobby a member of Congress or the congressional staff, expenditures for such an effort become allowable." With the Pentagon standing firm on its directive, Pryor introduced legislation, which was pending in 1982, to bar any reimbursement for lobbying activities. Calling the Pentagon-contractor lobbying relationship "tawdry affairs of military-industrial incest," Prior said it was unfair for taxpayers to be reimbursing contractors for lobbying expenses, especially at a time when cuts were being made in social programs and citizens were being asked to endure the recessionary and unemployment pressures of the early 1980s.

In addition to lobbying and entertainment costs, other "overhead" items passed on to the government and ultimately to the taxpayers are the costs contractors incur for paying high-priced lawyers to fight their claims for cost overrun payments on federal defense contracts. As James J. Cramer, reporter for *The American Lawyer* magazine and an authority on law firms specializing in federal contracts, put it, "In the last decade, lawyers have become as crucial to the United States defense contractor as a well-connected lobbyist."

The law firms specializing in defense contracting are so successful at winning cost overrun claims that, in Cramer's words, it is "the rare contractor who fears coming in over the bid price and risking a loss." Many of these lawyers previously served in the legal branches of the military and are therefore familiar with the government's strategy in fighting contractors' claims. Once in the law firms representing contractors, these same attorneys who in 1981 were charging rates in the range of $175 an hour, "create claims that can't be settled quickly, developing endless points of contention, obscuring the case," wrote Cramer. "The settlement that comes out of such a process is more of a horse trade than an intelligent estimate of the project's actual cost." Thus, on shipbuilding overrun claims settled for $1.1 billion in 1978, navy analysts felt that less than half that was justified—yet the navy paid up rather than continue to fight seemingly eternal, and costly, court battles.

In addition to the other costly benefits given defense contractors, the Pentagon and Congress have periodically bailed out financially troubled firms. The most-publicized instance of this was the $250 million federal loan guarantee to keep the shaky Lockheed Corporation in business in the early 1970s. (Lockheed was to experience even more bad publicity later in the decade when it was disclosed that it had made millions of dollars in overseas payments to influential figures in the Japanese and Dutch governments, among several others, to help it sell its commercial aircraft. In the best-publicized case, former Japanese Prime Minister Kakuei Tanaka was accused of receiving $2.17 million in bribes from Lockheed. As of mid-1982, two former top-level Japanese government officials had been convicted of receiving bribes from Lockheed, while the court case against Tanaka was still dragging on in Japan. Lockheed pleaded guilty in June 1979 to a United States charge related to $2.6 million in payments in Japan and was fined $647,000. Lockheed was among dozens of U.S. corporations that made illegal or questionable overseas payments in the 1960s and the 1970s. Among the others was its major competitor, Boeing, which in June 1982 pleaded guilty to federal charges of failing to disclose payments of at least $7 million, which it made in four countries in the early 1970s to help win $344 million in commercial aircraft orders. Boeing was fined $400,000, plus $50,000 in court costs.)

Less well-known than the Lockheed loan guarantee are the direct payments that have been made to financially shaky defense contractors. As the *New York Times* reported in early 1973, the Defense Department over the previous fifteen years had "used emergency authorizations to award tens of millions of dollars in outright grants to defense contractors"—often making such awards without the approval, or even the knowledge, of the secretary of Defense.

Pentagon documents indicated that 3,652 such bailout actions, totaling $85.9 million, had been taken since 1959 to assist contractors on the verge of bankruptcy. The actions had occurred after the firms had been declared to be "essential to the national defense." The *Times* investigation showed that many of the companies folded shortly after receiving federal financial aid, "some in questionable circumstances, or were absorbed by larger conglomerates."

In two instances, because the assisted companies could not work out their financial difficulties, the government ended up owning stock in the firms. In one case, in 1972, the government bought 17,414 shares of stock in the Gap Instrument Corporation, of Long Island; in another case the same year, a navy loan to Applied Devices Corporation, of Long Island, was converted to preferred stock, estimated to be worth about $2.6 million, which was then held by the government. Applied Devices (previously called Belock Instrument Corporation) had been the recipient of Pentagon financial aid since 1962 when the firm was making training devices for the army's Hawk missile system. The company received grants totaling almost $1 million from the army and the navy, plus a $3.2 million loan.

In another advantage given to contractors, Congress in 1980 amended a long-standing policy by allowing small businesses and universities to take title to inventions developed under federal contracts. By 1982, lobbying efforts were underway to, in the words of Admiral Rickover, "extend that giveaway practice to large contractors" and thereby "promote even greater concentration of economic power in the hands of the large corporations which already get the lion's share of the government's research and development budget."

Occasionally, officials of some major defense firms have criticized the corporations and the Pentagon for the special advantages given to contractors, and the cost overruns and lack of competition on contracts. Thomas V. Jones, chairman and chief executive officer of Northrop, wrote in late 1977 that defense contractors had failed "to assume the kind of management responsibility demanded elsewhere in the private sector" when they are working on defense programs. Rather than the government providing the contractor with plant and equipment for defense work, Jones said it should be the responsibility of "well-managed defense companies . . . [to] undertake investments in the high-productivity plant and equipment needed to meet military requirements effectively and efficiently." If this were done, Jones said, contractors' boards of directors would "become vitally concerned with such matters as technical risk and the resulting effect on product performance, schedule and cost commitments," as well as with modernization of plant and equipment to fulfill "their financial and legal obligations to deliver under the terms of the contract."

Government, for its part, "must evaluate defense companies the way companies in any other sector of our economy are evaluated— on the basis of the quality of their products, their performance record, their ability and willingness to make binding financial commitments." Prime contractors place these kinds of demands on their subcontractors, Jones said, but the government doesn't always make similar demands on its prime contractors. This "lack of discipline . . . leads to the expediency of government loan guarantees or, worse, increasing contract prices to cover cost overruns."

In addition to the problems already discussed, another disturbing aspect of Pentagon contracting is conflict of interest. For example, some companies have been awarded contracts to check on their own production work. One of many such examples occurred in late 1977 when the navy executed a contract with Lockheed to perform assembly checkout on the Trident 1 (C-4) and Polaris (C-3) missiles at the Polaris Missile Facility, in Charleston, South Carolina. To critics of this sole-source contract, here was a clear conflict of interest that also raised a national security issue. L.M. Pellerzi, then general counsel for the American Federation of Government Employees, contended that under its contract "Lockheed would in effect be checking out and accepting on behalf of the government missile components which it contracted to produce for the government." Pellerzi said the checkout work was clearly "critical to the agency mission and, as such, affects national security" and, therefore, it should have been performed by in-house government employees (whom the union represented). The navy defended the checkout contract, arguing that Lockheed, as the designer and manufacturer of the equipment, was best qualified to inspect it.

In the same vein, the Defense Contract Administration Services (DCAS) some years back instituted a program that removed quality control duties from DCAS personnel and placed them in the hands of the contractors who had done the work to be inspected. To qualify for self-inspection, a contractor had only to meet some minimal criteria: it had to have produced the same or similar items for at least twelve months; its contract had to be for $250,000 or more, and the contract had to have an expected life-span of at least six months. Union attorney Pellerzi protested the policy to General W.W. Vaughan, the director of the Defense Supply Agency, saying that it "violates agency regulations, is subject to inherent conflicts of interest and could well threaten this country's defense capabilities" because of inadequate inspections. Pellerzi said it was unreasonable to expect contractor employees "to serve both their corporate employer's interest in realizing management profits and the government's interest in rejecting all defective products and services."

Other types of conflicts of interest occur frequently in Pentagon contracts. In mid-1976, it was disclosed that the navy had twice retained a Virginia consulting firm to study the Condor missile, even though a founder of the firm also worked for Rockwell International, the missile's manufacturer. One of the founders, and first board chairman of Principia, Inc., the firm that received the consulting contracts, was Alan D. Simon. (Simon, incidentally, had picked up his knowledge of the Condor while working in the Pentagon's Directorate of Defense Research and Engineering.) In addition, Simon was also a partner in another consulting firm, Davis, Fubini, Simon and Kent.

Through that second firm, Simon served as a consultant to Rockwell at the same time Principia received its first contract to study the Condor.

Simon said he had heard about the navy's interest in a possible study of the Condor while he was visiting the Pentagon on other contracting business. So, Principia made an unsolicited proposal and in early 1976 received a sole-source contract for $69,962 to study the Condor's vulnerability to enemy attack. In its written justification for the sole-source arrangement, the navy stated that Principia was "the only firm available which has the unique knowledge and high-caliber personnel experienced in the Condor weapons system to perform this study within the time frame required. The loss of continuity, time and the already available expertise and talent provided by Principia would seriously jeopardize the success of the Condor program." A contract for a second study of the Condor program, this one to determine its cost-effectiveness, was awarded to Principia in mid-1976, four months after the first contract.

The Condor had been a highly controversial project since it was first contemplated, in 1963. It had substantial cost overruns and reliability problems. Many in Congress had criticized it as being obsolete. Its supporters touted the Condor, a television-guided subsonic missile, as being capable of getting past heavy enemy defenses to destroy ships and other targets. Favorable consultant studies, such as those provided by Principia, as to the Condor's cost-effectiveness and its lack of vulnerability, would provide ammunition against the Condor's critics—and no doubt result in additional contracts for companies with an interest in the project.

Because of all these issues, Senator Thomas Eagleton, D-Missouri, one of the Condor's main critics, asked the General Accounting Office for an evaluation of the first Principia study. The GAO produced a classified report showing, Eagleton said, the Principia study seemed to be "based on an erroneous model, and that the conclusion that Condor is survivable and cost-effective . . . is contradicted in the body of the report." In a letter to Senator John L. McClellan, D-Arkansas, who then chaired the Defense Appropriations Subcommittee, Eagleton said Principia's analysis of Condor's ability to penetrate enemy defenses was based on a scenario "most favorable to Condor."

Neither Simon nor Z.J. Kowalskey, Jr., the navy captain in charge of the missile program, said they saw any conflict involved in the awarding of the contracts to Principia. Kowalskey, it should be noted, had, under the Ford administration, been reprimanded by then-Defense Secretary Donald Rumsfeld for spending a weekend at a Rockwell-owned hunting lodge in Maryland. Rumsfeld also reprimanded and docked $3,200 in pay of another staunch advocate of the Condor program: Dr. Malcolm R. Currie, the Pentagon's director of defense research and engineering. Currie had taken a free fishing vacation at Rockwell's lodge over Labor Day in 1975.

Even on lower-priced military contracts, conflicts of interest often arise. For example, food services at Lowry Air Force Base, Colorado, were contracted out to a North Carolina firm that won the contract after hiring the master sergeant who had written the specifications for the contract a few months before he retired from the air force. According to congressional testimony, the sergeant wrote the specifications, then took a five-day leave and went to the company's headquarters in North Carolina to work on the firm's proposed bid on the contract.

Of all the potential conflict-of-interest problems in Defense Department contracting, none is more serious than the "revolving-door" issue already referred to. Perhaps the most remarkable use of the revolving door occurred in the decade or so following World War II, when many of the most famous United States generals and admirals from that war began to obtain positions with some of the nation's major corporations, many of which also happened to be important defense contractors. General Douglas MacArthur became chairman of the board of Remington Rand, Inc.; General Omar N. Bradley became board chairman of Bulova Research Laboratories; General James H. Doolittle was named vice president of Shell Oil; General Lucius D. Clay became chairman of the board of the Continental Can Company; Admiral Ben Moreell, Jr., was chosen chairman of Jones & Laughlin Steel Corporation; General Albert C. Wedemeyer was named vice president of AVCO Corporation. (General Bradley apparently took his new duties so seriously that he allowed his name to be used on a Bulova advertisement stating that a new tariff imposed on Swiss watch movements was justified on the grounds of military necessity.) As social critic C. Wright Mills has observed of this phenomenon, the high-ranking military men are sought by defense contractors "because of whom they know in the military and what they know of its rules and ways [rather] than because of what they know of finance and industry proper." Mills warned that this transfer of military leaders to corporations and corporate officials to the Pentagon, and the increased defense budgets, signaled "the great structural shift of modern American capitalism toward a permanent war economy."

Since those early days, the revolving-door activity has continued unabated. A 1981 study by the Council on Economic Priorities found that 1,672 former civilian and military employees of the Defense Department (between 1971 and 1979), and of the National Aeronautics and Space Administration (between 1974 and 1979), had gone to work for just the eight leading defense contractors. During the same period, 270 employees of these same companies went to work for the Defense Department and NASA. Other studies and reports in recent years have shown that 600 to 1,200 people of the rank of major and lieutenant commander and above move from the Defense Department to defense contracting companies each year, while the number of high-ranking Pentagon civilians (GS-13 and above) who make similar moves runs between 100 and 300 every year. Defense contracting company officials moving into Pentagon jobs have numbered between 150 and 400 annually.

One of the most prominent travelers through the revolving door in recent years was the Reagan administration's first secretary of State, Alexander M. Haig, Jr. Shortly after his mid-1979 retirement from the army as supreme allied commander in Europe, Haig became president and chief operating officer of fast-growing United Technologies, the nation's No. 2 defense contractor in 1981. Between 1971 and 1981, United Technologies' sales had increased sevenfold. During his year with the company before he became secretary of state, Haig presided over growth in the corporation's government contract dollars from $2.1 billion in 1979 to $2.7 billion in 1980. In the year after Haig left, United Technologies' government contract sales shot up to $3.8 billion.

During that same year, Haig received almost $900,000 in deferred compensation from United Technologies. When Haig resigned as secretary of State in June 1982, he was succeeded by another revolving-door traveler, former Treasury Secretary George P. Shultz, who was president of the Bechtel Corporation, the worldwide construction, management, and engineering firm and major government energy contractor, ranking 39th with $32.3 million from the Energy Department in 1980. Shultz became the second Reagan Cabinet officer from Bechtel, joining Defense Secretary Weinberger, who was formerly a vice president and member of the board of directors of Bechtel. Also moving to the government from Bechtel was another company executive, W. Kenneth Davis, who became the Reagan administration's deputy energy secretary. Three months after resigning as secretary of State, Haig was back at United Technologies as chairman of the corporation's new advisory committee on "global business policies." Company officials said Haig would consult on a "variety of domestic and international business matters" for United Technologies.

In addition to Haig, United Technologies boasted a number of other heavy hitters on its board of directors in the early 1980s, including two additional former Cabinet officers, William E. Simon (secretary of the Treasury) and Charles W. Duncan, Jr. (secretary of Energy). The company also had two officials with strong ties to Congress and the bureaucracy: Clark MacGregor, senior vice president for external affairs, and Hugh E. Witt, vice president for government liaison. MacGregor is a former member of Congress and a former campaign and White House aide to President Nixon. Witt is a former Defense Department official and former director of the Office of Federal Procurement Policy under the Office of Management and Budget.

Senator William Proxmire, D-Wisconsin, long a critic of the cozy relationship between the Pentagon and its contractors, has said that the various studies over the years indicate "the revolving door is not only open, but swinging wildly . . . breed[ing] conflict of interest with its constant companions—cost overruns, inefficiency, and reduced competition."

For example, syndicated columnist Jack Anderson reported some years back that an official of the Navy Materiel Command had handled eight consecutive procurement requests involving SEACOR, a navy contractor. Anderson reported that some of the contracts were dated after the official told the navy he was retiring. A week after the official retired, he accepted a job with SEACOR. When contacted for comment, the official stated that SEACOR "was only one of several firms that offered him a job" before he left the navy, and that there was no conflict of interest.

Anderson also noted that a common practice is for contractor personnel to be assigned temporarily in Pentagon procurement offices as secretaries, clerks, and even engineers. This practice gives the contract workers "access to secret information concerning their own companies" and permits them, on occasion, to "even write procurement requests for their own firms."

In one case, Anderson wrote, Admiral F.H. Michaelis, who became head of the Navy Materiel Command in May 1975, was disturbed that personnel loaned from private contractors doing business with the navy were working side by side with navy employees. In a letter sent by his top aide, Rear Admiral S.J. Evans, to other high navy officials, Michaelis warned that this situation could lead to "unwarranted access by contractor personnel to Navy files which may contain information that is sensitive, classified or proprietary." Evans wrote that the use of the contractors' employees interchangeably with navy personnel was improper, as well as illegal, under civil service regulations, and ordered the practice halted. But, Anderson reported his sources told him that this order "has been largely ignored."

Civilian sources interviewed at the Pentagon cited other similar practices. In one instance, a consulting firm working on Pentagon contracts managed to hire a retiring air force official. Then, in order to make room for him on the company payroll, the firm used its military connections to have one of its employees, who had been working on the Pentagon contracts for the company, placed on active duty. So, the firm's "former" employee continued to work on the same Pentagon contracts as a military officer.

In this vein, a story concerning E-Systems, Inc., of Dallas, Texas, which had former top government officials as its chief officers during a period when it experienced impressive growth based heavily on federal contracts, is particularly instructive. In fiscal year 1981, E-Systems, with $275 million in prime contracts of more than $10,000 each, was the 57th-largest defense contractor.

In 1974, the Memcor division of E-Systems received an army contract to provide mobile field radios. The contract had been revised and relet four times before E-Systems was able to come in with the low bid. After the many revisions, the contract grew in price from $2.8 million to $11 million. Representative Jack Brooks, D-Texas, chairman of the National Security Subcommittee of the House Government Operations Committee, which investigated the contract, later remarked that information received by the subcommittee "indicates that normal procedures may not have been followed and that favoritism toward the successful bidder may have been involved. The circumstances seem to point to a predetermination on the part of the Army that E-Systems would receive the contract."

When Brooks's subcommittee held hearings on the contract in mid-1976, Harold Brownman, assistant secretary of the army in charge of installations and logistics, defended the awarding of the contract. Brownman had been a vice president at E-Systems prior to 1974, but had had nothing to do with the contract negotiations because at the time it was awarded he was deputy director of the Central Intelligence Agency.

James Henderson, reporting in *The Washington Monthly* in late 1977, noted that E-Systems "is populated by men from the highest reaches of defense and intelligence agencies," including John W. Dixon, president, the former assistant comptroller for the Defense Department; L.K. Lauderdale, vice president, who spent six years with the Central Intelligence Agency directing the division of science and technology; W.F. Raborn, a member of the board of directors, who was director of the Central Intelligence Agency for fourteen months during the Johnson administration, and Eugene E. Berg, the man Brownman replaced in the Defense Department who went on to become a vice president of E-Systems.

In 1973 Dixon headed a group of investors who acquired E-Systems from Ling-Temco-Vought. In the next four years, E-Systems doubled its sales, with the "Army's generosity [vaulting] it from relative obscurity to preeminence in the communications and electronic warfare market," according to Henderson. During that period, E-Systems regularly seemed to be in the right place at the right time.

The army field radio contract was a telling example of this. A curious sequence of events surrounding the awarding of the contract began on November 27, 1973, when the Army Electronics Command asked bids on a contract for 6,990 radio units, known technically as AN/PRC 77, for U.S. forces, with an optional 10,000 sets for sales to foreign customers. Only three of the five bids received were determined to be valid, with Bristol Electronics low at $3,726,284. Next came Electrospace, Inc., followed by E-Systems with the high bid of $5,588,515.

Bristol didn't get the contract. Instead, the army made slight changes in the specifications and asked for new bids. None of the bidders made any changes in its bid amounts. Still, Bristol did not get the contract. The army first negotiated with Bristol and then, without making any changes in the specifications, again asked for new bids. The other two bids remained the same, but E-Systems managed to lower its bid to $4.4 million, which now made it the second-lowest bidder after Bristol.

Still, Bristol didn't get the contract. The army instead changed the specifications again on February 21, 1974, deleting quality assurance provisions and asking the bidders for cost impact statements on the change. None of the firms altered its bids. Four days later, the army made another change in the proposed contract, which, as Henderson noted, "by any production logic, could be expected to alter the unit prices upward." This was because the army deleted 1,526 radio units from the contract proposal, lowering the amount sought to 5,464 units. The lower the production run, the higher the cost, so as expected Bristol increased its unit cost. But, inexplicably, E-Systems was able to drop its unit cost by $150, which put it $5 under Bristol's original unit cost proposal.

Thus, in the three months since the army had first asked bids on the contract, E-Systems had reduced its unit price from $799.50 to $528: a decrease of slightly more than one-third of its original bid. This occurred despite no major change in the design specifications (which might lower the unit cost) and a decrease in the number of units—a situation that generally could be expected to raise unit costs.

With E-Systems for the first time in the position of being the lowest bidder, it was awarded the contract on March 14, 1974. This sparked an immediate protest from the Bristol firm. Four months later, the

General Accounting Office sustained the protest and ordered the army to rebid the contract. But the army, even though it had itself delayed awarding the contract for three months because of its repeated specifications changes, said the radios were urgently needed and urged the General Accounting Office to permit the contract with E-Systems to proceed.

The General Accounting Office acceded to the request but made it conditional upon an army agreement not to exercise the contract option for the 10,000 radios to be sold overseas. As Paul G. Dembling, the General Accounting Office's general counsel, explained later to Brooks's subcommittee: "We made that recommendation in the belief that such action would eliminate the gravamen of the protest and any possibility of windfall profits by E-Systems on the option quantity. The Army informed us that because of our recommendation it would not exercise the option."

But the army, a few weeks after agreeing to the General Accounting Office's request, pulled a semantical maneuver and achieved a windfall for E-Systems. The army "modified" the contract (rather than "exercising the option") and ordered the 10,000 additional units—at substantially higher prices than under the contract it signed with E-Systems the previous March. That contract, with its price of $528 per unit, was modified to provide for unit prices up to $943 for the additional 10,000 units. The subcommittee deduced from this that E-Systems had been able to lower its unit prices for the original contract in anticipation of greater rewards later on.

Brooks attacked the army for this subterfuge, saying: "The army, being somewhat resourceful in getting what they want done, did not exercise the option. They accepted modifications, and ordered another 10,000 of those radios. They did not exercise the option. They just got 10,000 more. It is called semantics. The Army apparently ignored this [GAO] recommendation. It modified. That's a new word for change. It's a brand new word. They got one of those thesauruses and looked it up. Did this action not circumvent clearly the recommendation of the GAO?"

To which Dembling replied, "It would appear that it did, yes sir."

Brooks responded, "You make a good judgment. You make a good decision. Then they just play games with you like you're in the third

grade and they run right around you and go and do as they please."
When Assistant Secretary Brownman and other Pentagon officials
appeared before the subcommittee, they attempted to justify the
army's actions. Noting that the army was getting the radios at $528
each but was requiring its foreign customers to pay up to $943 for the
same item, Brooks told the Pentagon officials: "I would feel like I
would not want you to buy anything for me. I will just shop for myself,
thank you."

In August 1976, Brooks's subcommittee issued a report saying that,
by selling units to the army at $528 each, E-Systems stood to lose $150
per set, or more than $800,000 on the original contract. But, whereas
the contract as originally awarded was worth $2.8 million, the addi-
tion of the extra 10,000 sets, at prices up to $943 per unit, boosted the
overall contract value to $11 million. Said the report: "E-Systems or
any other bidder who could have suspected such an escalation of
business might have been induced to lower its bid significantly in
anticipation of ultimate gain." The report added that the questionable
atmosphere surrounding the awarding of the contract, and the subsequent price escalation, "arouse suspicions that someone in the Department of Defense was intent on favoring E-Systems."

With more certainty, Brooks added, "It seems clear the army was
determined to award the contract to E-Systems."

Eugene E. Berg was an assistant secretary of the army who went
on to become a vice president at E-Systems after resigning his Pentagon post on July 15, 1974, four days after the General Accounting
Office made its decision on the Bristol protest of the contract award.
It wasn't until a year later that he assumed his post at E-Systems; he
recalled having nothing to do with the radio contract and said he had
"never heard of E-Systems until well after that."

Nevertheless, the Brooks subcommittee turned up a memorandum,
dated March 13, 1974, which was written by Colonel Robert D.
Worthen, acting deputy director for materiel acquisition, to the U.S.
Army Materiel Command. The memo cites a letter from the Materiel
Command seeking authority to award the contract to E-Systems prior
to a General Accounting Office decision on the Bristol protest. It
notes that the Materiel Command letter was "hand delivered" to Berg
and goes on to state that "The request is hereby granted by direction

of the Assistant Secretary [Berg]. . . ." The memo was written one day before the contract was awarded.

E-Systems has been involved in other controversial contracts. For example, a contract to supply field radios to the South Korean Army, an agreement that needed U.S. Army clearance, also took a number of curious twists and turns before being awarded to E-Systems. The chain of events began in 1969 when Electrospace, Inc., a New York City radio manufacturer with just three hundred employees, began negotiating with the South Korean government to provide the field radios to the Korean Army. In 1971, although no contract yet existed, an agreement was reached under which the Oriental Precision Company in Seoul was to assemble components produced in New York by Electrospace. Early the following year, officials of Oriental Precision visited the Electrospace facility, and its appeared certain that Electrospace would get the contract.

But sometime in the next few months, the U.S. Defense Security Agency's foreign military sales desk said that the contract would have to be bid competitively because, as the Pentagon press office was to explain later, the South Koreans would be purchasing the sets with U.S. military grants, which require competitive bidding.

Instead of opening up the bidding to the dozen or more United States companies that would have been qualified to handle such a contract, the U.S. Army Electronics Command on May 4, 1972, solicited planning bids from only Electrospace and E-Systems—even though E-Systems had not previously been in the picture at all, and there was no apparent reason for it to have been designated instead of any of a dozen other firms. The planning bids, which are a preliminary step prior to solicitation of formal bids, indicated that Electrospace had the lower price and seemed likely to be the low bidder when formal bids were taken.

On July 26, 1972, the U.S. Military Assistance Group in Korea asked for formal bids to be delivered by August 25. Then, eight days before the bid delivery deadline, representatives of the Defense Security Agency and the Electronics Command, Headquarters U.S. Army Logistics, met in the Pentagon and determined that competitive bids were unnecessary after all. The South Korean government could choose any contractor it wanted, they said, because U.S. military grants were not going to be used for the purchase after all, but rather repayable loans in the form of "military credits" would pay for the radios.

Electrospace still hoped to get the contract, but soon determined after a meeting with Korean officials in Seoul that it was not to be. On July 13, 1973, the Korean Defense Ministry agreed to provide a noncompetitive contract to E-Systems for $8.4 million worth of radios. Of this, $2.6 million was actually to come from U.S. military grants, which, as noted earlier, should have required competitive bids.

Two months after the South Koreans decided in favor of E-Systems, Lieutenant General Robert Nelson Smith resigned as Chief of Staff of United Nations Command/U.S. Forces in Korea, and assumed the post of director of Far East Operations for E-Systems. Smith was not reported to have been involved in the awarding of the E-Systems contract.

While revolving-door situations raise questions concerning subsequent contracts awarded to a firm that hires former Pentagon officials, they also sometimes lead to allegations of illegal acts committed by contractor or government employees. For example, in March 1982, five employees of General Research Corporation, of McLean, Virginia, a subsidiary of Flow General, Inc., were charged in a federal indictment with conflicts of interest and conspiring to defraud the government in the awarding in 1980 of a $2.6 million contract to computerize the army's assignment system for enlisted personnel.

The indictment alleged that a senior vice president of General Research and another firm official offered and later provided jobs and pay increases to one military and one civilian employee of the army —in return for information the two men were to provide to the company before they left government employment at the Army's Military Personnel Center in Alexandria, Virginia. Both men were working on the personnel computerization plan for the government, the indictment alleged. The information, according to the indictment, ensured that General Research would receive a higher evaluation score in its bid for the contract against two competitors. The contract was awarded in September 1980 but was canceled two months later after a competitor made allegations of improprieties. The indictment stated that the two army employees went to work for General Research shortly after the contract was awarded. In a plea bargaining arrangement, charges against the individuals were dropped, and the company pleaded guilty to conspiracy and corruption charges in May 1982 and was subsequently fined $30,000.

Former navy procurement official Gordon Rule has said that the revolving-door problem and the closely related cost overrun abuses continue because government officials and contractor personnel are seldom punished for unethical conduct. "If one admiral or general, or any other officer, was court-martialed and dismissed for conflict-of-interest violations," Rule said, the Pentagon's procurement system and credibility "would be immediately enhanced." With the proliferation of big-money Pentagon contracts, "corporate, political and individual morality [have] reached the choke point with all these billions of the taxpayers' money being up for grabs." Noting the illegal payments many defense contractors had admitted making to overseas officials during the 1970s, Rule said it was foolish to believe these corporations would have one standard of ethics abroad and a completely different one in the United States.

Obviously unimpressed with the multitude of revolving-door problems over the last decade, the Reagan administration asked Congress in 1982 to eliminate the regulation that requires persons leaving the Defense Department to work for defense contractors, or persons leaving a defense contractor to work for the Pentagon, to fill out a one-page form listing their current and former positions. Department officials complained that the regulation was too costly and burdensome to administer. Although Common Cause, the public interest group, said it takes only a few minutes to fill out the form, the organization found many noncompliers in early 1982, including such notables as Defense Undersecretary Richard DeLauer, former board member of TRW, Inc.; Deputy Defense Undersecretaries Donald Latham, former executive of RCA Government Systems Division; T.K. Jones, former products evaluation manager for Boeing; and Navy Undersecretary James Goodrich, former board chairman of Bath Iron Works.

As all the revolving-door activity indicates, the major defense contractors clearly view themselves as something more than mere armaments producers. When the LTV Corporation (the No. 31 defense contractor in fiscal year 1981) made its late 1981 bid to take over the Grumman Corporation (the No. 9 defense contractor), Grumman strongly opposed the move. Grumman took to radio, television, and newspapers a massive advertising campaign, the point of which was that the takeover was "not in the national interest" and could lead to "a weaker defense capability" for the United States. (In all, Grumman spent $1.5 million in legal fees and $600,000 on advertising to fight LTV's takeover bid.)

In testimony in Grumman's suit to block the LTV bid, Admiral Elmo R. Zumwalt, the former chief of naval operations, testified that if the LTV bid were successful, there would be lessened competition for defense contracts and the result would be "very negative from the viewpoint of the government and national defense." Zumwalt's position was undoubtedly correct, but at the same time the argument he made underscores the point that defense contractors are no longer (and haven't been for several decades) neutral manufacturing enterprises that produce war items. Rather, these companies are so intimately bound up with the Defense Department that they are seen by themselves and the military experts as being an extension of the government and the "national interest." LTV, incidentally, subsequently withdrew its takeover bid.

Although the emphasis thus far in this chapter has been on major contractors, it is not just the contracts for weapons systems that are problem-laden. Many other types of Pentagon contracts—for studies and analyses, management support, consulting services of various sorts, construction, operation of military installations, and missile test ranges, overhaul and maintenance, and various blue-collar jobs—have also lacked competition, produced excessive costs, and raised questions concerning accountability and the loss of Pentagon in-house expertise to perform certain functions vital to national defense.

For example, serious questions have been raised in Congress concerning certain consulting and management support services contracts awarded for work that, by its very sensitive nature, should be performed in-house by Defense Department personnel.

In one case, Systems Research and Applications, Inc., received a $155,262 contract in fiscal year 1979 to assist in developing a war mobilization plan for the Defense Supply Service of the Office of the

Secretary of Defense. The contract, later modified to double its total cost to $304,018, required Systems Research to develop improvements in the Defense Department's management of its manpower mobilization system, to devise the "framework for a Mobilization Plan," and to assist "in planning and preparing for a specific mobilization exercise." Awarded without competitive bidding, the contract was justified by Defense on the ground that the department lacked the in-house capability to perform such duties. Perhaps a major reason the Pentagon purportedly lacked the in-house expertise was the fact that many of its qualified personnel had gone to work for contractors. For instance, Systems Research had on its payroll a number of former high-ranking military officials, including an air force general, a vice chief of the army, and a deputy assistant secretary of the army.

When a congressional committee in 1981 looked at this and similar defense contracts, panel members voiced astonishment at the degree to which private contractors were formulating defense planning in such vital areas as mobilization and war planning. Representative Geraldine A. Ferrarro, D-New York, a former prosecutor, subjected Pentagon officials to some especially tough questioning at a hearing of her Human Resources Subcommittee of the House Post Office and Civil Service Committee.

Ferraro got Dr. Benson Adams, from the Office of Secretary of Defense, Atomic Energy, to admit not only that the Pentagon lacked in-house mobilization expertise, but that defense planners for years had been planning only for nuclear or other wars of short duration. "I know it may sound fantastic in 1981 that the Defense Department lacks expertise about mobilization," Adams said, "but the fact remains that for a long time the nature of the assumptions we made about war suggested a short war where industrial-based mobilization would not have a role since the war would be so short or it would go nuclear." Adams contended that "for a number of years, planning assumptions made by the Defense Department have downplayed the whole question of mobilization because [different] views have been held about the length, duration, nature, and types of wars we might have to fight. Because of other priorities and these assumptions about conventional war, issues related to mobilization, logistics, and manpower were given lower priorities than in the past." Adams's testimony can hardly be of comfort to those concerned about either defense preparedness or the prospects of nuclear war.

The General Accounting Office, in an early 1981 report on defense management support contracts, underscored the problem that the loss of expertise within the Pentagon leads to the likelihood that the nation's defense capability is weakened. Of 256 contracts reviewed, the GAO concluded that 183—or 71 percent—were for functions that most likely should have been performed by government personnel because they appeared to be intimately involved with the defense mission. As the GAO observed, "several of the contracts have preempted [Defense's] prerogative in directing national defense and management and direction of the Armed Services." Walton H. Sheley, Jr., director of GAO's mission and analysis and systems division, later in 1981 testified to a congressional committee that GAO had determined the Defense Department "at one time had the in-house capability for much of the work currently being contracted out. This is apparent from the involvement of former Defense officials and employees in contracts included in our review." In addition to this loss of some expertise through the "revolving-door" to contractors' firms, Sheley said Defense was "not adequately considering the in-house capability it already has" and was often unnecessarily contracting-out for studies, management support, and other services.

The loss of in-house expertise has added to the concern of contracting critics who fear that outside organizations have too much influence over formulation of defense policy and strategy.

For example, the nation's best known think-tank, The Rand Corporation, has as its major sponsors of research the U.S. Air Force, the Office of Secretary of Defense, the National Security Council, the Central Intelligence Agency, as well as more than a dozen other federal agencies, including the Department of State, the Agency for International Development, and the Department of Housing and Urban Development. One-third of all of Rand's research is carried out for the air force. A typical Rand brochure noted that the organization was studying United States' security interests in Europe and Asia; was formulating plans that would provide for U.S. troop reductions in Europe while at the same time "still meeting current U.S. goals for conventional NATO defense"; was working on projections of China's future military potential; was studying the effects of Chinese economic and military developments on the Soviet Union and Japan, as well as looking at "alternative concepts of tactical nuclear warfare, attempting to identify areas where advanced technology can improve tactical nuclear capabilities."

In the area of policymaking and technical expertise, the General Accounting Office has questioned whether the Defense Department had further eroded its in-house capacity by farming out too much work to The MITRE Corporation, of Bedford, Massachusetts. MITRE is one of nine federal contract research centers, which are private nonprofit organizations that do work primarily for the government. In reviewing three projects assigned to MITRE by the Electronic Systems Division of the Air Force Systems Command at Hanscom Air Force Base, Massachusetts, the GAO found that the air force did not even consider whether the work could be done in-house before turning it over to MITRE—despite the fact that the Electronics Division's regulations require MITRE not be used if the government can do the work itself.

MITRE's government contracts brought together its systems analysts and engineers with high-level policymakers at the Pentagon and at a number of other civilian federal agencies. While its prime sponsor is the air force, MITRE's other clients include the Defense Department, the army and navy, the National Security Council, U.S. Postal Service, and the Departments of Commerce, Transportation, Energy, Justice, and Treasury, among others.

In addition to the direct influence it wields, MITRE also has "former officers and legmen . . . in permanent and appointed positions throughout government," says *Federal Times*, a newspaper that writes exclusively about government and the bureaucracy. Instead of MITRE working for the government, the newspaper contended, many federal employees and officials feared that MITRE exercised policymaking direction, and even control, of many of the government operations with which it is involved, and that it undermines the civil service by taking over so many functions traditionally handled by federal workers.

Increasing dependence on private firms and universities for research and development, discussed in an earlier chapter, has prompted concern by some federal officials and contracting critics that the Department of Defense has diminished its capability to deal with emergencies or to evaluate properly the work of its outside contractors. Despite such concern, the Pentagon in the mid-1970s began a further reduction of in-house research and development, starting with an initial cutback of 4,000 civilian personnel. The money released by cutbacks in in-house programs was to go to fund research and development efforts in private industry and universities.

Sheley, of the General Accounting Office, noted a number of sometimes overlapping problems uncovered in GAO's 1981 study of management support services contracts. He pointed out that 102 of the 256 contracts studied had resulted from unsolicited proposals.

"All too often," Sheley said, unsolicited proposals "are being used to subvert the competitive process, encourage work that may not be important relative to . . . mission needs and priorities, abrogate [Defense's] responsibilities over the scope of work related to defense management, and are not truly unique or innovative."

Once these unsolicited proposals result in contracts, the contractor then is in a good position to win additional work in the same area—and to use the work done on its first contract as the basis for obtaining another contract on a noncompetitive basis. For example, the navy awarded Flight Systems, Inc., a noncompetitive $824,756 contract for its unsolicited proposal to provide various technical services in connection with the F-18 fighter plane project. Flight Systems had been working on several aspects of the F-18 program since 1975, and in fiscal years 1977 and 1978 had helped develop the F-18 program master plan and the production readiness review plan. Then, in late fiscal year 1978, Flight Systems submitted its unsolicited proposal for a three-year technical and management assistance contract in preparation for production of the F-18. The navy said the new contract was warranted because Flight Systems' experience on its previous contracts made it "uniquely qualified" for the new contract.

In the same 1981 General Accounting Office study, in a stark illustration of the revolving-door problem, Sheley said that 131 of the 256 contracts reviewed were obtained by contractors that had former military and civilian employees of the Defense Department "in capacities of top management as well as various technical levels." Sheley said this extensive contract involvement of former military and civilian personnel with the agency for which they formerly worked raised questions as to the extent Defense "uses the skills of former employees to perform functions similar to those performed while employed by [Defense], the objectiveness of work performance by former employees in areas where they were formerly involved, and the degree of influence used by former top level [Pentagon] officials in securing contracts."

One such contract, for $73,576, was awarded by the navy to PRB Associates, Inc., for engineering analyses in connection with the navy's anti-submarine warfare program. PRB, in its unsolicited proposal, stated that the navy no longer had the in-house expertise to perform certain functions, but that the contractor did have such expertise in the persons of two former employees of the navy's Anti-Submarine Warfare Operations Center Program—a project engineer and a program manager. Both had left the navy when PRB was formed and were principals in the firm.

The General Accounting Office also found that the Defense Department was wasting money by contracting for services and information that it may not need. This was reported to be the case in 44—or 17 percent—of the 256 contracts studied by GAO. The 44 contracts were valued at $6.8 million. GAO's Sheley told Congress that these possibly unnecessary contracts were ones in which "the subject matter of the contract indicated that the information should already be available in the federal government; the questions raised which justified the study could or should have been answered by the service itself and/or other [Defense] activities, or the contract results appeared to be of questionable use" to the Pentagon.

One example cited by Sheley was a $30,000 navy contract, $23,000 of which was for data on technical aspects of a naval test range. The information was to be used in making a decision on the relocation of the test range. Sheley said naval officials told GAO "that the technical data was available and could have been obtained directly from the naval facility operating the range." However, the activity was not contacted because its objectivity was considered questionable. Instead, a contractor, Doty Associates, Inc., "was paid to obtain the data from navy sources."

Just as questionable was the government providing a six-figure payment for engineering and management support to a contractor for a project that had already been canceled. In fiscal year 1979, such a contract, for $124,529, was awarded by the navy to MAR, Inc., for engineering and management support for shipbuilding. Then, Congress canceled the program, and the Defense Department halted the prime ship development contract. With the program canceled, there obviously was no need for engineering and management support, but Pentagon logic dictated otherwise. Instead of canceling MAR's contract, the navy programmed an additional $96,000 for engineering and management support for the terminated project. As Sheley told the House Human Resources Subcommittee, "program officials advised us that at the direction of higher officials they were urged to continue" MAR's efforts. Sheley said the end-run around the program's cancellation was undertaken by the navy "in an effort to obligate, rather than lose any portion of the program's $4.1 million fiscal year 1980 budget"—that is, spend it all, rather than return any of it to the federal treasury.

As we have seen in an earlier chapter, this rush in the last quarter of the fiscal year to spend all budgeted funds results in hundreds of costly, unnecessary contracts government-wide every year. To federal officials, unspent money is a clear invitation to Congress to cut back on an agency's budget in the next fiscal year. In the Defense Department, 88 of 256 contracts reviewed by the General Accounting Office in early 1981 were awarded in the last 90 days of a fiscal year. The 88 contracts totaled $21.8 million; in addition, $16.7 million in modifications to others of the 256 contracts were also awarded in the last quarter. For 26 of the contract procurement requests originating in the last quarter, the GAO determined that these "appeared to result because of the availability of funds near yearend" and not because of any need for the service.

For example, 26 days before the end of the fiscal year, on September 4, 1979, the navy awarded Litton Industries an $830,000 noncompetitive contract for engineering support for a shipbuilding project. More than a year later, on September 28, 1980, just two days before the fiscal year ended, only about $300,000 in work had been assigned to Litton under the contract. The following day, GAO reported, "three new task orders were issued and the scope of the previous task was increased for a total of $530,000," thereby using up the full $830,000 provided for in the contract. Later modifications almost doubled the amount of the contract to $1,633,313.

The fiscal year 1979 yearend rush to dispose of unspent air force funds resulted in at least a $104,850 overcharge on a $714,000 contract with the Martin Marietta Corporation for 34 modular instrumentation packages. In addition, government investigators found in 1981 that the contractor's proposal was incomplete and provided no substantiation for $268,000 in costs, that the proposal was negotiated by telephone beginning 17 days before the fiscal year ended, and that the government (contrary to regulations) failed to make a cost or technical evaluation of the proposal.

The General Accounting Office also found that once a company obtained a contract, it seldom let go of it. Of the 256 contracts it reviewed, 146 (57 percent) were repeatedly renewed for periods of up to 28 years. For example, the Battelle Memorial Institute had had since 1951 a sole-source contract with the air force to provide, among other things, detailed studies of Soviet and People's Republic of China research and development facilities and resources. The contract, for $1,624,037 in fiscal year 1978, was modified three times and its performance period was extended four months, bringing the cost up to $2,922,037. The GAO, suggesting the work could have been done by air force employees, reported that program officials said there had been no studies undertaken to determine the relative costs of doing the work in-house versus contracting for it.

As Sheley told Congress, "We found few cost studies that justified contracting-out as the least-costly alternative," especially for engineering and technical services. "The failure to consider the in-house costs of performing work of a continuous nature," Sheley said, may result in the Defense Department "paying significantly more for services which are essential to accomplishing [its] mission."

The list of problems uncovered by GAO also included cost increases caused by overruns, additions to the scope of work covered by the contract, and extensions of time to complete the contract. Of the 256 contracts studied, 176 were modified a total of 735 times. The modifications almost doubled the value of the contracts from $84.6

million to $158.5 million. The GAO also found that work was not completed on time in 45 percent of the contracts, with late completions ranging from one to thirty-one months.

One particularly noteworthy series of modifications, for Hawk missile system engineering services, shot the cost of an original army contract from $6,278,981 to $33,278,640—a 425 percent increase. The contract, with the Raytheon Corporation, was modified 60 times, increasing the scope of work from about 160,000 hours to almost 790,000 hours. The Raytheon contract was no one-shot deal; the company has performed engineering services for the army since 1956, and over-all in fiscal year 1981 had almost $1.7 billion in Pentagon contracts. Army officials said they expected to continue the relationship with Raytheon as long as the Hawk system is used, which was expected to be at least until the early 1990s.

Turning to another type of contract, government investigators have determined that millions of dollars are wasted annually through unnecessary maintenance work on army helicopters at both in-house depots and contract facilities. In recent years, contractors have performed just under 30 percent of the depot maintenance for the army's approximately 8,000 helicopters. The army's approach to helicopter maintenance has been to bring in the machines for extensive overhaul and maintenance at specific scheduled times—regardless of whether the craft needed the work. Consequently, the General Accounting Office found in 1979 that army depots and contractors were overhauling some engines that had no defects and others that could be repaired at less cost. For fiscal year 1978, an estimated $9.6 million was wasted on helicopter overhauls alone.

In addition, many helicopters with minor defects that could have been repaired in the field for a minimal cost were instead being sent to army depots or contractor facilities for full overhauls. For example, in fiscal year 1977, the center service engine deck on 12 army UH-1D/H helicopters split. This was the only defect on any of the 12 machines, yet army regulations required that they be sent in for overhauls. This contrasted with air force regulations, which permitted less costly field repair or replacement of the center service engine deck. The air force thus was able to repair its helicopters with center service engine deck problems at a field cost of $6,500 per machine, compared to the army's cost for depot or contractor maintenance of $135,500 per machine. This $129,000 difference in repair costs meant that the army needlessly incurred more than $1 million in costs on just this one type of helicopter problem during one fiscal year. In addition, the army procedure clogs repair depots and contractor facilities and causes delays in repairs and maintenance for other helicopters that need more serious work.

Insufficient army planning has also raised questions of just how helpful private contractors would be in helicopter maintenance operations if mobilization for war were required. The General Accounting Office reported in 1979 that the army did not know how much contractor helicopter maintenance support would be available in the event of mobilization and was, therefore, "unable to plan for organic mobilization support." The army did say that it planned to have contractors handle about 17 percent of its helicopter maintenance in a mobilization situation, but this seemed an unrealistic figure because it was far below the 29 percent that contractors were handling in a peacetime situation. Here was one area where it appeared the military should have been planning for a possible increase in the use of contractors, but uncharacteristically was trying to minimize contractor involvement.

As with helicopter maintenance, ship overhaul contracting has been plagued with cost overruns, missed completion dates, and poor government management. Overlaying this is an issue that cannot be talked about in mere dollars and cents—namely, preparedness. Problems with ship overhauls, particularly in private shipyards, have produced concern by many members of Congress that the navy would not be able to respond adequately in an emergency situation.

As Representative Charles E. Bennett, D-Florida, chairman of the Seapower and Strategic and Critical Materials Subcommittee of the House Armed Services Committee, has observed: "There are examples, from time to time, of ships being, for all practical purposes, worse off in an operational sense following an overhaul than before. There is finger pointing by all sides: that is, the navy and the private sector, as to why an overhaul goes sour." Bennett noted that there had been allegations "that the private sector does not have the requisite skills to do more than simple overhauls" and, conversely, "that public sector overhauls are too costly and wasteful of tax dollars."

Representative G. William Whitehurst, R-Virginia, a member of the House Armed Services Committee, said he was concerned about reports that, on ship overhaul contracts, contractors would deliberately bid low to get the contract, knowing that the navy had funds available to cover future cost escalations. Also, he was disturbed over allegations that contractors deliberately flood the navy contract administrator with change order proposals, that navy contract personnel lack the expertise to deal knowledgeably with change order proposals and so approve items that should not be approved, and that many change orders are priced after the work has been done, instead of before as sound budgetary procedures would warrant.

A General Accounting Office study of ship overhauls in early 1982 bore out many of the concerns of Whitehurst and Bennett. Although noting some improvement in recent years thanks to navy management initiatives, the GAO concluded that contractors' cost growth and missed completion dates continued to plague the navy by wasting fiscal resources and lessening fleet readiness "by not providing fully serviceable ships when needed."

Looking at private contractor ship overhauls for the three-year period ending January 1980, the agency found that these overhauls were delayed an average of 64 days and had cost overruns averaging 62 percent for frigates, 55 percent for auxiliary ships, and 29 percent for amphibious ships. Cost rises due to increases or changes in the scope of work were all handled by the navy on a sole-source basis, putting the navy at a severe disadvantage in insuring that it was getting the best price for the new or revised work.

The navy spends more than $800 million annually for ship overhauls by private contractors. While the navy's in-house facilities have been handling overhauls for the more complex ships—submarines, aircraft carriers, cruisers, frigates, and guided missile destroyers—the less-expert private contractors have usually been assigned to less intricate ships such as amphibious and auxiliary ships and some of the less complex surface warships. With substantial increases planned in the number of navy ships during the 1980s, it was expected that private shipyards might do more work on complex ships because of the crush of work being handled by the public shipyards.

But as the General Accounting Office noted, there is much concern in Congress that, based on past performances, the private shipyards will continue to lack the expertise to handle the more complex ships, and, therefore, any work they undertake is likely to miss completion schedules and be subject to numerous change orders, greatly adding to the cost.

The General Accounting Office said that, often, unqualified shipyards deliberately submitted low bids to "buy in" on a contract, later submitting numerous change orders, which run up the cost of the contract. In addition, the agency said the navy was often unable to define properly the work that is needed, with the result that competent as well as unqualified contractors have had to perform extensive and costly changes later on.

Representative Whitehurst has, over the years, raised questions about ship maintenance by both contractor and in-house yards. "I've screamed bloody murder about it," he said, but he didn't know if there had been any real improvements in recent years. The difficulty for members of Congress trying to deal with such problems, he said, "is there is so much going on up here in Congress all the time. You raise these things and assume something is happening, then you go off to some other issue. When you get back to the original issue a few years later, you discover nothing has changed." The navy does not get its money's worth on ship repairs, he said, but the even more vital issue is whether "these ships will be ready to sail in case of emergency. It's a question of preparedness." The navy's ship overhaul program is so burdened with delays and unsatisfactory work that it "poses grave questions about our country's ability to continue as a dominant sea power in the world." Retired Navy Captain Lou Kriser, a Whitehurst aide who investigated ship repair problems, said he had determined from interviews with workers that quality assurance programs, particularly in the private shipyards, were "just paperwork programs designed to meet contracting requirements."

Despite the importance of overhaul and maintenance work to the preparedness issue, Congress, when it has looked for areas to cut in the defense budget, has generally spared major, costly weapons systems and has instead reduced operations and maintenance funds used for programs directly related to the military branches' capability to respond to emergencies. Weapons systems, of course, are more politically appealing than operations and maintenance, especially in those congressional districts where defense contractors and subcontractors are located. Also, while advocates of greater defense spending warn ominously of Soviet weapons buildups, comparatively little is said about the less glamorous issue of overhaul and maintenance. Yet, in President Reagan's proposed fiscal year 1983 budget, operations and maintenance is by far the major defense spending category—$67.3 billion, compared to $55.1 billion for weapons and equipment procurement—and thus, more so than weapons systems, a likely candidate for cuts.

Given the choice between weapons systems and operations and maintenance, Congress invariably makes the cuts "exactly where they should not be, in the operations and maintenance account that funds readiness," said Representative Les Aspin, D-Wisconsin, a member of both the House Budget and Armed Services committees.

Even during the Vietnam War years, spending for major weapons systems, which had little to do with fighting a guerrilla war, took precedence over operations and maintenance, often with drastic consequences for U.S. forces in Southeast Asia. As a prime example, in the *Mayaguez* incident in 1975, then-Defense Secretary James R. Schlesinger ordered every ship near the Gulf of Thailand to aid the U.S. merchant ship *Mayaguez,* which had been seized by the Cambodian government. However, because of maintenance problems, none of the ships could move at full speed; one ship had power-supply problems, while a helicopter carrier and an aircraft carrier never reached the scene.

Incidents such as these made Representative Patricia Schroeder, D-Colorado, wonder in an early 1982 interview whether the increasing use of contractors for ship, aircraft, and weapons maintenance is wise from a security standpoint. In the event of emergencies, she said, military personnel must have the expertise in maintenance and repair work when it isn't possible to send machines to contractors' facilities. A Pentagon study, disclosed in early 1983, voiced the same concern, noting that if key contract personnel "should choose not to work in crises, the effect on weapon system material readiness could be devastating."

Representative Whitehurst, along with other House and Senate members of varied liberal, conservative, and moderate views, in 1981 formed the Military Reform Caucus in an effort to ensure that what money the Pentagon pays for weapons is wisely spent. Basically put, they favor "simpler, cheaper, and more weapons over complicated, expensive, and fewer weapons" in an effort to increase U.S. preparedness and hold down costs they see the American people unwilling to bear beyond a certain point. Although Whitehurst, himself, has gone after some wasteful contracting practices, this is not the main purpose of the group. Rather, said Senator Gary Hart, D-Colorado, a caucus member and Senate Armed Services Committee member, the caucus doesn't "quarrel with individual budget items" but attempts "to bring about a different outlook, a different way of looking at things" and of controlling the Pentagon—"the biggest bureaucracy in America, and in the world."

While Hart is generally described as a liberal, or "neo-liberal" in the jargon of the day, and has been generally skeptical of Pentagon spending over the years, some self-described military "hawks" were also going after what they saw as uncontrolled defense spending and planning in early 1982. Representative John J. Rhodes, R-Ohio, a conservative and former House minority leader, commented that "Eisenhower was obviously right when he said that the military-industrial complex needed to be watched. It does. And it isn't being watched to the point that it must be in the future."

Also, said Rhodes, in regard to the arms race with the Soviet Union: "This whole idea: the more they build, the more we build, the more we both build, the more dangerous it gets. I'm worried about the economy and, well, I'm worried about the future of mankind." Rhodes said he knew "that sounds a little bit Boy Scout of me, but I am, I really am, worried about all this talk of nuclear war." With the goal of reducing international tensions and cutting costs, Rhodes made several proposals, including withdrawing the 350,000 American troops in Europe and scuttling the B-1 bomber in favor of the Stealth bomber, a manned aircraft designed to evade radar so skillfully that, its advocates say, it is almost invisible. Like other members of Congress, Rhodes was catching the message of the burgeoning grassroots nuclear weapons freeze campaign, as well as the concerns of recession-

and unemployment-plagued constituents who were becoming increasingly reluctant to give a blank check on military spending, especially when programs designed to ease the plight of the poor, and others to assist the middle class, were being cut back.

Given the huge amounts of waste in defense contracting, one might have expected that those members of Congress who demand strict accountability for social programs would have the same standard for the Pentagon's legions of contractors. With a few exceptions, this has not been the case. Instead, members of Congress from states having large numbers of defense contractors and subcontractors see Pentagon contracts as a shot in the arm for their local economies.

However, there is ample evidence, according to a number of studies, that accelerated defense spending, rather than bolstering the United States economy and creating jobs, instead adds to the nation's fiscal woes and generates additional unemployment over-all.

Employment Research Associates, a Lansing, Michigan, study group, contends that for every $1 billion increase in the military budget in 1977 and 1978 there was a net loss of 10,000 jobs throughout the United States. Twenty-one states showed employment gains due to military spending, while twenty-nine experienced losses. In its study released in September 1981, Employment Research said that one reason for the military budget's failure to alleviate unemployment nationwide is that, as weapons systems become more complex and more costly, a greater share of the defense dollar is spent for technology and less of it for hiring people. By 1982 major defense contractors were turning increasingly to labor-saving machinery, experimenting with computer-aided manufacturing and robots to increase productivity—moves that seemed certain to eliminate jobs in the future.

The economic research firm argued that, because a dollar can be spent only once, spending it on defense is less helpful in creating jobs than spending it almost anyplace else in the economy. For example, the company's report stated that for every $1 billion spent on the MX missile program, about 17,000 jobs would be created; the same $1 billion would produce 27,000 jobs in private industry, 48,000 jobs for hospital workers, 62,000 jobs in education, and 65,000 jobs in retail trades. Thus, when a decision is made to spend more money for defense, it is also a decision to forgo greater job creation in the private and other public sectors of the economy.

The report concluded that "The deep problems of the American economy cannot be ameliorated until the military budget is cut, and the money either left in the hands of citizens through tax cuts or spent on economically productive activities by the government—federal, state or local." Marian Anderson, the author of the report, said that the Reagan administration's proposals to increase spending in the most unproductive area of the economy—defense—"directly undermines the stated goals of the administration" to curb inflation and end the recession and the widespread unemployment that was approaching 11 percent by 1983.

Although military spending produces benefits for some areas of the country, these are often of a short-run, boom-and-bust variety. Once the contracts run out, or a program is canceled, thousands of people can be suddenly tossed out of work because the plant does not have enough other government or private-sector work to do. Lloyd J. Dumas, associate professor of political economy at the University of Texas in Dallas, emphasized this point in early 1982 when he argued for increased planning for conversion of military-industrial facilities to civilian-oriented activities. "Such planning," Dumas said, "would insure the corporation against the vagaries of what has always been a shifting military market, in which weapons contracts and related projects are sometimes canceled and are frequently reshaped," with the result that workers are often "precipitously and unceremoniously" laid off and the local communities suffer sudden serious tax and income losses.

In addition, Dumas said, the nation since World War II "has paid an increasingly high price for its military spending. In the last decade alone, diversion of large numbers of engineering and scientific personnel to military-oriented research has seriously drained our ability to develop the technology needed to produce machinery, equipment and consumer goods." The result is that, in relation to countries such as Japan and West Germany, which produce goods mainly for civilian markets, the competitiveness of U.S. industry has been steadily deteriorating. Noting that the Reagan administration had pledged national reindustrialization, Dumas said such a program could not succeed as long as defense budgets continued to exceed the after-tax profits of all United States corporations, as they had in every year since 1951.

What is needed, Dumas said, is civilian industry access to additional capital and technological personnel, which could be accomplished only through a coordinated program of economic conversion that takes into account both the nation's real military needs and the economic needs of industrialized areas. "Restoring the nation to economic vitality would do more to strengthen our security and international influence than building yet another set of multibillion-dollar missiles or adding more militarily irrelevant nuclear warheads to an already mind-boggling stockpile," Dumas said.

While criticism of defense spending has been somewhat standard fare in some liberal and intellectual circles for years, the business community and its allies have been overwhelmingly supportive of ever-larger defense budgets and the contracts such spending produces. By 1982, however, some segments of the business community, alarmed by mounting federal deficits linked chiefly to military spending, were beginning to have serious doubts that increased defense outlays would have over-all positive effects on a recession-wracked economy.

Jack L. Rivkin, president of the research arm of Paine Webber Mitchell Hutchins Inc., one of Wall Street's largest brokerage houses, wrote President Reagan in early 1982 with the warning that "the level of defense spending proposed in the fiscal year 1983 through 1987 budgets is beyond the capacity of the defense industry to absorb and will ultimately lead to a failure by this administration to achieve a lower inflation rate, renewed capital investment in the private sector and its other economic goals." In the mid-to-late 1970s, Rivkin said, the rapid rise in inflation was mainly due to an excess demand for manufactured goods. He added that Reagan, through his military spending plans, was "now proposing to substitute the defense industry for basic industry as the engine to fuel inflation in the 1980s."

Likewise, the Council on Economic Priorities reported in a March 1982 study that the Reagan administration's five-year defense spending program of $1.6 trillion would produce larger federal deficits, greater unemployment, and slumping economic growth, and would put the United States at a further disadvantage in the international economic community. The Council said that, in studying the economic performance of a dozen other Western nations over the last twenty years, it had determined that the countries with comparatively small military budgets had larger increases in economic growth, productivity, and investment.

In addition to the other negative effects of increased defense contracting, it is clear that the process does nothing to trim the size of the Pentagon bureaucracy. While some agencies of government in the early 1980s could argue that, by contracting for more services they could reduce the number of civil service employees, the Pentagon could make no such claims. In addition to the contracting boom anticipated as a result of the Reagan administration defense spending proposals, the Defense Department was also the only major federal unit being allowed to increase its civilian work force. The number of Defense Department civilian employees increased from 990,000 in fiscal year 1980, before Reagan came into office, to 1,025,000 in fiscal year 1982 during Reagan's first full year as president. More increases were expected after the military services, in late 1981, requested that 72,000 additional civilians be hired over the next five years to help carry out the expanded defense spending programs.

Even though the Pentagon has been spared personnel cutbacks over-all in recent years, the trend toward greater use of contract employees has continued unabated for the last three decades. A study for the Defense Department by the influential think-tank, The Rand Corporation, determined that in 1956 contract-hire employees made up 11.9 percent of the Defense Department's total personnel; by 1978, the figure had climbed to 33.1 percent. In 1956 there were fourteen military personnel on active duty for every contract employee; by 1978 the ratio had shrunk to less than four to one. Noting the trend toward greater use of contract employees, Rand (which itself received $20.5 million in defense research and development contracts in fiscal year 1981) recommended that it continue. Given the Reagan military program, the day may not be far off (if it hasn't arrived already) when contract employees comprise more than one-half of the Defense Department's total personnel.

Given the widespread problems with defense contracting, it is disturbing to note that, compared with other major government entities, the Pentagon has made little in-house effort to clean up the monetary waste and other abuses in its contracts, much of which has been uncovered by its own investigators (as well as those in Congress and the General Accounting Office).

Between 1978 and 1982, Congress established by statute the post of inspector general in fifteen civilian federal agencies. The inspectors general, appointed by the president with the consent of the Senate, are mandated to combat fraud, waste, and abuse (in both contract and non-contract matters) and to keep Congress informed of their activities. Despite the importance of such positions to the agencies' fiscal and ethical integrity, the Defense Department, the biggest-spending federal unit of them all, still did not have a similar post established by statute by mid-1982. The Pentagon in 1981 did establish the post of assistant to the secretary of Defense for Review and Oversight and appointed to it Joseph H. Sherick so that he could serve as a watchdog over departmental fraud, waste, and abuse. However, the position was established not by statute but by Defense Secretary Weinberger, and Sherick did not have to undergo any Senate screening process nor did he have any specific reporting duties to Congress.

Also, according to an aide in the Office of the Secretary of Defense, Sherick's post does not entail any specific investigative functions; instead, he relies on reports prepared chiefly by the Defense Contract Audit Agency. After reviewing such reports, he then can make recommendations to the Defense secretary on dealing with some problem of fraud, waste, or abuse.

The Defense Contract Audit Agency, for its part, is involved in the contract monitoring process—but usually in the period before the contract is awarded. The General Accounting Office in 1982 concluded that the DCAA served "more of a procurement support function than an audit or review function." Often, too, DCAA findings of questionable charges on potential contracts have been ignored by contracting officials.

Legislation to create a statutory inspector general (or auditor general) in the Defense Department was passed by the House of Representatives in May 1981; identical legislation was pending in the Senate in 1982. The Reagan administration supported a watered-down measure that would limit the Pentagon's inspector general to examining only "financial and policy decisions." The limited bill would also allow the secretary of Defense to veto any investigation. Given the widespread past abuses in Pentagon contracting, and the rapid proposed increase in defense contracting under the Reagan administration, creation of the post with powers and independence equal to that of the inspectors general of other federal agencies takes on even greater importance.

The Reagan administration did take an apparently important step in August 1982 to try to clean up some of the abuses in defense contracting. At that time, a joint Justice Department/Pentagon special investigative unit was established to prosecute fraud in procurement of defense goods and services. The unit was to concentrate on cases in which the Defense Department is fraudulently charged for goods and services, cases in which illegal payments are involved, and cases in which materials contracted for are shoddy or do not meet the standards agreed to in the contract. Justice and Defense officials said the unit was being created specifically in response to public criticisms that the administration's growing defense budgets will open up greater opportunities for fraud by contractors.

Reports prepared by Sherick's office every six months suggest there is considerable activity to investigate. Sherick's reports are drawn mainly from the records of the Defense Contract Audit Agency (DCAA). During the six-month period ending September 30, 1981, for example, the report states that the DCAA questioned contractors' proposed and incurred costs exceeding $12 billion, of which $3.5 billion was sustained by contracting officials.

During the period, auditors referred 33 cases of alleged fraud to various defense investigative units, while defense investigators submitted 27 cases to the Justice Department for possible prosecution. Among the pending cases (for which no names of contractors were given) was one in which a contractor allegedly mischarged $500,000 in non-contract costs to its Pentagon contract; another in which a service contractor overbilled the government by $750,000 for labor costs; another in which a contractor allegedly obtained $1.2 million illegally by submitting fraudulent progress payment claims to the government and by furnishing substandard goods. These were typical of the cases then pending before a grand jury or in the Justice Department.

In its report for the six-month period ending March 31, 1982, the Defense Contract Audit Agency questioned $8.6 billion in contractors' proposed or incurred costs, of which $3.7 billion was sustained by contracting officials. More than 250 cases of fraud in defense programs were referred to the Justice Department for possible prosecution during the period. Over the years, Justice has decided to prosecute only about 13 percent of all cases referred to it by Defense Department auditors and investigators. In this six-month period, the percentage was higher—23 percent—as Justice accepted 40 cases for prosecution and declined 131. There were 15 federal convictions during the period, which resulted in almost $5.7 million coming back to the government in the form of fines, penalties, and restitutions.

Despite the well-documented and costly contracting abuses in the Pentagon over the years, Defense Secretary Weinberger said in late 1981 that he could see little "waste or inefficiency or ineffectiveness in what we're doing." A. Ernest Fitzgerald, the air force civilian cost expert who has been a longtime critic of Pentagon waste, sees it differently.

"People outside the Pentagon always ask me, 'how can we cut costs?' " Fitzgerald said. "It's not difficult. Right now, the money sack is open at both ends for contractors. We could cut spending if there were the will and determination to do so. And one way is to stop the handouts to contractors." Fitzgerald said he had never seen anyone in government get fired for failing to hold down contract cost overruns or for allowing needless, wasteful contracts to be awarded. Holding Pentagon officials accountable for contract waste would be one way of cutting costs considerably, he said.

Fitzgerald, to many Pentagon critics, is the living embodiment of what happens when defense officials do try to combat waste. In November 1968 Fitzgerald, then air force deputy for Management Systems, testified before a Senate subcommittee that there was a $2 billion cost overrun on Lockheed's C-5A cargo plane program. For disclosing what had theretofore been a secret overrun, Fitzgerald became the target of air force harassment.

Twelve days after his Senate testimony, Fitzgerald's job was reclassified and his career tenure revoked, without explanation. This meant he could be fired from his post without cause and that he would not have civil service protection. He was removed from overseeing significant programs, such as the C-5A, and was assigned to monitor bowling alley construction in Thailand and food service costs in mess halls. The Pentagon's Office of Special Investigations investigated him, as did Richard Nixon's White House.

One year after his testimony on the C-5A, Fitzgerald was subjected to a one-man reduction-in-force (RIF, in government parlance) and was out of a job. In 1973 he was finally restored to an air force post after a favorable Civil Service Commission ruling, but he was given duties in which he seldom had access to documents that might contain information embarrassing to the air force or its contractors. He sued the air force in 1974 in order to win back a position with the same duties as he originally had. Finally, in the spring of 1982, the air force agreed to let Fitzgerald have back his original job, which would enable him once again to review costs of major air force acquisitions. His treatment by the air force for more than thirteen years could hardly be encouraging to other potential Pentagon whistleblowers. "Nobody is going to get out and do what I did when they see what happened to me," Fitzgerald said after his settlement with the air force was announced.

During his long battle with the air force, Fitzgerald continued to set the example of what a good public servant should be by assisting congressional committees looking into waste and other Pentagon foolishness. Before his firing, even when he was assigned to the relatively mundane task of monitoring bowling alley construction in Thailand, the irrepressible Fitzgerald took his work most seriously. He discovered cost overruns on that project, too, and raised questions as to why air force funds were being used for such a dubious purpose. His air force superiors promptly removed him from that project, too, and told him to concentrate on mess halls.

In an early 1982 interview, Fitzgerald said that those government contracts that substitute contract employees for federal workers are usually not entered into for reasons of cost effectiveness. Such contracting, he said, constitutes "a deliberate attempt to whack bureaucrats but not to save money. The system was brought to perfection under the Carter administration, and the Reagan administration has improved upon it."

As long as the federal bureaucracy is made the scapegoat for government waste and inefficiency, the contractors—which are the source of a significant portion of needless government spending—will continue to get a free ride. Until as much attention is paid to the documented contracting abuses as is given to bureaucratic excesses, programs to eliminate wasteful federal spending are not likely to achieve far-reaching results. Given the Pentagon's contracting record over the last three decades, it seems safe to suggest that neither social programs nor other projects run by federal bureaucrats can match the waste involved in defense contracts of all types.

5 · A Company
Called TRW

"A company called TRW" is truly an American success story. Since the inception of the R-W portion of TRW in 1953 as a tiny consulting firm "with a desk, a telephone, and three or four good people," TRW, Inc., by the current decade had grown into a versatile technological giant with net sales of more than $5 billion annually and 92,000 employees worldwide.

While not exactly a household name such as Exxon or General Motors, TRW was by the 1980s a prominent enterprise involved in everything from computers and spacecraft, to components for motor vehicles, to equipment for oil exploration and production. What was less well-known about the company was that it was also running key operations of the federal government. TRW's rise to wealth and prominence is an instructive case history of how financial empires and control of major functions of government can be built on federal contracts.

TRW, which bills itself as "a company called TRW," is a diversified, technically oriented company that provides to industry and government a dazzling array of goods and services: advanced systems engineering; research and technical expertise; electronic systems, components, and services; computer-based and analytical services; and a variety of managerial and consulting skills.

Motor vehicles that Americans drive, the clothes they wear, the buildings they work in—all have something in them developed or produced by TRW. For cars, trucks, buses, and farm equipment, TRW provides components—in the steering, hydraulics system, gears, valves, chassis, and in the safety, suspension, and electrical systems. Nearly every engine manufactured in the United States, for everything from automobiles and jets to lawnmowers, uses TRW parts. For clothes, TRW supplies fasteners. A subsidiary of TRW is the major computerized credit reporting service in the country.

For the energy industry, TRW provides technical services and products—including valves, pumps, pump parts, drilling tools, submergible electrical pumping systems, power cable for secondary and tertiary petroleum production—which are used in oil and natural gas pipeline transmission and in exploration and production. On the trans-Alaska oil pipeline, TRW provided one oil company with a system to control oil gathering and production and developed the valves that controlled the oil flow through the pipeline. TRW-produced tools were also widely used in construction of the 800-mile-long line. In 1981 TRW contracted with the People's Republic of China to provide products to assist that nation with offshore petroleum exploration. TRW also supplies components for nuclear reactors.

The corporation has played a major role in space exploration and in providing the Pentagon and the Central Intelligence Agency with super-secret spy systems in space. It has built more than 100 unmanned spacecraft for the National Aeronautics and Space Administration (NASA), as well as subsystems and components for other space vehicles. TRW's Pioneer I, launched in 1958, was the first spacecraft designed, built, and launched by a private company. The company's Explorer 6, in 1959, transmitted the first photographs of earth from space. In NASA's manned space flight program, TRW provided mission analysis, trajectory simulation, and computer software support. More recently, the second manned space-shuttle flight, in November 1981, carried a TRW-designed payload for monitoring the earth's air pollution from outer space. TRW also set up the biological laboratories on the Viking spaceship for the Mars probe, provided communications systems for space satellites, has studied the earth's atmosphere, magnetosphere, and ionosphere for the space shuttle program, has built tracking and data satellites, and has been chosen to develop NASA's next-generation astronomical satellite. On the military side, TRW has been involved in anti-submarine warfare and undersea surveillance projects, laser technology, an electro-optical deep-space surveillance system, and the Thor, Atlas, Titan I, Minuteman, and MX missiles. In 1981 the company received many significant and secrecy-shrouded military contracts, including one for $34 million for a "very high speed integrated circuit program which is intended to make significant advances in the state of the art of military microelectronic technology" and another for $76 million for a military reconnaissance system.

TRW has also developed a computerized dispatching system for the Bonneville Power Administration, has designed electronic terminals at supermarkets so that funds are automatically withdrawn from savings and loan accounts and put into the customers' supermarket accounts, and has provided the valves in the heating and cooling systems for most of the buildings that make up Atlanta's skyline. If one only looks, TRW is everywhere.

After its modest beginning in 1953 as an independent consulting firm, Ramo-Wooldridge prospered rapidly, achieving $2 million in sales in 1954 and $43 million in 1957. After it merged in 1958 with Thompson Products Company, of Cleveland (making it Thompson-Ramo-Wooldridge), the company's meteoric rise continued. By 1968 net sales were up to $1.5 billion; by 1973 the figure was $2.2 billion; by 1976, more than $2.9 billion; by 1979, almost $4.6 billion; and by 1981, almost $5.3 billion. TRW's total income was just under $632 million for 1981, which was also the tenth consecutive year that the company showed higher sales, profits, and dividends. By 1981 its total assets stood at $3.2 billion, of which $1.1 billion was in other countries: Argentina, Australia, Brazil, Canada, France, Italy, Japan, Spain, Switzerland, the United Kingdom, and West Germany. The company has more than 100 U.S. manufacturing facilities, and more than 90 abroad.

Although owing its creation and early successes entirely to government contracts, primarily with the Pentagon and NASA, TRW by 1963 had diversified enough so that nonfederal work comprised about half of its annual net sales. The percentage of federal sales continued to decline (while actual dollar amounts increased), reaching 25 percent in 1971 and then leveling off in the 19 to 22 percent range for much of the rest of the decade. By 1980 the percentage had inched up to 24, and in 1981 it climbed even higher, to 27 percent, which means that about $1.4 billion of the company's sales came from the government in 1981.

Almost half of TRW's government sales in 1981 were to the Defense Department, with NASA and the Energy Department being its other main federal customers. Its three main private-sector customers are General Motors Corporation, Ford Motor Company, and United Technologies Corporation; they accounted for 5 percent, 5 percent, and 3 percent, respectively, of TRW's over-all sales in 1981. All three are also major defense contractors, with General Motors No. 27, Ford No. 33, and United Technologies No. 2 in the Pentagon's listing for fiscal year 1981.

TRW is regularly in the top 50 defense and energy contractors. In fiscal year 1981, the company was 34th among defense prime contractors with $516.6 million in contracts; among defense research and development contractors, TRW was 7th with $270.2 million in contracts. Among energy contractors, TRW was 42nd in fiscal year 1980 with $30.7 million in new contracts. In the first 13 months of the Reagan administration, TRW substantially boosted its number of new energy contracts, receiving awards totaling almost $140 million during that period. When the contract list is divided into services and goods, TRW is usually near the top of the Energy Department's roster of support service contractors. For example, in fiscal year 1978 TRW was No. 1 among Energy Department service contractors with $16.9 million. On the *Fortune* 500 list of leading corporations, TRW ranked No. 71 in 1982. Worldwide, it is in the top 150 manufacturing enterprises.

TRW's three major sales areas have in recent years been fairly evenly balanced in earnings. In 1981, for example, 38 percent of TRW's sales came in the area of electronics and space systems; 32 percnet, in motor vehicle parts and components; and 30 percent, in industry and technology.

To show how TRW rose to wealth and influence in federal policymaking requires a look at the origins of TRW and its history as a government contractor.

As one writer has noted, the founders of the Ramo-Wooldridge Corporation, Drs. Simon Ramo and Dean E. Wooldridge, "were until 1953 obscure and moderately paid aerospace scientists" with Hughes Aircraft Company. Ramo had been director of research electronics for guided missiles and vice president and director of operations at Hughes; Wooldridge had been director and then vice president of electronics research and development at Hughes. Both left Hughes in 1953 to form Ramo-Wooldridge. Within five years—thanks to lucrative air force contracts and the subsequent merger with Thompson Products—the two men "had been transformed into multi-millionaires and captains of industry."

Or, as the House Government Operations Committee, which investigated TRW's contractual relationship with the air force, put it in a 1959 report, the company's spectacular rise was "intimately tied to and largely a result of its work for the Air Force."

Ramo's and Wooldridge's work for the government began in 1953 when their newly formed firm was awarded an air force contract that was to set the stage for its eventual controlling role in the United States missile program. The contract designated Ramo-Wooldridge as the technical staff to an air force advisory group that was to come up with recommendations for establishing an intercontinental ballistic missile (ICBM) development program.

With Ramo-Wooldridge's help, the advisory committee, formally called the Strategic Missiles Evaluation Committee, recommended that the development and deployment of ICBMs be given the highest priority. Continuing its association with the program, Ramo-Wooldridge in May 1954 won a key contract to perform a one-year engineering and design study to determine how extensive the ICBM program would be. This contract put R-W "at the decision-making center of future development" of the strategic missiles systems and led to a subsequent contract giving the new firm over-all authority for systems engineering and technical direction of the program.

At least one member of the Strategic Missiles Evaluation Committee objected at the time to giving the crucial design and engineering study to Ramo and Wooldridge. F.R. Collbohm, president of The Rand Corporation, said he felt that R-W had "no demonstrated competence" and that its involvement presented an "unworkable" arrangement that "would tend to separate responsibility and authority." Also, he said, he felt the air force could have established the in-house capability itself to handle the functions assigned to R-W. Panel member Jerome Wiesner had tried to get the California Institute of Technology to assume the role that the air force assigned to R-W, but other members said no university or corporation was equipped to handle the role. Given these concerns by panel members concerning R-W's role, the air force appointed a special three-member committee to evaluate the matter. The panel determined that the arrangement with R-W was "logical and sound and should be continued."

In connection with obtaining the initial air force contracts, Ramo-Wooldridge developed a close working relationship with Thompson Products, a manufacturing company, founded in 1901, that had prospered initially by providing valves to the budding automobile industry. Under a complex arrangement worked out in 1954, Ramo and Wooldridge each put up $6,750 and received 51 percent of the voting common stock of Thompson Products; they were given seats on Thompson's board of directors. The Thompson firm, which was also an air force subcontractor, pumped in $20 million to spur R-W's development.

In October 1958, R-W and Thompson Products formalized their agreement and merged. Under the terms of the merger, Ramo and Wooldridge each showed paper profits of more than $3.15 million on their original investments of $6,750 apiece. One result of the merger was that both Ramo and Wooldridge removed themselves from operations of the Space Technology Laboratories, the R-W division that worked on the major air force missile contracts. As contracting critic H.L. Nieburg pointed out, through the merger "the government lost the services of the men who were the bases of the original source selection."

During those early years of success, R-W's contracts with the air force contained a "hardware ban," which prohibited the firm from engaging "in the physical development or production of any components for use in the ICBM" unless given permission to do so by the Assistant Secretary of the Air Force for Materiel. Despite the ban, some members of Congress later contended TRW had received some hardware contracts, but the air force reported this was not the case.

But, even more crucial was the fact that the air force permitted all contractors on the ICBM project to subcontract with Thompson Products. And since R-W substantially determined who the other contractors on the ICBM project would be, its critics felt it was in a position of ensuring that Thompson Products would receive a substantial share of the subcontracts.

Ramo-Wooldridge's rise to eminence with the air force did not come without controversy. In 1959 the House Committee on Government Operations looked into R-W's initial role on the Strategic Missiles Evaluation Committee and the multimillion-dollar benefits that later flowed from that privileged position. The committee reported: "Considering the decisive impact of the Strategic Missiles Evaluation Committee report on the future course of the ICBM program, the distinctive management arrangement that evolved from it, and the continuing contractual role of the Ramo-Wooldridge Corporation in the program, the question naturally arises as to the degree of Ramo-Wooldridge participation in developing the report. To the extent that Ramo-Wooldridge authored the report . . . they became in a certain sense the beneficiaries of their own handiwork."

The committee's report said that TRW had so much control over the air force missile programs that "this contractor alone sits at the very seat of government and wields an enormous influence on the course and conduct of multimillion-dollar missile programs." TRW officials, the report stated, "are regarded as performing those supervisory or directing functions which Air Force personnel themselves otherwise would perform." There was also concern among other missile contractors that TRW, in its supervisory role, was learning too much about the other contractors' technical operations and could turn the knowledge to its own advantage on later contracts. There was even, the House report said, "a question as to whether the conflict-of-interest statutes apply to the [TRW] personnel who have responsibilities similar to those normally exercised by government personnel."

(Twenty years later, echoes of those earlier criticisms of TRW's arrangement with the air force could be heard in the concerns voiced by congressional committees and the General Accounting Office over TRW's contracting arrangements with the Energy Department.)

One reason Congress took a look at TRW in 1959 was that many

of the company's competitors had become increasingly unhappy—
and vocal—about the favored position TRW enjoyed with the air
force. At the same time, President Eisenhower, his scientific advisers,
and the army were growing concerned about the air force's increasing
control over aerospace weaponry and felt it necessary to clip the air
force's wings. This was done by creating the National Aeronautics
and Space Administration to handle civilian aspects of space programs and by establishing in the Pentagon a centralized research and
development contracting authority. The result of all this for TRW was
that in 1960 it gave up the missile management contract to the Aerospace Corporation, a nonprofit systems engineering firm that was
created specifically to replace TRW in the key missiles program position. TRW's role in the program thus "was reduced from preeminence
to equality" with other major contractors, which meant it continued
to receive substantial contract awards from the air force, as well as
from other military services and NASA.

TRW's government influence was so notable by the late 1950s that
it is credited with helping get Dr. T. Keith Glennan, president of the
Case Institute of Technology, selected as administrator of the newly
formed NASA. Among those promoting Glennan's candidacy was
Frederick C. Crawford, chairman of the Case Institute trustees, who
was also chairman of the board of TRW. Through its systems engineering contracts with NASA, TRW also had substantial influence on
the space program, just as it had earlier with the air force.

Continuing concern over federal research and development contracting practices and potential conflicts of interest embodied therein,
prompted President John F. Kennedy in his first year in office to
appoint a special study commission on government research and development contracting. The commission, in its 1962 report, sharply
criticized the original relationship between Ramo-Wooldridge and the
air force. The commission, headed by President Kennedy's budget
director, David E. Bell, stated that, "The kind of situation . . . exem-
plified some years ago by the Ramo-Wooldridge position is improper." The Bell Report added that no private firm, such as R-W,
should "be simultaneously offering technical advice to the government on an activity and in a position to benefit from that same
technical advice" through later government contracts. In the subse-

quent two decades the government, particularly in the defense and energy fields, continued to place contractors in positions of authority where they could influence future policies and thereby possibly benefit.

This was not to be the last criticism against TRW by a governmental unit. The company was also cited in 1961 House hearings for excessive markups of 110 percent on armatures for fuel pumps, for B-47 aircraft, it had sold to the Pentagon. Then, in 1964, the General Accounting Office charged that TRW had deliberately violated the law requiring it to report any patents it developed under government R&D contracts. The GAO contended that TRW had not disclosed to the Defense Department eighteen inventions developed during the previous three and a half years under Pentagon contracts. One purpose of the law was to insure that inventions developed under contracts would be readily available for other contractors to use in their government work. But, by failing to disclose its patents, "TRW put itself in the position to claim sole-source status for new contracts, or could charge other contractors and the government royalties for the patents' use," according to contracting critic Nieburg.

Later in the 1960s, TRW became involved in other controversies concerning government contracts. In 1967, for example, the General Accounting Office reported that TRW had obtained expensive government equipment, purportedly for Pentagon contracting work, but had actually used it—without government permission—mostly for its nongovernment commercial work. The accounting office said that TRW received from the government a $1.4 million, 8,000-ton mechanical force press after telling federal officials that the older government-owned presses in the TRW plant "were inefficient and unable to handle all the government orders for jet-engine midspan blades." Yet the accounting office found that TRW, from 1962 to 1965, had used the large press for its own commercial work 78 percent of the time, while using the supposedly inadequate smaller presses for most of the government contracting work.

In the following decade, TRW disclosed in a filing with the Securities and Exchange Commission in late 1977 that some of its employees, consultants, and sales representatives had made $125,000 in questionable payments to officials or employees of foreign governments, and another $50,000 in questionable payments to nongovernment personnel in connection with TRW's foreign business. Also, over the previous five and a half years, TRW reported that a division of the company and several of its foreign subsidiaries had, at the request of "a limited number of foreign customers or sales representatives," structured certain business transactions in such a way as "to avoid foreign government business regulation applicable to such transactions." These transactions included paying "legitimately owed sales commissions" to sales representatives in countries other than those in which they lived, and overinvoicing certain exported products "with ultimate remission of the over-indexed amounts" to foreign customers in countries other than those in which they lived.

The company stated that no director or member of the company's senior management "participated in, authorized or had prior knowledge of any of the payments," indicating the payments were approved at middle-management levels. Some of the payments may have resulted in TRW failing to pay "a negligible amount" of income taxes to the United States government, and the company said it had so advised the Internal Revenue Service. According to TRW's statement to the Securities and Exchange Commission, the company was taking "vigorous steps" to insure that no more questionable payments would be made in the future. TRW had undertaken the investigation of its overseas payment policies during a period beginning in the mid-1970s when there were numerous disclosures and allegations that many United States companies had made illegal and questionable payments in the pursuit of business in other countries. In response to this situation, the Securities and Exchange Commission established a voluntary disclosure program under which corporations could publicly report questionable payments they had made. TRW personnel conducted the internal investigation that uncovered the questionable payments.

TRW encountered other difficulties in early 1979 when the Federal Trade Commission ruled that the company and its former board chairman and chief executive officer, Horace A. Shepard, had violated a provision of federal antitrust law that bars interlocking directorates among competing companies. The commission said the violation covered the period 1971–75 when Shepard simultaneously served on the boards of directors of both TRW and the Addressograph-Multigraph Corporation (which later became AM International). The agency ruled that TRW and Addressograph competed in the sale of various banking and credit authorization equipment, and that, therefore, no one who sat on the board of one of the companies could also sit on the board of the other firm.

TRW was fined $10,000, but would not be required to pay it unless the firm again violated the interlocking directorate ban in the following ten years. The commission's decision also ordered TRW to obtain from its other directors a list of corporate boards on which they sat, and a list of the products and services offered by those other firms in order to ensure there were no additional interlocks among competing companies. Shepard had left the Addressograph board in 1975 and stepped down as TRW's chief executive in 1977; he continued to serve on TRW's board of directors as late as 1982. TRW denied that it and Addressograph were in any way competitive and said there had been no violation of the law.

In the mid-1970s, TRW even had its own spy saga involving incidents that raised questions about its abilities (as well as those of other government contractors similarly situated) to handle top-secret material and data. The tale involved a TRW employee, Christopher John Boyce, who had obtained a $140-a-week job as a code room clerk at TRW's Defense and Space Systems Group in Redondo Beach, California. Boyce received a top security clearance and was given access to spy satellite data and a secret code room linking TRW with Central Intelligence Agency headquarters in Virginia and with the CIA's Rhyolite surveillance system's principal ground station near Alice Springs in central Australia. TRW has been one of the major suppliers of surveillance systems to the CIA.

Boyce later began passing top-secret information on CIA codes and surveillance systems to a friend, Andrew Daulton Lee. Lee, a convicted drug dealer, in turn passed the information to the Soviet Embassy in Mexico City in return for about $77,000 over an 18-month period. Boyce and Lee were arrested in January 1977 and later indicted on a variety of espionage charges. Both were convicted; Lee received a life prison term, while Boyce was sentenced to forty years. Boyce, a personable young man who was well-liked by most people who met him, said he turned over the secret data because of disillusionment with CIA activities abroad and with the arms race. Federal prosecutors claimed he did it for thrills and money.

The tale became even more dramatic when Boyce in early 1980 used a complex plan to escape from the maximum security prison in Lompoc, California. Boyce initiated the escape plan by asking to be assigned to a job with a prison maintenance crew. Then, another prisoner obtained a blank work order form that he used to submit a forged work assignment to clean an underground drainage tunnel away from prison yard checkpoints and near a "blind spot" for prison guards, close to two ten-foot-high chain link fences that ran parallel to each other near the rear of the prison yard. After cleaning the tunnel, the rest of the work crew left, but Boyce stayed behind in the tunnel. Also left behind with Boyce was a small wooden ladder, which another prisoner had made in the prison shop, and a pair of metal-cutting shears, which yet another prisoner had stolen from the shop.

Boyce was to remain in the tunnel until dark, then use the ladder to climb to the top of the fence, and cut through the razor-sharp wire at the top of the fence with the stolen shears. To complete the scheme, another prisoner placed on Boyce's prison bunk a papier-mâché dummy, which Boyce had made in a prison art class. Boyce had even cut off some of his own hair to put on the dummy. So, when guards looked into his cell on the day of the escape, they saw what they thought was Boyce sleeping in his bed.

One prison acquaintance said just after the escape that Boyce had said he was heading for Arizona to pick up more top-secret Central Intelligence Agency documents he had stashed there before his arrest. After a 19-month international manhunt, Boyce was finally captured, thanks to an informer's tip, in a rural area of Washington State. Boyce had supported himself during that period by robbing several banks in the U.S. Northwest; he eventually pleaded guilty to robbing five banks and received a 25-year sentence on top of his espionage term.

After his conviction on the spying charges, Boyce was quoted as saying that "Security at TRW is a joke." Although employees were barred from discussing their particular secret project with persons not working on the project, Boyce found this security stricture was regularly breached. One worker told him, according to Robert Lindsey's book, *The Falcon and the Snowman,* "about a secret project . . . to build a new satellite that would be used to shoot down other satellites with a superhigh-energy laser beam." Boyce also regularly, without difficulty, used a tiny camera to photograph documents in the "black vault," the supersecret communications center for the spy satellite operations. Later, he took documents home with him at night and returned them the next morning after photographing them. Employees, sometimes using courier pouches that were supposed to be used to carry National Security Agency and CIA documents, regularly smuggled liquor into the black vault, where they had many drunken parties. One employee used lunchtime breaks to show pornographic movies in the plant, while another employee "took bets on the horse races over the secure telephone lines in the TRW War Room." A marijuana plant grew in the black vault. As Boyce had stated, security did, indeed, seem a joke, and certainly raised questions about the company's ability to adhere to strict security provisions on its other government contracts.

The Boyce affair wasn't the only time TRW had security problems at one of its principal facilities. In late 1976, six men were convicted in federal court in Los Angeles on charges that they worked with a clerk at TRW Credit Data, the nation's largest consumer credit bureau, to doctor computerized credit reports on hundreds of poor credit risks. The purpose of the scheme was to find people with poor credit records and then charge them fees of between $300 and $1,500 to "improve" their credit ratings by changing records on the computer.

TRW's contracts with the CIA have earned it an inside position with access to top intelligence information, as has its representation on various Pentagon and presidential advisory panels. In this regard, President Reagan in late 1981 reactivated the President's Foreign Intelligence Advisory Board, which President Carter had abolished, and selected nineteen persons to serve on it, including John S. Foster, Jr., a former Pentagon official who was TRW's vice president. Foster had previously served on the board before it was abolished. The panel, headed by economist Leo Cherne, who had also served on the board under Presidents Nixon and Ford, was to evaluate the reliability of United States intelligence gathering operations.

TRW was also well represented in the highest circles of the Carter administration by one of the company's founders, Simon Ramo, who served on the President's Committee on Science and Technology. The versatile Ramo is also the author of books ranging from topics as disparate as the United States' decline in technology *(America's Technology Slip)* to tennis instruction *(Extraordinary Tennis for the Ordinary Player)*. In his well-written, often philosophical, essays on technology, Ramo comes across, as one reviewer put it, "more like an earnest and concerned scientist than like a millionaire industrialist."

Down through the years, Ramo has had the ears of various presidents and Cabinet officers through his appointments to a number of influential advisory posts. During both the Nixon and Ford administrations, he served as a member of the White House Energy Research and Development Advisory Council and as a member of the State Department's Committee on Science and Foreign Affairs; during the Ford administration alone, he was a member of the advisory committee to the Secretary of Commerce, a member of the consulting roster to the administrator of the Energy Research and Development Administration, and chairman of the President's Committee on Science and Research. Ramo has also been a director of the United States Chamber of Commerce and of several corporations, and is the former president of the Bunker-Ramo Corporation.

During the transition period between President Reagan's election and the day he took office, Reagan selected Ramo for the choice spot of co-chairman of a Science and Technology Task Force that provided advice to Reagan's transition team on technical issues. Panel members advised, among other things, that Reagan strengthen programs in military, industrial, and space technology to increase the nation's economic and military might.

Wooldridge served as president of Ramo-Wooldridge from 1953 to 1958 and then took over for four years as president of the newly formed TRW company. He served as a member of TRW's board of directors until 1969, and since then has held no official company post. Since 1962, he has been a research associate in engineering at the California Institute of Technology and has written several scientific and technical books on such subjects as the brain and the physical basis of intelligent life. While Ramo's views often have appeared in the popular press, Wooldridge's writing has been more confined to scientific and technical publications.

This discussion of Ramo's and Wooldridge's background helps shed some light on TRW's success. Another key to its success is that, throughout its three-decade history, the company and the Pentagon have periodically exchanged personnel. As a prime example, Richard D. DeLauer, upon his retirement as a navy commander in 1958, came to TRW and held a number of executive posts. He was also a member of a major Pentagon advisory panel, the Defense Science Board, and was chairman of the board's manpower panel. In early 1981, he left his executive vice president and director positions at TRW, upon his selection by President Reagan to return to the Pentagon as undersecretary of Defense for research and engineering, one of the key Defense Department posts. At the Pentagon, DeLauer was responsible for weapons development and acquisition, a position that assumed even greater importance in light of President Reagan's $1.6 trillion, five-year defense spending program initiated in 1982.

John S. Foster, Jr., who came to TRW in 1973 and by 1982 was vice president for science and technology, had served at the Pentagon as director of defense research and engineering from 1965 to 1973. TRW's chairman and chief executive officer in 1982, Ruben F. Mettler, had served as an aide to the assistant secretary of Defense for research and engineering in 1954–55. Stanley C. Pace, TRW's president in 1982, had been an air force colonel when he left the military service in 1953, and TRW vice president Neal A. Pritchard had served as a navy commander in both World War II and the Korean War.

In July 1982, questions were raised in Congress concerning DeLauer's role in setting up an eleven-member task force of the Pentagon's Defense Science Board to evaluate a proposed new computer procurement policy. Of the defense contractor members on the task force, only TRW had two members: Barry W. Boehm, of its defense and space systems group, and John G. Weber, of its military electronics division.

The task force became the focus of controversy when the General Accounting Office reported that seven of the eleven contractor members had a financial interest in one or more of the firms that would benefit from the proposed new policy, which pertained to standardizing computers purchased for military purposes. Two of the members did not even submit their financial disclosure forms until after the task force made its recommendations. Although the accounting office did not name the seven members of the companies, it was subsequently disclosed that TRW and its officials were among them. TRW already had an army contract, under a joint venture with General Electric Company, to develop an advanced computer. Among the other seven on the list were representatives of Control Data Corporation, Texas Instruments, Inc., and MITRE Corporation.

DeLauer and one of his top aides had, according to Representative Jack Brooks, D-Texas, chairman of the House Government Operations Committee's National Security Subcommittee, "picked out all of the members" of the task force. Because of the conflicts-of-interest question, Norman R. Augustine, chairman of the Defense Science Board, refused to approve the task force's report, pending an internal Pentagon review of the issue.

In testimony before Brooks's subcommittee, the top accounting office official, Comptroller General Charles A. Bowsher, said that "the tilt of task force membership toward interests that support the proposed policy" meant its conclusions "cannot reasonably be looked upon as having been objectively reached, irrespective of the merits of those policies." Bowsher said he would forward his information to the Justice Department for a determination of whether the conflict-of-interest laws had been violated.

A number of task force members, including Weber, contended that there were no conflicts involved. One task force member, George H. Heilmeier, of Texas Instruments, was quoted in the press before the hearing as saying that in his ten years on the Defense Science Board he had "never seen anyone vote their own special, selfish interest. I reject the inference that because a person works for a company that is in the computer business that individual is totally and hopelessly biased." It was then disclosed at the Brooks' subcommittee hearing that Heilmeier had written Texas Governor William P. Clements, Jr., to get him to pressure Brooks to "behave like a true Texan" and drop his "witch-hunt" regarding the Defense Science Board. Clements, according to Brooks, never contacted him on the matter. Clements was deputy defense secretary in the Nixon administration.

The proposed computer policy, which was also endorsed by Defense Secretary Caspar W. Weinberger, could result in billions of dollars worth of contracts to the firms that end up providing the standardized computer system to the Pentagon. The policy was opposed by a number of commercial computer firms that have both private sector and government customers and would stand to lose Pentagon contracts under a shift to the standardized system. In later testimony before Brooks's subcommittee, Deputy Defense Secretary Frank C. Carlucci said the Pentagon had been "sloppy" in not requiring the advisory panel members to file financial disclosure statements before the panel decided on the computer issue, but he insisted, nevertheless, that no conflict of interest was involved. In December 1982, the Justice Department said it had decided there was "no prosecutable violation of Federal law."

By the 1970s, the fast-growing TRW firm, in addition to its major defense work, had established itself as a significant force in the government's energy programs. Little-publicized congressional investigations determined that the company was, in effect, running portions of federal energy agencies by performing functions that were governmental in nature and properly should have been carried out by federal bureaucrats and not by employees of profit-making firms. TRW and other consultants and contractors were shown through these investigations to be playing key roles in the operation of, first, the Energy Research and Development Administration, and then its successor, the Department of Energy.

The Energy Research and Development Administration (ERDA) was established in 1975, when the old Atomic Energy Commission was reorganized and divided into ERDA and the Nuclear Regulatory Commission.

About the same time, stories that TRW and other contractors and consulting firms were running some of the energy agency's operations came to the attention of members of Congress. On March 11, 1976, Representative Ken Hechler, D-West Virginia, then-chairman of the Subcommittee on Energy Research, Development and Demonstration (Fossil Fuels) of the House Committee on Science and Technology, wrote to Comptroller General Elmer B. Staats, the head of the General Accounting Office, concerning TRW's relationship with the

Energy Research and Development Administration. The subcommittee was concerned, among other things, about TRW's access to vital ERDA information that Hechler said raised the likelihood of a conflict of interest conceivably able to give TRW the inside track on future contracts. The subcommittee was also disturbed by the "use of contractors to perform tasks, which involve ERDA program formation and budgets, normally performed by government employees." Hechler asked the General Accounting Office to "look into this situation and the extent to which TRW is performing such tasks."

On April 15, 1976, another congressional panel, the Conservation, Energy and Natural Resources Subcommittee of the House Committee on Government Operations, also asked Staats' agency to investigate TRW's relationship with the energy agency. In a letter signed by Chairman William S. Moorhead, D-Pennsylvania, the subcommittee noted that the Energy Research and Development Administration "has moved to the device of service contracts outside the government in order to have certain administrative and program functions performed." Added Moorhead: "This committee is concerned about the speed and direction with which this administrative technique has expanded within a number of executive agencies, but particularly as it has been adopted by ERDA. The relationship and the responsibilities of the ERDA to consultant groups outside the government is extremely sensitive. . . ."

Moorhead requested that the General Accounting Office "review this adopted administrative policy of ERDA, to determine whether such contracting efforts represent a sound arrangement for the performance of ERDA functions, and whether this device poses any danger of minimizing development of in-house ERDA administrative capability." The chairman said the subcommittee was concerned that the contracts "may further remove ERDA administrative capability from its day-to-day oversight and management of the agency's fossil energy program responsibilities."

On September 21, 1976, the General Accounting Office issued a report confirming the two subcommittees' worst fears that contractors were substantially controlling programs at the Energy Research and Development Administration. The GAO found that, as of July 1976, eighteen months after ERDA began operations, its Fossil Energy

Organization had awarded thirty-six management and technical support contracts—that is, contracts intimately involved with key operations of the agency—worth $27 million. In addition, Fossil Energy had assumed jurisdiction over twelve other such administrative contracts, valued at about $16 million, which had previously been awarded by the Interior Department's Office of Coal Research, one of ERDA's predecessors.

The General Accounting Office further noted that ERDA had contracted out "basic functions for planning and management of its programs." The net result of this, the accounting office stated, was "to dilute the agency's ability to retain essential control over the conduct of its programs and to assure the Congress that its programs are being carried out in an efficient and economical manner." The report went on to recommend that ERDA "reduce its dependence on management and technical support contracts." Throughout the investigations of TRW's energy contracts, the General Accounting Office and congressional committees made it clear that there were no questions of TRW's competence to do the work; rather, it was a matter of who controlled the vital functions of the energy agency.

The Federal Energy Administration (FEA), before it also was assimilated into the new Department of Energy, was, like ERDA, found to have turned over key aspects of its basic mission to private contractors. Criticism of FEA came in the Senate Appropriations Committee's report on the fiscal year 1977 supplemental appropriations bill. The report noted that the FEA, in its budget request, anticipated it would have 45 contracts for data gathering, 12 contracts for operation of regulatory programs, 23 contracts for conservation programs, and another $4.5 million for contracts for "innovative conservation programs." Criticizing the use of contractors in such key areas, the committee stated it "believes that necessary analyses and studies in these areas should represent the best independent views of the agency itself." In addition, the committee asked that "to the extent possible, the agency . . . develop sufficient in-house capabilities to meet some of the needs for which contracting is recommended."

The 1976 General Accounting Office report on ERDA contractors focused on one contract for $4.9 million that had been awarded to TRW on a sole-source basis for the period of February 1975 to May

1976. The technical and management support services provided by TRW under this contract covered a wide range of functions essential to the energy agency's mission. It appeared from the language of the contract that TRW, and not the civil service bureaucracy, was running the Energy Research and Development Administration.

Under the contract, TRW was assigned to review and revise the fiscal year 1977 budget justification to insure its compatability with ERDA's national plan for energy research, development and demonstration; to study and report to the Fossil Energy Organization on various government incentive plans to encourage commercializing synthetic fuels; to update the strategies and objectives for the coal gasification program; to evaluate other contractor's unsolicited proposals for their technical merit; to develop work statements for proposals solicited from other contractors; and to assist in developing a program to identify and develop a detailed research strategy for resolving health hazards associated with fossil energy technologies.

Significantly, the General Accounting Office found that a look at the Energy Research and Development Administration's budget would not give a true picture of the type of managerial work TRW and other contractors were performing at ERDA. The corporations' support services contracts were "funded from program research and development appropriations and are not specifically identified in the ERDA budget request as support service expenditures." In addition, the General Accounting Office found that TRW had subcontracted much of its managerial work at ERDA to 22 other companies. These subcontractors included such corporate giants as Battelle, General Electric, and McDonnell Douglas.

Energy Research and Development Administration officials contended that the agency needed the contracts with TRW and the other firms because of manpower shortages, an unusually heavy workload, and time pressures. But ERDA officials also defended the delegation of their agency's authority on other grounds.

The deputy assistant administrator for fossil energy told the General Accounting Office that "even if additional Civil Service personnel were hired, there would still be a need for such contracts as the TRW contract." The official explained that "in most cases TRW was assigned tasks of limited duration that required an expertise not readily available within Fossil Energy." The GAO said it did not investigate whether ERDA truly lacked the in-house personnel to perform the tasks assigned to TRW. However, if the energy administration truly lacked this expertise, then the agency had clearly lost control of its own operations to the outsiders of the contractor bureaucracy.

The same energy administration official felt that contractors, rather than civil service workers, were needed for "the work done on evaluating various government incentives that would encourage industry to construct and operate commercial scale synthetic fuel plants." He said this assignment "required financial and economic expertise" that "was not readily available within Fossil Energy." The General Accounting Office countered that, while it "did not conduct a manpower utilization study to determine whether or not Fossil Energy could have done the tasks assigned to TRW," it was clear "that such work should be done whenever possible by ERDA."

The General Accounting Office noted that in order to deal with its purported in-house personnel deficiencies, the energy administration had contracted with Arthur Young and Company for a manpower utilization study. Under this contract, the Young firm was to determine to what extent the agency would have to rely on support service contractors such as TRW. The GAO apparently failed to see the irony in having another contractor, and not agency staff, determine the future role of contractors at the energy administration.

In its study, the General Accounting Office also considered the question of whether TRW had a conflict of interest or had gained unfair advantage over its competitors as a result of its managerial contracts with the energy agency. The GAO report said ERDA's conflict-of-interest restriction on TRW was inadequate. Addressing TRW's access to the energy administration's private records, the report stated that the agency's fossil energy unit had "submitted certain information to TRW which was not available to the public at the time the information was in the possession of the contractor. This included budget and planning data, unsolicited proposals, and 'confidential' project information on H-coal gasification process." Submission of this data to TRW "could possibly have put TRW or its subcontractors in an unfair competitive advantage over other contractors unless properly screened" before being given to the company.

Yet, such proper screening was unlikely because "Fossil Energy does not have an established procedure for screening material sent to support contractors."

TRW, in its energy agency role of reviewing other companies' unsolicited proposals for contracts, had been given ten proposals for review. None of the proposals had been screened in advance by energy administration officials to see if TRW or its subcontractors might have had a conflict of interest in reviewing these suggested projects. In fact, TRW admirably took it upon itself to return two proposals without reviewing them, because it saw a problem concerning related work it was carrying out. Energy Research and Development Administration officials reported that both the MITRE Corporation and Gilbert Associates had also evaluated unsolicited proposals, and that the energy agency "generally . . . agreed with the consensus in deciding whether to accept or reject the proposals." In other words, TRW and other contractors decided which proposals should proceed to the contract stage, thus raising not only the conflict-of-interest issue but also the troubling prospect of private firms determining the direction government-subsidized energy research and development would take.

The General Accounting Office wondered how TRW came to achieve expertise in preparing a federal agency's budgets and in overseeing what GAO called "the critical area of congressional budgeting and program review procedures"; it found that TRW had gained the capability through prior similar contracts with the Interior Department's Office of Coal Research. In other words, TRW had gained enough experience to help manage portions of one federal agency by previously having helped manage another.

The sharply critical GAO report prompted additional congressional criticism of the energy administration's contracting-out practices. The late Representative Leo J. Ryan, D-California, then-chairman of the Conservation, Energy and Natural Resources Subcommittee of the House Committee on Government Operations, focused on twenty of TRW's subcontracts, totaling $900,000, which he said "present an excellent case study in ERDA decision-making."

In lamenting the policy of giving contractors increasing authority over energy agency operations, Ryan observed that the Energy Research and Development Administration had its contractors and subcontractors "doing all sorts of things," and that certain consulting firms "are deeply involved in the development of the ERDA fossil fuels research and development program. The question is, how deeply involved?" Ryan also wondered why TRW and other contractors were "participating in budgetary decisions and have been assisting in evaluating the success of various demonstration projects being funded by ERDA." Even more peculiar, Ryan said, was that "TRW has even been hiring subcontractors to obtain basic information for ERDA that is available in other federal agencies. One wonders why ERDA must go through one contractor to hire another to get information that could be obtained free from another federal agency. It just doesn't make sense."

Ryan saw as "particularly objectionable" one $10,000 subcontract that had been awarded to the Washington-based consulting firm, Don Sowle Associates, Inc. The subcontract was for preparing "a draft of regulations regarding the award of incentives to builders of commercial demonstration facilities." Ryan said the "writing of official government regulations is traditionally a task that is performed in-house by qualified government employees," and that ERDA had no business allowing such a function to be delegated to private firms that could themselves be affected by, or have clients affected by, the resulting regulations.

Norman G. Cornish, staff director for Ryan's subcommittee, said in an interview that the energy administration's relationship with its contractors was rife with potential conflicts of interest. "We began to be disturbed that so many line functions of ERDA were being put into the hands of private contractors," Cornish said. "Policy analysis was being contracted-out to the same contractors who were bidding on other agency contracts. You could have situations where they would be bidding on contracts which they had put themselves into." Cornish noted that the energy agency had contracted for certain studies, even though the information sought was already in the hands of other federal agencies.

"The U.S. Geological Survey had coal maps, yet TRW received a contract from ERDA to do a study on coal reserves," Cornish said. Also, he said the energy administration's contract with TRW for a study on coal gasification technologies "was well within the competence of the Environmental Protection Agency to provide." Cornish felt that a major problem with the widespread contracting-out of the agency's key functions is the loss of what others have referred to as "the corps of competence" within the agency. He said that some of the work contracted-out by the energy agency had been performed "extremely well." But reliance on contractors "meant that ERDA didn't have any institutional memory over there. And that's very important. When key people would leave ERDA, other people at ERDA wouldn't be able to tell you how certain policies or decisions were arrived at. Instead, you would have the situation in which, as happened to me, you would call ERDA and ask for information and they would say, 'hold on a minute, let us call TRW and find out.' "

Robert C. Ketcham, counsel to the Subcommittee on Energy Research, Development and Demonstration (Fossil Fuels) of the House Committee on Science and Technology, echoed Cornish's views. "TRW was very successful in getting ERDA money to do things for ERDA, rather than ERDA doing things for itself," Ketcham said in an interview. "That was repugnant to us on the committee as to what should be the role of the government employee. TRW was even preparing ERDA's budget, and this clearly was a function for government employees." ERDA, he said, allowed contractors to "abuse their role."

Despite the congressional focus on TRW and similar support services contractors, the newly formed Department of Energy (DOE) ignored the controversy over the Energy Research and Development Administration's contractors. One of the Cabinet-level department's first acts, shortly after it was formed in late 1977, was to announce that it had awarded TRW a new $4-million contract "to provide technical support services for Fossil Energy." These services were for almost exactly the same kinds of key agency functions that had been attacked by the General Accounting Office and the congressional committees: "Data gathering and analysis, program evaluation and review, special studies and general staff assistance."

The reborn Fossil Energy division within the Department of Energy wasn't going to depend solely on TRW to run its shop. It also announced in November 1977 the awarding of a $501,615 contract to MITRE Corporation "for analysis and technical services to prepare a programmatic environmental impact statement for the coal research, development and demonstration program." Another early departmental contract, for $1.6 million, went to Energy & Environmental Analysis, of Arlington, Virginia, for "engineering and technical support services." Many similar contracts followed.

In late 1977, the department announced a major contract for another division—of oil, gas, and shale technology—which sounded as if that division also were turning over key functions to private enterprise. The $4,076,170 contract, to Booz-Allen & Hamilton, of Bethesda, Maryland, called for that firm to provide "data gathering, analyses and special studies; program development, planning documentation and reporting; program issue analyses and project reviews; economic and econometric studies, analyses and projections; environmental studies, impact statements and assessments and general management support." Given the scope of this contract, it appeared there was little left for the Energy Department's oil, gas, and shale technology division's in-house personnel to do.

When TRW's $4.9 million contract, which had been the subject of the General Accounting Office investigation, expired, the energy administration assigned many of TRW's previous duties to another firm, Energy and Environmental Analysis (EEA), under a $2-million contract. The duties assigned EEA were so intimately concerned with the agency's operations that even Energy Secretary Charles W. Duncan, Jr., acknowledged in late 1979, after reviewing the contract, that there was basis for a contention that the contract gave EEA the authority to "run the government." The myriad tasks provided for in the contract required EEA, among other things, to assist in semi-annual revisions and editing of the fossil energy research program; to prepare materials for the energy agency's annual report to Congress, including "strategy statements, special issue analysis, program implementation plans;" to review program cost estimates and prepare program cost proposals, including five-year cost forecasts for an annual report to Congress; to review unsolicited proposals from other contractors; and to "prepare long-range strategy and guidelines related to industrial developments, institutional and resource constraints for fossil energy development."

Reagan administration policies also seemed sure to increase the

Energy Department's reliance on contractors for fossil fuels services. In July 1982 the energy agency sent out notices firing or reassigning 173 of the 213 workers in its Office of Fossil Energy. With more than 80 percent of its work force cut, the division would have no place to go—other than to contractors—to get necessary work done.

TRW's loss of the major management support services contract to EEA did "not mean that TRW was out of work" at the Energy Department, as was made clear by a comprehensive late 1980 report by the staff of the Senate Governmental Affairs Committee. Rather, TRW received two other support services contracts "as large as the one that had expired." Under the two contracts, which totaled about $13 million over a three-year period, TRW was again assigned tasks that put it in charge of various fossil and synthetic fuels operations.

For example, TRW prepared congressional testimony for Energy Department officials; monitored fossil energy contracts; prepared budget materials and statutorily mandated reports to Congress; and drafted departmental policy statements and prepared fossil energy plans, such as the 1980 "Coal Cogeneration System Development Plan." The department gave no indication in the reports and testimony to Congress that a contractor, rather than departmental personnel, had prepared the materials. So important was TRW to Energy Department operations that the agency itself bluntly noted, in awarding a noncompetitive synfuels contract to the company in 1980: " . . . TRW has a long history of close involvement with DOE and its predecessors in development of most of the major ongoing DOE programs."

TRW had been involved in synthetic fuels planning since 1975 when, under its contract with the Energy Research and Development Administration, it served on an interagency task force to study alternative fuels programs for the United States. The task force's subsequent four-volume report recommended that the nation undertake an alternative fuels program. In connection with that work, TRW produced a number of publications, including various reports recommending a synthetic fuels commercialization program. In subsequent years, TRW received more than $2 million in synthetic fuels support services contracts. Under these contracts, TRW performed a number of managerial functions, such as reviewing and evaluating proposals for multimillion-dollar synfuels projects, and producing strategy documents for coal gasification and liquefaction projects.

When Congress in 1980 passed legislation providing more than $2 billion to the Energy Department for alternative fuel projects, TRW and other contractors—Hudson Institute, Don Sowle Associates, Booz-Allen & Hamilton, Rand, MITRE, Stanford Research Institute —were hired for managerial support. TRW, according to Energy Department officials, was called upon because it had unique experience unavailable within the department.

For its part, TRW by October 1980 had a staff of more than twenty persons working on the synfuels program under a task order issued under one of its existing contracts with the Energy Department. The initial cost of the task order was an estimated $150,000; Senate investigators found this was revised three times over the next five and a half months, raising the cost to approximately $1,049,000. Generally, TRW was to provide "support" to the assistant energy secretary for resource applications, who had primary responsibility for the synfuels project. The duties performed by TRW included establishing the rules by which the assistant secretary for resource applications would make funding decisions, helping design a plan for the energy resources on Indian-owned lands, preparing semi-annual reports to Congress on the synfuels program, and helping prepare program memoranda that summarized resource application programs.

In the case of the report to Congress and the recommendation for policy on Indian lands, Senate Governmental Affairs Committee staffers found that neither contained any reference to TRW's work on them, and the department's "final, 'official' product . . . was derived by simply removing the TRW cover" and submitting the documents as the department's own.

The Senate investigators reported that Energy Department officials maintained they had reviewed and edited TRW's early drafts of these reports, and, therefore, the documents truly reflected the position of the agency and not of TRW. Since the reports "consisted primarily of summaries of policy and action, and boilerplate," the Senate staffers wondered why Energy Department employees couldn't have done the work themselves without TRW assistance. And, asked the staff report, if TRW had such unique expertise for these reports, "how does the apparently substantial official review effort reflect on the expertise referred to in the employment of the contractor?" TRW either wasn't needed in the first place, or TRW's expertise in this field wasn't all that it was cracked up to be, the report suggested.

The staff report's section on synthetic fuels concluded that the "potential problems caused by excess reliance on private contractors are posed most starkly in the case of synfuels—a case where the federal government is giving out billions of dollars for complex technical projects. . . . The issue posed is not whether . . . the public should provide billions of dollars in grants and contracts for synthetic fuels projects . . . [but] whether the country, if it wishes to make such expenditures, should also contract out the planning and management functions required to direct and control them."

Despite the critical reports by the General Accounting Office and the Senate Governmental Affairs Committee, the Energy Department by 1982 was still contracting-out basic managerial, policy, and planning functions to TRW and other contractors and consulting firms. Near the end of fiscal year 1981, TRW had active Energy Department contracts totaling $113 million, with many of these for support services of the type that had been repeatedly criticized by General Accounting Office and congressional investigators.

On the one occasion when TRW was given the opportunity to answer formally the contentions that it and other contractors were running portions of the Energy Department, the company not so subtly refused, as did another management consulting giant, Booz-Allen & Hamilton. Officials of both firms had been invited by Representative Herbert E. Harris II, D-Virginia, chairman of the Human Resources Subcommittee of the House Post Office and Civil Service Committee, to testify in August 1980 concerning their support services contracts at the Energy Department, and concerning legislation Harris had proposed to tighten up regulation of such contracts.

Giving almost identical reasons, both companies refused to testify. Booz-Allen responded that "vacation schedules and other previous commitments make it impossible for us to accept your invitation at this time." TRW responded: "Because there is such a short time between now and the hearings, and because of unavailability during the month of August of many of the TRW officials who would be involved in preparing the statement on our behalf, we will not be able to meet your . . . deadline for response. . . ." TRW said it would submit comments on the proposed legislation, but none arrived in time for the hearings. Its only statement at the time came to the press. Robert H. Shatz, TRW's vice president for energy systems planning, said he couldn't comment on specifics, but added, "I don't think contractors should run DOE and I know they don't. DOE runs the contractors."

Harris was appalled at TRW's and Booz-Allen's refusals to testify. "I think it is extraordinarily important," he said at the hearing, "that those consulting firms that are in fact operating as agencies of our government be prepared to present testimony in this subcommittee. I would like to indicate on the public record this subcommittee's tremendous concern about people that have been vested with the authority of submitting reports to Congress and still do not see the need to come before the subcommittee and testify with regard to their activities. This, I think, presents a rather remarkable hole in our government's activities." Later during the hearings, in an exchange with representatives of contractor trade associations, Harris said that certain contractors' refusal to testify "demonstrates an arrogance" and makes it "extremely difficult for Congress to conduct the type of oversight it intends to."

In joint hearings earlier that summer by Harris's subcommittee and Senator David Pryor's Civil Service and General Services Subcommittee of the Senate Governmental Affairs Committee, various committee members focused on potential conflicts of interest among companies, such as TRW, that have private energy company customers, while at the same time involved in managerial and policy activities with the federal agency responsible for planning for the nation's energy future.

Harris, on that occasion, noted that multimillion-dollar support services contracts were held by firms with close ties to oil and utility companies. Yet these same contractors were used throughout the Energy Department "to perform crucial planning, budgetary and policy development activities . . . to write congressional testimony and to prepare reports to Congress." While at the same time these contractors were acting as "essentially an extension of [the Energy Department's] staff," they were also working for utilities, oil companies, and even the Organization of Petroleum Exporting Countries' oil companies.

In the case of TRW, Harris said, the Energy Department had made no formal determination of possible conflict of interest. And yet the company had private energy clients while at the same time holding federal contracts under which it did such things as preparing suggested additions to the Coal Pipeline Act of 1980, evaluating state-of-the-art technical and economic factors relating to the commercial viability of specific slurry pipeline technologies, and drafting reports to Congress—such as one on the Energy Department's fuels production program. Harris said this federal work posed a possible conflict with TRW's production for energy companies of various types of equipment—pumps, valves, pump parts, drilling tools, and parts—for oil and gas exploration and handling, and pipeline transmission.

"I do not know how I could assure the American people that TRW does not have a major financial interest in affecting the energy policies of this country," Harris said. "The demand for its products is directly related to the very policy which it assists in formulating." Harris said that the Energy Department had told him it had not performed a conflict-of-interest determination on TRW because the contracts had been awarded before the department formulated its conflict regulations.

The joint hearings did not single out TRW for criticism, but rather focused on several major support service contractors. Also cited was Booz-Allen & Hamilton, which, despite its key federal contracts in the areas of fossil energy, solar energy, nuclear power, utility regulation, and geothermal power, also had clients that put the firm in possible conflict-of-interest situations. These included such major oil companies as Exxon, Gulf, ARCO, Texaco, Mobil, Standard Oil of Indiana, and Standard Oil of California, as well as OPEC oil producers, such as the Arabian American Oil Company, the Government of Libya, National Iranian Oil Company, Abu Dhabi National Oil Company, and Sonatrach-Algerian National Oil Company. Booz-Allen's work for the OPEC oil producers "was by no means limited to incidental or narrowly technical assistance," Harris said, "but included defining long-range objectives, plans and organization" for Sonatrach, long-range planning for Iran, assistance in the organization of hydrocarbon industries for Libya, and a broad range of management and technical consulting services for Abu Dhabi.

Although Booz-Allen in its publicity brochures made no secret of its ties to OPEC oil producers, it did not formally make this known to the Energy Department at the time it was seeking contracts at the agency. When Eric Fygi, the Energy Department's deputy general counsel, was asked at a July 22, 1980, congressional hearing about possible conflicts between Booz-Allen's government contracts and its work for domestic and OPEC oil producers, Fygi responded that he had not been aware of that situation until that very morning.

Regarding TRW, Harris noted that the company had taken the position with the Energy Department that it was not an energy firm, and, therefore, presumably would have no conflicts of interest in that area. In response to questioning, Fygi conceded that TRW "probably" is an energy firm, but added that this in no way had any bearing on the company's eligibility for Energy Department contracts. Harris said that wasn't the point; the real point was full disclosure, and TRW's contention that it isn't an energy company hardly meets the criteria of complete disclosure.

Concerning TRW's work in preparing additions to the Coal Pipeline Act of 1980, Fygi said he "was surprised and a little shocked to learn that apparently they had been asked to work on legislation as part of their contract. In my judgment, that would not on . . . sound policy grounds . . . be an appropriate use of the contractor and, at the risk of sounding parochial, I had rather thought we lawyers in the general counsel's office were the ones that drafted legislation."

The failure of the Energy Department to examine prospective contracts for potential conflicts of interest appeared to violate 1977 laws making the secretary of Energy, through his contracting officers, responsible for requiring such contractors to disclose possible conflicts. According to the General Accounting Office, the laws prohibit the secretary from entering "into any contractual arrangement until he finds either that a conflict of interest is not likely to exist or that conditions can be written into the contract which will avoid or mitigate the conflict."

The joint hearings also produced information that TRW and other contractors had even been allowed to write their own task orders—

that is, to assign themselves more work of various types at the Energy Department. The hearings further disclosed that a contractor, Don Sowle Associates, helped establish the Energy Department's conflict-of-interest guidelines for contractors and produced a manual to help train top department officials about contracting.

Other disclosures included ones that Booz-Allen and Planning Research Corporation both helped manage the department's solar programs—even though their enthusiasm for solar energy was a little suspect in the minds of some joint committee members, considering that PRC's annual report said that it "serves every major oil company in the free world," while Booz-Allen's report boasted it served twenty-seven of the fifty largest utilities in the United States.

The hearings also disclosed that TRW drafted the official Energy Department organizational plan; that Price Waterhouse, the auditor for Exxon and other major oil companies, had helped prepare oil-pricing regulations and had prepared a study to justify sizable increases in propane prices; that Booz-Allen prepared a training manual to implement the Civil Service Reform Act; and that Booz-Allen told the Energy Department it didn't have enough employees to handle the task of defining the jobs of departmental officials, and so was permitted to go outside its own firm to hire additional consultants—mostly former government personnel experts—to help it. This latter case prompted Senator Pryor to observe that the Energy Department "paid a private contractor a fee to locate and employ former government officials to define the work of present government officials."

In addition, the hearings produced information that contractors were operating the Energy Department's contract file rooms, as well as preparing the basic terms of contracts, devising advertising campaigns, typing, preparing budgets, answering phone calls, and drafting speeches and response letters to House and Senate members who had written to Energy Department officials for specific information. It was also learned that many basic contract documents—work orders, work products, and sometimes the contracts themselves—were missing from departmental files.

An exasperated Senator Pryor, noting all of the functions contractors were performing for the Energy Department, commented during the hearings: "Why does DOE hire firms with conflicts? Why does

DOE hire the same firms to set policy for this country that are employed by the major oil companies? . . . Why are tens of millions of dollars spent without competitive bidding . . . ? And why are consultants and contractors today being used [for so much] in the Department of Energy . . . and what, actually, is there left for the employees of the Department of Energy to do?" And the final question, he said, is, "who, today, is running the Department of Energy?" Ultimately, Pryor's staff concluded, in its official report, that TRW and other firms, through their contracts to provide technical, managerial, and policy and planning expertise, appeared to be "running" the department.

Despite the congressional and General Accounting Office criticisms of its energy contracts and its activities on the Defense Science Board, TRW has taken a low profile rather than becoming embroiled in a public debate over its role in the government—as witnessed by its refusal to testify at the Harris subcommittee hearings in 1980. It rejects the notion that it has been "running" operations of government, instead emphasizing its expertise to perform certain technical and management functions that federal agencies are unable to do for themselves.

Michael L. Johnson, TRW's media relations manager in Cleveland, said in July 1982 that the company had come to expect it would be the subject of controversy from time to time because of its federal contracts and had learned to take the criticism in stride. At the time Johnson was contacted for this book, stories were just breaking in the press concerning the allegations referred to earlier of possible conflicts of interest involving TRW and other members of a Defense Science Board panel on computer technology.

"To tell you the truth, I don't see people around here getting too excited about these stories," Johnson said. "The fact is, there are only a relatively few companies that have expertise in the kinds of areas we're involved in, so it shouldn't be too surprising" if TRW or other companies are advising federal agencies in areas in which they might later make more sales to the government. Regarding the Defense Science Board controversy, Johnson said he saw nothing in it that "was very earth-shaking. But I'm not so blasé or naïve to think it couldn't become earth-shaking, but no one around here really sees any problem."

The policy of TRW has been to restrict its public comments on controversies in which it has been involved. In this regard, Johnson said TRW has never developed a formal, detailed response to any of the criticisms of its energy contracts by congressional committees and the General Accounting Office. He noted that when CBS's muckraking television show, "Sixty Minutes," was investigating government consulting contracts in 1980, it had contacted TRW about setting up interviews with company officials concerning its Energy Department management support contracts. TRW said it would only allow the interviews if "Sixty Minutes" agreed to certain terms, including giving TRW editing authority. CBS refused, and no interviews were ever done. The program was broadcast and did include a brief discussion of some TRW work for the Energy Department.

Johnson, in talking with this author, said he assumed that the book would be focusing on controversial aspects of government contracting, rather than saying the system was working well, and that TRW officials would not want to be interviewed for such a book. "You wouldn't sell a lot of books if you said everything was right with the system," Johnson said. Consequently, "You're just not going to find people around here jumping through hoops to get you a response to these issues that have been raised."

Johnson said he realized that Congress and the General Accounting Office were not questioning TRW's expertise; rather, he said, "they question the relationship" between the contractor and the federal agencies. "I know you don't want a lot of motherhood and apple pie talk," Johnson said, "but to the best of my knowledge, TRW has tried to behave in an ethical fashion over the years."

In this regard, Johnson offered a humorous example to show that when TRW has had ethical problems it really wasn't very newsworthy. Back in 1977, Johnson said, when an internal company investigation produced information that some of its lower-level employees had made questionable overseas payments, the firm decided to go first to *The Wall Street Journal* with the news. This, of course, was at the time when major corporations, under a Securities and Exchange Commission voluntary disclosure program, were coming up with reports of hundreds of thousands or even millions of dollars in questionable overseas payments. When TRW officials called the *Journal,* a reporter asked how much money was involved in the company's payments. When the officials told him it was $175,000, the reporter said, "That's not enough, we're not interested."

Johnson said that the reason TRW and other companies were performing important functions for the Energy Department was that the agency lacked the expertise to do the work in-house. Perhaps the department should have some of this expertise in-house, he said, but without it, it was logical for the agency to turn to TRW and others to provide it. Asked about congressional and General Accounting Office criticism that TRW had stepped over the line that separates giving advice from managing agency programs, Johnson said, "Go ask the government."

In sheer numbers, the extent of the Energy Department's reliance on contractors is staggering. In fiscal year 1980, the department spent 87 percent of its $11 billion budget on contractors and had only 20,500 employees in-house compared with an estimated 200,000 or more contract employees. Cost of salaries and benefits for in-house employees was $640 million—less than 6 percent of the total agency budget. In its field operations offices, the department had about 3,800 in-house employees compared with 111,000 contractor employees. Contractor employees at contractor-operated laboratories alone totaled almost 54,000.

One of the department's predecessors, the Energy Research and Development Administration, in mid-1977 had 8,283 civil service employees and an estimated 110,200 contract employees: a 13-to-1 ratio. Two years earlier, the General Accounting Office reported that 94.44 percent of ERDA's $3.27 billion budget authorization that year went to private contractors. In actual dollars, ERDA spent two and a half times as much for contractors as did the Department of Health, Education and Welfare, whose $100 billion budget was thirty times greater than ERDA's.

Daniel Guttman, a Washington, D.C., attorney and coauthor of a book about consultants' roles in shaping government programs and policies, has been one of the most persistent and effective critics of government contracting practices. In late 1979 testimony to a Senate subcommittee hearing on Energy Department contracting, Guttman observed that the department "has called on private contractors to such an extent that, were there a 'truth in government' law, the [energy] agency would be listed on the stock exchange rather than in the government organization manual." And, he said, were the identity of the energy agency's contractors widely publicized, people would realize that the agency "has chosen to employ the energy industry, rather than to regulate it." Yet, Guttman noted that the Energy Department has "hidden its reliance on contractors" while contracting-out "the management of government lock, stock and barrel."

The extent to which the Energy Department has relinquished authority to contractors has been largely hidden from public view because the agency usually does not disclose those instances when it adopts a contractor's policy proposals as agency policy. Legislation to require federal agencies to make such disclosures has been pending in Congress in recent years, but has never been enacted into law.

A major effect of the Energy Department's extensive reliance on contractors for management support work is that it creates confusion and doubts in the minds of many organizations and individuals having to deal with the agency. A vivid example of this was given by attorney Jack A. Blum, general counsel for the Independent Gasoline Marketers Council, a trade association of small gasoline retailers. Testifying before the Senate Governmental Affairs Committee on proposed contractor reform legislation in August 1980, Blum said that the Energy Department's use of contractors to perform vital governmental functions was "intolerable" to the small companies he represented and to others doing business with the agency. The growing use of contractors "means that we no longer have access to the levels of government where policy is made. It means that when we deal with government there is no certainty that our views will be considered in a neutral and unbiased fashion."

As an illustration, Blum noted that to his clients, "gasoline rationing, if it is ever imposed, is a life and death issue" because the manner in which such a rationing plan is structured "will determine whether a business will survive." When the Energy Department began to develop such a plan, using outside contractors, Blum said that officials of his trade group were visited by representatives of one of the contractors, Price Waterhouse Company, a prestigious accounting firm.

Price Waterhouse "was drawing up the fundamental framework for the rationing system."

Blum, himself a former congressional aide, said his clients were wary of cooperating with Price Waterhouse because that firm was the accountant for five of the top seven international oil companies. "We frankly do not trust them to render an independent judgment on the issues involved in rationing or any other petroleum issue," Blum said. "That lack of trust will continue regardless of Price Waterhouse's promises and no matter what we are told by the Department of Energy about the protection for us in the government contract. Would you be willing to give your confidential data to a consulting firm which works for your largest competitors and which you could never hope to employ?"

Blum characterized the in-house employees of the Energy Department as a "skeleton crew." "It is misleading advertising to say that the Department of Energy has 20,000 employees," he said. "We really believe it has closer to 200,000 employees [including contract workers] and that at least half of these should be on the government payroll." This lack of in-house expertise causes problems, Blum said, because the government has relied on outside firms with ties to the energy industry for its data, leaving members of Congress and citizen activists to feel—as they did in past energy crises—that the information was being manipulated in the energy companies' favor. Blum was adamant on the point that the Energy Department must have in-house "its own independent analytical capabilities and data base" so the public can have some measure of confidence in the information used for legislative and regulatory purposes.

Energy Department officials, in testimony before a number of congressional hearings in recent years, have generally rejected the criticism that there are serious problems with the agency's contracting policies. At one joint hearing of House and Senate subcommittees in 1980, John A. Hewitt, Jr., chief financial officer for the Energy Department, gave some typical departmental testimony concerning conflicts of interest. On the surface, Hewitt said, there might be the appearance of conflicts in some cases, but the Energy Department "goes through extraordinary steps to insure, before we let such contracts, that there is not a real conflict." Also, he said the firms offering managerial support to the Energy Department were professional, well-respected firms that did objective work in response to specific requests for help, and there was no real need to worry that conflicts existed.

The Energy Department's Inspector General's Office presented a far less rosy picture. In a series of late 1979 reports to the Energy Department, the inspector general pinpointed a number of problems related to conflicts of interest, overpayments on contracts, and contractors performing functions that should properly be handled by in-house Energy Department employees.

For example, the Inspector General determined that the Planning Research Corporation (PRC), the principal management support contractor for the department's Office of Solar Applications, was paying its consultants at rates of up to two and a half times as much as would be allowable if the consultants worked directly for the department. Also, the inspector general found that PRC was performing many activities—such as budgeting, coordinating programs, and establishing priorities—that "appeared to supplant policymaking and managerial functions that should be handled by Department of Energy staff." In addition, the inspector general said an appearance of conflict of interest existed among some of PRC's consultants who also had their own private firms. These consultants, by virtue of their work for PRC, "may have an unfair advantage in obtaining Department of Energy funding for projects proposed by their own firms."

Planning Research and other contractors were also running the Energy Department's solar programs. A Senate Governmental Affairs Committee staff report in December 1980 disclosed that, from the time of the creation of the Energy Department in late 1977, the contractors were running the solar programs because the in-house solar bureaucracy was in serious disarray. In its first thirty months of existence, the department's Conservation and Solar Energy Division had an assistant secretary overseeing it for only about half that time. The division was twenty-six months old before it even had an approved organizational structure. Consequently, the office was unable to be fully staffed, and there were a large number of vacancies.

Nevertheless, as the Congressional Office of Technology Assessment reported in 1980, pressures were mounting on the division to implement such new legislation as the Energy Policy Conservation Act, the Energy Conservation and Production Act, and the National Energy Conservation Policy Act. Into the breach stepped PRC and other skilled management support services firms called upon to help plan, manage, and analyze the over-all solar and conservation programs, including selecting and overseeing other contractors' work.

Planning Research in 1979 alone provided more than one hundred professional and technical personnel to the solar program. One contract, for $7.8 million, was awarded for three years in 1977. As the Senate committee staff report put it, that contract placed Planning Research "at the day-to-day heart of the Solar Applications Office." The company's work "was not only located in every nook and cranny of the Solar Applications Office but, most significantly, was often indistinguishable from that produced by officials." Such work included "a catalogue of the work that might be expected to be normally done by civil servants"—responses to inquiries from Congress and the public; memoranda; materials for transmission to Congress; plans and drafts of plans; status reports on all aspects of the Solar Applications Office's activities; reviews of contractor work; speeches, briefings, and press materials to be presented by officials; and handling contracting requests, including justifications for sole-source contracts and work statements.

In addition to calling on PRC, the solar office also used TRW, Booz-Allen & Hamilton, MITRE, and the Aerospace Corporation to help it with similar solar planning and management support efforts. The control of solar program management by private firms raises the same kinds of conflict problems already discussed, because these same firms have as their private clients many of the major energy companies and utilities. Through their Energy Department contract evaluation and policy recommendations, these firms are in a position to benefit their private sector clients.

And, in the field of solar energy, the department's contracts have consistently favored the energy giants and major corporations over smaller, often more innovative firms. In fiscal year 1980, for example, only 14.5 percent of all federal solar energy contracts went to small businesses, continuing a long-standing pattern. Several Energy Department solar program officials justified awarding most of its contracts to major corporations, telling the General Accounting Office that "relying on small businesses to accomplish program objectives is generally more risky" than using large, established firms. Other officials said they had difficulty finding small firms with the particular technical capabilities needed, while others said they were concerned with getting the job done, and not whether the contractor was large or small. Of no concern, apparently, was the prospect that major energy companies would gain a stranglehold on the promising solar energy field.

By 1981, there were more than 900 companies producing an estimated 17,000 solar devices, but the major energy, electronic, and utility companies were coming to dominate the field—with government help, in the form of research and development contracts. Of the ten largest solar photovoltaic companies in the early 1980s, six were controlled by oil companies and three others by major corporations. The once-independent and innovative solar companies had been bought up over the last decade by Exxon, Atlantic Richfield, Amoco, American Smelting & Refining, and other giants. In the words of the Citizens Energy Project, a Washington, D.C.-based public interest organization, Exxon and Arco "have a firm grip on nearly half the solar cells industry."

This grip has prompted concern among solar activists and some members of Congress. Senator Gary Hart, D-Colorado, wondered whether Exxon "hopes that solar stays under wraps until the world's fossil fuel markets are exhausted." Senator Edward M. Kennedy, D-Massachusetts, contended that "the prospect for cheap solar is jeopardized since petroleum companies have entered this market through the acquisition of solar energy development interests." And, cautioned Alfred Dougherty, director of the Federal Trade Commission's Bureau of Competition in 1980, by controlling substantial amounts of alternate energy sources, the oil companies "may slow the pace of production of alternate fuels in order to protect the value of their oil and gas reserves." With small firms squeezed out through a lack of federal contracts and through acquisitions by larger companies, solar energy development is coming increasingly into the hands of the same interests that already control the nation's other major sources of energy. Instead of cheap solar power, which solar activists say could come about if the field is not controlled by the energy giants, the nation will instead have gold-plated systems, which most people will not be able to afford—thus leaving oil and natural gas as our main sources of energy.

Federal energy officials over the years have also been particularly close to the nuclear power industry—an industry created largely through federal subsidies that, by 1980, totaled roughly $40 billion. In the days before nuclear power became a matter of widespread public concern, the Atomic Energy Commission was even using contract personnel to perform nuclear facility licensing operations.

As in the Defense Department, support services and management consulting firms with Energy Department contracts often overcharge the government. Diane Cleemput, who has worked as a researcher for various management consulting firms in the Washington, D.C., area, said that on one energy conservation contract on which she worked for a private firm, the company "falsified employee time records to back up its phony billings." The contract called for fulltime work from herself and another researcher, and from a company vice president who was to manage the project. While she and the other researcher did most of the work, the vice president's time was spent mainly developing new business for the firm—and he charged the time spent on this task to various government contracts. Cleemput said company employees always billed 40 hours of work each week to government contracts, regardless of how much time they actually put in on federal work. She recalled that one time the vice president in charge of her project asked her to revise her time sheet for a week she had worked on a Small Business Administration contract and to bill her time instead to the Energy Department contract. "When I asked why," Cleemput said, "he said it was nothing for me to worry about, just an internal matter."

Cleemput said she learned that time for several nonexistent employees had been billed by the company to its contract with the Community Services Administration. Also, she noted that consulting firms for which she had worked charged to the government overhead rates ranging from 35 to 170 percent of the salaries it paid. Some overhead items that she recalled had been charged to the government included "a long-term lease on a Cadillac for the firm's president," rents on two townhouses, health club memberships, "and even a pair of Gucci shoes" with which to navigate long corridors in government buildings.

In addition to excessive overhead costs, also causing soaring contract costs is the lack of competition for most energy contracts. For example, the Energy Research and Development Administration in fiscal year 1976 initiated or renegotiated 714 contracts, of which only 36—or 5 percent—involved competitive bidding. Of its 426 consulting contracts, not one involved competitive bidding. In March 1978, the fledgling Energy Department reported that it had in force at that time 2,899 noncompetitive contracts, worth $5.3 billion, while just 1,290 contracts, worth $1.6 billion, were competitive.

More recent government studies have shown the same noncompetitive trend in the Energy Department continuing, with resulting waste of many millions of dollars annually. An April 1982 report by the General Accounting Office stated that in fiscal year 1980 the Energy Department awarded 390 new sole-source contracts, of which 330—or 84 percent—could have been awarded competitively. Among the examples cited were noncompetitive contracts for $1.2 million for an advertising campaign to promote basic energy conservation, for $35,-000 to produce a film showing the history of United States energy production and consumption from 1776 to the present, and for $218,-000 to study a process for determining the amount of oil remaining in an abandoned reservoir.

In fiscal year 1980, the Energy Department, as the largest civilian contracting agency in the federal government, awarded $9.6 billion in contracts out of its total budget of $11 billion—which meant that 87 percent of the agency's budget went to contractors. Of the $9.6 billion, 77 percent—or about $7.4 billion—was awarded noncompetitively. Using the Office of Federal Procurement Policy standard that as much as one dollar in four can be saved through the use of competition in contracting, this raises the possibility that as much as $1.8 billion may have been wasted on the Energy Department's noncompetitive contracts.

Money has also been wasted on Energy Department contracts because of the agency's failure to do adequate cost comparisons. Office of Management and Budget Circular A-76 requires that, when an agency is contemplating a contract for a service expected to last more than a year, the agency must do a study to compare the costs of doing the service in-house versus the costs of contracting it out. The late 1980 report by the staff of the Senate Governmental Affairs Committee, however, found that the Energy Department "has apparently performed virtually no such cost comparisons" for the management support and consulting contracts examined by the committee.

Before Horace A. Shepard retired as chairman of the board and chief executive officer at TRW, he castigated "big government" in one of his annual messages to stockholders. However, he said, there were "encouraging signs . . . that the public is becoming aware of rapidly rising costs of government and their impact on all citizens," and that people were calling "for less rather than more government at local and state as well as federal levels." Seen from a perspective different from Shepard's, the growth of big government over the last three and a half decades can be attributed in great measure to the contractor bureaucracy that TRW and other corporations helped to foster.

In light of contractors' control over the Energy Department, the complaints of energy corporations about their mistreatment at the hands of the agency's bureaucrats take on a somewhat hollow ring. In dealing with the Department of Energy, the energy giants should remember the words of the immortal Porkypine, in the comic strip *Pogo:* "We have met the enemy, and he is us."

6 · Reagan:
Business As Usual

In August 1981, the Reagan administration's Office of Management and Budget (OMB) submitted to the Senate Governmental Affairs Committee its views in opposition to proposed legislation designed to reform federal consulting contracting practices. The following month, Laura Henderson, representing the National Council of Professional Services Firms, a trade organization that favors increased federal contracting, testified against the legislation during a hearing of the committee's Expenditures, Research and Rules Subcommittee.

This was certainly not the first time the budget office and a pro-contracting organization had joined forces to oppose a measure that sought to regulate some aspect of federal contracting by law. Both the Office of Management and Budget and various contractor trade groups have long opposed enactment of new statutes to deal with contracting abuses, preferring instead to rely on agency regulations or OMB guidelines to control such practices. What made this situation unusual is that many of the key points in both the budget office's position paper and in Henderson's testimony were, word-for-word, virtually identical.

To critics of federal contracting practices, the incident—plagiarism and all—symbolized the Reagan administration's attitude toward both government contractors and business in general.

Henderson's testimony, although not presented until September

1981, had been based on a written legal opinion prepared by her organization's general counsel the previous April. So, the organization's position on the legislation predated the budget office's written views by about four months. At one point in her prepared testimony, Henderson stated: "Section 205 . . . is replete with unworkable requirements that will substantially reduce the ability of federal agencies to obtain professional services of the highest quality." The budget office document stated: "Section 205 is replete with unworkable requirements that will substantially reduce the ability of federal agencies to obtain professional services of the highest quality." The following six paragraphs in both OMB's statement and in Henderson's testimony were virtually identical, with only a word or two occasionally changed or a phrase moved from one part of a sentence to another.

To some critics in Congress, the identical testimony raised the specter that contractors not only see eye-to-eye with the Office of Management and Budget in opposition to reform proposals, but that they might also even be preparing the agency's testimony.

When the similarities of the statements were brought to light at the subcommittee's hearing on September 18, 1981, the budget office's Fred Dietrich said, "As far as I know, there was no collusion. We read a lot. Sometimes things that sound good we use whether we paid for it or not." Dietrich also said that perhaps someone at the budget office had incorporated the contracting organization's legal opinion into the OMB statement without knowing its source.

Senator David Pryor, D-Arkansas, the sponsor of the legislation, wasn't convinced. "I think it's unlikely that OMB didn't know where it came from. Highly unlikely," he said. Pryor said he could not imagine someone at the budget office using a legal opinion without knowing its source. The identical comments by OMB and the contractors' group "proves better than anything else my concern that there is an incestuous relationship between federal agencies and private outside consultants."

Pryor then fired off a letter to Budget Director David A. Stockman, saying that the budget office's use of a private organization's legal view seemed to be right in line with the findings of earlier congressional hearings and reports of the General Accounting Office that contractors often "are actually making the policy to be carried out by the federal government." Pryor said, "It has to be more than mere coincidence" that the statements of the Office of Management and Budget and the contractors' organization were almost identical in several parts. Pryor said he was "insulted by this 'coincidence' " and that it didn't matter whether "the consultants are now writing your agency's testimony . . . or whether your agency is now writing testimony for consultants." There either is "collusion between OMB and consultants or gross negligence on the part of your agency."

One month later, Stockman wrote to Pryor with an assurance "that there is neither collusion between OMB and consultants, nor have consultants been hired to prepare Congressional testimony for either me or members of my staff." Rather, Stockman acknowledged that OMB had committed "plagiarism," but that "regardless of the particular words included in our comments . . . they are consistent with our current thinking, were thoroughly reviewed, and stand on their merits."

Stockman explained that on April 7, 1981, the budget office began reviewing Pryor's proposed legislation. Two weeks later, he said, his agency's Office of Federal Procurement Policy received a copy of the comments of the general counsel for the National Council of Professional Services Firms. Then, on June 3, the Office of Federal Procurement Policy submitted to the budget office's Legislative Reference Division its comments on the legislation. The comments included language, not attributed to the lobbying organization, that had been extracted almost verbatim from the organization's statement and were then incorporated into the budget office's statement on the legislation which was submitted to the subcommittee on August 14. "Neither those who consolidated nor those who received the comments knew of the plagiarism," Stockman wrote.

While saying that plagiarism "*is not* and *will not* be condoned in this administration [his emphasis]," Stockman also said that applicable law permitted the Office of Federal Procurement Policy to solicit "the viewpoints of interested parties in the development of procurement policies, regulations, procedures and forms." The budget office, therefore, in obtaining the contractor organization's comments, was doing it in conjunction with "developing balanced, government-wide procurement regulations and policies."

Interviewed three months after the receipt of Stockman's letter, Pryor by then was over his initial astonishment at the admitted plagiarism and was more amused by the incident. Still, he said, the episode illustrated that, regardless of how the plagiarism occurred, there had been such a convergence of views between the budget office and the contractors that it had reached the point where the agency would unquestioningly adopt as its own the opinions of a party with a direct financial interest in the legislation.

During its first eighteen months in office, the Reagan administration took a number of steps designed to increase the government's reliance on contractors, particularly in the defense area. Some of the administration's proposals seemed to be helping mainly large and medium-sized businesses, while other proposals—specifically, a cutback by nondefense agencies in consulting contracts—were hurting mainly small and medium-sized firms with no defense expertise, which were, therefore, unable to cash in on the administration's five-year, $1.6 trillion military buildup program.

The Reagan administration also was promoting a policy of persuading state and local governments to turn over more of their services to private contractors. The leading advocate of this policy was Emanuel S. Savas, assistant secretary for policy development and research in the Department of Housing and Urban Development. As Savas put it, "I'm just trying to find ways of making government work better for people. Government should do those things it does best, like national defense, and the private sector should do those things it does best, including the delivery of many municipal services." Savas's agency in June 1982 sponsored a "privatization roundtable" to discuss ways of "assigning to the private sector greater responsibility for the delivery of public services." Savas told participants—who were all business and academic advocates of greater contracting-out of government services—"we want you to help us lay out what we should do to push privatization." Other HUD-sponsored conferences to promote privatization were scheduled in vavious parts of the country over the next year.

Just as in federal contracting, much is at stake in industry's efforts to obtain more state and local governmental contracts. In 1980 state and local governments contracted for an estimated $66 billion worth of goods and services. As one of the key architects of the Reagan administration's plans for the nation's cities, Savas was in a good position to influence local governments to increase their contracting for municipal services. In mid-1982, Savas stirred up a storm of protest from many mayors and other local governmental officials when the draft of the administration's first statement on national urban policy—which he was in charge of—became public. The draft contended that many urban problems were caused by the cities having too great a dependence on the federal government and called for a reduction in federal aid to local governments for such items as water supplies, sanitation, and street repairs. Under fire, Reagan stated that the Savas report was merely a draft—not official administration policy. Savas's views were omitted in the final report.

In early 1983, Savas encountered major controversy. He was placed on administrative leave, pending a departmental investigation of a number of allegations, including ones that he had charged personal trips to the government and had improperly awarded a consulting contract to a former research associate. Savas denied any wrongdoing.

During his campaign for the presidency, Reagan time and again pledged to reduce government spending, to remove bureaucratic roadblocks and regulations that he said were thwarting the growth and productivity of American business, and to root out "fraud, waste, and abuse in government." Once in office, Reagan began to make good on many of his pledges, undertaking a counterrevolution to overturn what he saw as the debilitating welfare state programs initiated by President Franklin D. Roosevelt in the years of the Great Depression. Thus, Reagan's Cabinet officers and other top agency personnel were drawn largely from the ranks of business, or from intellectuals at universities and conservative think-tanks who were known for their espousal of loosening government controls over business.

The early Reagan administration's programs and budget proposals reflected the tilt toward business, particularly big business: a tax cut program benefitting primarily large corporations and the wealthy; lessening of enforcement of antitrust laws; a plan to dismantle the

Department of Energy and put most of its functions in the Department of Commerce to eliminate what Reagan saw as overregulation of the energy industry; an attempt to repeal the law that prohibits overseas bribery by United States corporations; proposed or actual reductions in the oversight and monitoring of health and safety conditions at United States factories, mines, mills, nursing homes, and other businesses; proposals that industries monitor some of their own polluting activities; reductions in enforcement of certain clean air and water standards; emphasis on a number of "privatization" programs to put more federal land, resources, and government operations in the hands of private enterprise through oil and mineral leases on federal lands and offshore, sales of federal land and property, and contracts for services; the $1.6 trillion, five-year defense spending program that would provide lucrative contracts for major defense industries, research and development firms, management consulting organizations, and think-tanks; proposed new subsidies for the faltering nuclear power industry; and reductions in the federal workforce, with an expected corresponding rise in the use of contract employees to take up some of the slack left by the departing workers.

The administration's decided tilt toward big business was best symbolized by Interior Secretary James G. Watt, characterized by his foes as one of the "rape, run, and ruin boys," who believes that more government land and resources should be developed by private interests. Under Watt, the Interior Department launched unprecedented massive leasing, contracting, and land sales programs to put more of the nation's resources into the hands of private enterprise. (Watt's activities will be discussed further in the next chapter.)

The Reagan administration's connection with the Bechtel Group, Inc., and particularly its appointments of Bechtel officials to top government posts, is a good illustration of the president's philosophy that executives of major corporations are best equipped to run the affairs of the country—whether it be in government office, or by contract.

Bechtel is one of the world's largest construction, engineering and project management companies, as well as being a government contractor. It has been involved in building an impressive list of projects worldwide since its inception in 1898 by Warren E. Bechtel, "who hired out with his team of mules to help build a railroad in the Indian Territory that is now Oklahoma."

In addition to its business expertise, Bechtel has had excellent connections with oil-rich Arab nations, with Republican administrations, and, some suggest, with the Central Intelligence Agency—connections that have won it political influence and government contracts, but have also often made it the focus of controversy, despite its image as a secrecy-shrouded company.

Bechtel has had many key government contracts, including one to design a defense nuclear waste depository in New Mexico, another to write three major sections of the Ford administration's energy plan, and a previously mentioned one to advise the government on building a coal slurry pipeline from Wyoming to Arkansas. (The contract was controversial because Bechtel failed to disclose its financial interest in a company planning to build the pipeline, prompting Congressional accusations of conflicts of interest.) In the first eleven months of the Reagan administration, Bechtel received more than $67 million in Energy Department contracts—more than double its Fiscal year 1980 total.

Because Bechtel is a privately held company, controlled by Bechtel family members and some sixty senior executives, it is not required to file documents with the Securities and Exchange Commission nor to make public its financial data. Industry analysts have said that, based on their observations, Bechtel would probably be in the top twenty-five of the *Fortune* 500 if its financial records were public. What is known is that Bechtel in the early 1980s had annual sales of $8 billion and was involved in more than 100 major projects in almost two dozen countries. Its operations have been likened to those of sovereign states with Stephen D. Bechtel, Jr., who has been running the company in recent years, often being received by heads of state as a virtual equal. With an apolitical stance when it comes to business overseas, Bechtel has found it perfectly comfortable to deal with all kinds of leaders of both democratic and nondemocratic nations—conservatives, liberals, communists, military dictators, and monarchs.

With no requirement that it file public documents, Bechtel has given out little information about its operations. Some publications have even suggested that its close association with former top Central

Intelligence Agency officials has also helped smooth the way for company operations overseas and that, in turn, Bechtel may have done some favors for the CIA.

Such speculation can be traced partly to the relationship between Stephen D. Bechtel, Sr., one of the sons of the original founder of the company, and former CIA director John A. McCone. Bechtel and McCone had been friends and classmates at the University of California and then later formed a business partnership, Bechtel-McCone, which won World War II contracts as part of a joint venture to build Liberty ships and tankers for the Pacific theater at shipyards in Los Angeles and Sausalito, California, and an aircraft-modification center in Alabama. When McCone after the war was nominated for a top Defense Department post, the Bechtel-McCone partnership was dissolved.

At his Senate confirmation hearing, McCone was accused of having profited excessively on the shipbuilding contracts. Investigators contended that the participants in the Los Angeles shipbuilding venture alone made $44 million on a $100,000 investment. Ralph Casey, of the General Accounting Office, testifying at the hearing, stated that "at no time in the history of American business, whether in wartime or in peacetime, have so few men made so much money with so little risk and all at the expense of taxpayers, not only of this generation but of generations to come."

After leaving the Defense Department, McCone went on to become chairman of the Atomic Energy Commission and later, in 1961, director of the Central Intelligence Agency. At the Atomic Energy Commission, he reportedly was instrumental in helping Bechtel obtain the contract to construct the nation's first commercial nuclear power plant in Dresden, Illinois. The project gave Bechtel a leg up in the fledgling commercial nuclear power industry, and over the next two decades the company was involved as builder or engineer, or both, in construction of almost half of the nation's sixty-eight commercial nuclear facilities.

Mother Jones magazine has reported that there has been a "flow of men back and forth" between the CIA and Bechtel, and that one former Bechtel vice president set up a small Washington, D.C.-based energy-consulting firm that was a CIA proprietary—or front—operation. A company like Bechtel, with its ready access to heads of state, combined with its projects throughout various and often politically unstable Third World countries, was in an excellent position to pick up all kinds of political information and, according to the magazine, would share such data with the CIA. Bechtel also between 1965 and 1969 provided cover for at least two CIA agents in Libya, where Bechtel constructed a pipeline from the Sahara Desert to the Mediterranean for Occidental Petroleum, the magazine reported. Adding to the speculation about Bechtel's CIA relationship was its hiring in the late 1970s of Richard Helms, the former CIA director and ambassador to Iran. This continued the Bechtel tradition begun with McCone; also, another later CIA director, Allen Dulles, was a Bechtel consultant during World War II.

In addition to Bechtel's overseas connections, both Stephen D. Bechtel, Sr., and his son, Stephen, Jr., have developed strong ties to United States governmental leaders and have been appointed to various important federal advisory panels over the years. But never did the company's political clout more clearly manifest itself than during the Reagan administration.

Initially in his administration, Reagan appointed Caspar W. Weinberger, then a Bechtel vice president and board member, to be his secretary of Defense. Weinberger had been secretary of Health, Education and Welfare under both Presidents Nixon and Ford. In his first year at the Pentagon, Weinberger received from Bechtel $93,183 as "compensation for past services." Also moving into the Reagan administration was another Bechtel executive, W. Kenneth Davis, who became the deputy secretary of Energy.

Then, when Alexander M. Haig, Jr., abruptly resigned as secretary of State in June 1982, Reagan again turned to the Bechtel corporation to designate George P. Shultz, Bechtel's president, as his new secretary of State. Shultz had served as secretary of the Treasury in the Nixon administration.

Shultz was overwhelmingly confirmed by the Senate for the Cabinet post in July 1982, but he came under sharp questioning at his confirmation hearing from a number of senators concerning his position at Bechtel. The questioners expressed concern over Bechtel's extensive projects in Arab countries, while it had none in Israel; over its role in an alleged effort to undermine President Ford's policy on restricting exports of nuclear technology to Brazil; over its lobbying in support of the Reagan administration's decision to sell airborne warning and control system (AWACS) equipment to Saudi Arabia in 1981; over its major work in nuclear power development and how this would affect Shultz's role in efforts to control nuclear proliferation; over the 1977 accusation by the Justice Department that Bechtel had participated in the Arab nations' boycott of companies doing business with Israel; and over how, in a crunch, Shultz would react concerning Israel and Saudi Arabia (where Bechtel has undertaken major construction and energy projects).

Shultz's only show of temper during the hearings came when Senator Alan Cranston, D-California, produced letters written by another Bechtel executive to Brazilian officials in 1975 after Shultz had already come to work for Bechtel. Cranston said the letters expressed Bechtel's willingness to offer Brazil "the entire gamut" of nuclear technology. Cranston contended that this represented an effort by Bechtel to undercut President Ford's policy of stopping West Germany from providing Brazil with advanced technology that could lead to the production of nuclear weapons. An obviously angry Shultz responded: "I resent what I regard as kind of a smear on Bechtel. I think it is a marvelous, law-abiding company that does credit to our country here and all over the world." He went on to say that he became aware of the letters to Brazilian officials "long after the fact" and that the contact with Brazil had been initiated by "an overenthusiastic business development person." The effort was inappropriate, he said, and was halted after he heard about it.

To most of the other questions about his Bechtel connections, Shultz said he foresaw no conflict because of his association with the company. He also said he would divest himself of his investments in Bechtel and place the proceeds in a blind trust.

The extent of Bechtel's influence within the Reagan administration again became an issue just a few weeks later when it was disclosed in late July 1982 that Philip C. Habib, President Reagan's special Middle East envoy, was also serving as a private consultant to Bechtel. The disclosure came at a time after Israel had invaded Lebanon and Habib was deeply involved in efforts to restore peace and to get both Palestine Liberation Organization and Israeli troops out of Lebanon. If Bechtel were any ordinary company, the disclosure of Habib's ties to it would have scarcely caused a flutter. But, since it had become well-known during the Shultz confirmation hearings that Bechtel had much influence in the Arab world through its work on major projects there, and that Bechtel does no business at all in Israel, concern was expressed by some members of Congress that Habib's private loyalties might influence his position in deliberations over the Middle East peace.

Senator Larry Pressler, R-South Dakota, called for Habib's resignation from the Middle East post. Pressler said Bechtel "actively lobbies for pro-Arab causes" and that Habib thus "cannot be effective now that it has been revealed that he is a paid consultant" to that company. Pressler said he also felt "betrayed" by the failure of Shultz to mention during his confirmation hearings earlier that month that Habib also worked for Bechtel. Pressler noted he had spent more than an hour at Shultz's confirmation hearings "asking questions about Bechtel and who was in government for Bechtel. By omission, I feel Mr. Shultz was not candid with me. I want an explanation." Pressler also stated Bechtel was "a classic example" of an "international conglomerate with too much power" and too many people in key positions in the Reagan administration.

Bechtel officials explained that Habib had been hired in 1981 by Shultz to be a consultant on the Pacific Basin area—Australia, New Zealand, Southeast Asia, and the Pacific Islands. They said they were uncertain whether the company had ever used Habib's expertise on matters affecting the company in the Middle East. A Bechtel spokesman said Shultz and Habib were long-time friends, and that Shultz felt Habib's knowledge of the Pacific basin area was especially important to the company because, he said, "This is an area of great developmental possibilities, an area where Bechtel has more major projects than in the Middle East." The spokesman would not divulge Habib's compensation, saying it was company policy not to disclose salaries or fees paid to its employees or consultants. Habib, who resigned as under secretary of State for Political Affairs in 1978 after having a heart attack, was receiving no salary for his work as Reagan's Middle East envoy; his reimbursement was limited to daily expenses.

Within a few days, the controversy over Habib's ties to Bechtel appeared to have blown over. White House deputy press secretary Larry Speakes said Reagan had "the utmost faith in [Habib's] ability and integrity" and was not concerned over his relationship with Bechtel. The State Department likewise praised Habib, and an earlier critic of Shultz's ties to Bechtel, Senator Cranston, said that Habib's "value to our country and to the cause of peace" should "not be impaired by his Bechtel connection." Also, Thomas A. Dine, executive director of the American Israel Public Affairs Committee, said it was unfortunate that Habib's connection with Bechtel had not become public knowledge earlier, but that he had "the highest respect for Ambassador Philip Habib's integrity and for his skills as an ambassador and a negotiator." Dine, whose organization consisted of 11,000 United States citizens who support Israel, said he was "fully confident that [Habib] will carefully fulfill all of his responsibilities independent of any commercial concerns."

Throughout the controversy, Habib issued no statement. A Bechtel spokesman said that although Habib's ties to Bechtel may not have been general public knowledge when he first went on a Middle East mission for Reagan in May 1981, he had disclosed this connection to the administration upon his formal approval as Middle East envoy in November 1981.

Habib's personal integrity was not really the issue. Rather, the controversy shows vividly the problems that arise when corporations have their former or present employees in an administration in positions in which they have control over issues of vital interest to all United States citizens—defense policy, foreign policy, energy policy, and the Middle East.

Despite his obvious faith in the need to apply business techniques to government, Reagan did take a small step in his first week in office that gave some federal contracting critics hope that the private sector would not be spared in the new administration's efforts to cut federal spending. In those early days, Reagan ordered a 5 percent reduction in contracts for consulting services, as well as imposing restrictions on the purchase of office furniture and on unnecessary office remodeling jobs. (The restriction on office remodeling was widely ignored by Reagan's Cabinet officers, as at least six of them undertook renovations of their offices, or bathrooms and dining rooms, during their first several months in office.)

Because of varying definitions of the term "consultant" throughout government, a relatively small number of services were actually covered by this term, so the reduction did not have a major dollar impact. Also, it affected mainly smaller to medium-sized firms, rather than established leaders in the field—such as Booz-Allen & Hamilton and TRW—and, over the long haul, hurt mainly those firms that had had contracts primarily in social program areas, which experienced the most severe budget cuts. Still, the reduction did indicate a possibility that an administration on record as opposing fraud, waste, and abuse in government might be willing to look at the problems of the contract bureaucracy as well as those of the civil service bureaucracy.

Despite the promising start, the approach of the Reagan administration to contracting policy reform in its first year in office could be characterized as one designed to increase substantially the use of government contracting without insuring that many of the types of previous contracting abuses would be dealt with.

On the positive side, the Office of Management and Budget proposed new regulations designed to bring more control over the awarding of contracts for consulting, management and professional services, special studies and analyses, and support services for research and development activities. A proposed revision of existing OMB Circular A-120 prohibited most unsolicited sole-source consulting contracts, limited the types of functions that could be provided to the government by consultants, and imposed tighter restrictions on extending consulting contracts beyond one year. The proposed revision spelled out more specifically the kinds of government functions that could not be contracted out: i.e., management of programs requiring value judgments, such as directing national defense; management and direction of the armed forces; selection of program priorities; the handling of monetary transactions; and the conducting of "in-house core capabilities in the area of research, development and testing." The revised circular also required that, when an unsolicited proposal is received, the agency cannot make a sole-source award but must instead solicit competing offers from qualified contractors.

Other steps by the Reagan administration were designed to contract-out even more government services. In Reagan's third month in office, the Office of Management and Budget called for government agencies to make a major effort to increase the use of federal contractors for commercial and industrial services. The agency said there were some 92,000 jobs being performed by government workers that could be turned over to contractors, in line with agency policy of "reliance on competitive private enterprise to supply the products and services needed by the government," as OMB Deputy Director Edwin L. Harper put it. Harper urged agency heads to become "vigorously involved and provide the overall leadership" in contracting-out more commercial and industrial services.

By the spring of 1982, the Office of Management and Budget had followed up on this earlier initiative by drafting guidelines to step up the pace of contracting-out for commercial and industrial services. The guidelines went beyond those of previous administrations that had also emphasized turning such services over to the private sector. Government commercial and industrial services are those for which there exist firms in the private sector doing the same or similar work. Thus, the definition would include such services as maintenance of military equipment and government buildings and vehicles, printing, guard services, clerical functions, automatic data processing and computer services, operations of recreational areas and storage facilities, photography and movie-making, human and animal health services, and various manufacturing and testing operations. By 1982 private firms were estimated to be performing about $6 billion worth of such services annually for the government, while some 400,000 federal workers were performing similar work in-house—work that contractor lobbying groups have been attempting to get for their members for years.

Unlike similar programs advanced under the Ford and Carter administrations, the Reagan administration plan provided that agency officials could in many instances contract-out for such work without doing any cost comparisons to see whether the service could be performed at less cost in-house. The plan exempted from cost comparisons any activity involving twenty-five or fewer in-house employees. Previous programs provided for cost comparisons for all contracting-out efforts for commercial and industrial services—although agency heads, in practice, often have ignored this requirement. The plan would also require agencies to justify by 1983 their intentions to keep any of these commercial or industrial functions in-house. By mid-1982 the proposal was being revised by the Office of Management and Budget, following criticism by members of Congress and government union officials.

In pushing for greater reliance on contractors for commercial and industrial services, the Reagan administration held out the Defense Department as a model. Between 1979 and 1982, the Pentagon contended that it had saved $70 million a year by contracting-out commercial and industrial functions it had previously handled in-house. In some cases, the Pentagon said, government employees had reorganized their operations and had shown they could perform the functions at less cost in-house, resulting in an additional saving of $14 million annually. Several Pentagon officials opposed to full-scale contracting of commercial and industrial services said that the Defense Department had allowed in-house personnel to restructure their own operations, to try to show they could do a job at a lower cost than could contractors, in only a small number of cases. Usually, they said, cost comparisons were made on the basis of what the job currently is costing in-house, as opposed to what a contractor says he can do the job for.

In a much more far-reaching plan, the Pentagon under the Reagan administration pushed a program to move its military personnel out of jobs that civilians can do and to move as many civilian jobs as possible into contractors' hands. Under a five-year Pentagon plan, the military services were instructed to examine the work done by more than 90 percent of their civilian employees—both blue-collar and white-collar—with an eye toward replacing them with private contractors. Drawing some conclusions in advance of the study, the plan suggested that probably 50 percent of the jobs of more than one million Defense Department civilians could be eliminated and replaced by contractors.

If successful, the Reagan plan would mark the most radical restructuring of Defense Department personnel in the nation's history. Given the previously discussed control that contractors already exert over the Defense Department, one can only imagine the stunning amount of leverage such contractors would hold if they replaced 500,000 civilian employees of the department by 1988. Yet, other than complaints by a relative handful of members of Congress, and the expected protests of government employees' unions whose members stand to lose jobs whenever services are contracted-out, the revolutionary Pentagon proposal had stirred little public debate or editorial comment by 1983. The loudest congressional response to the Pentagon's contracting-out plan was a call by the House Armed Services Committee, in its report on the Defense Department's fiscal year 1983 authorization bill, for a one-year moratorium on the cost comparison studies that are undertaken prior to contracting-out government work. The committee contended that the administration "has lost sight of priorities in its headlong rush to contract out a large number of federal jobs."

The major contracting initiative put forth during the first two years of the Reagan administration (although it had been in the works before Reagan took office) was an October 1981 proposal by the Office of Federal Procurement Policy for a uniform federal procurement system. The proposal called for sweeping changes to "put federal procurement on a more systematic, professional and businesslike basis." If implemented, the proposal would require the Defense Department, which has always had a separate procurement system, to follow generally the same rules that govern civilian agencies while at the same time retaining its own system.

The proposal traces its origins to a high-level study of government procurement performed by the Congressional Commission on Government Procurement between 1970 and 1972. The commission, a twelve-member bipartisan panel with government and private sector members, submitted 149 recommendations in its 1973 report, including a basic one to create the Office of Federal Procurement Policy "to provide leadership in the development of the government-wide procurement policy." Legislation creating the office was passed in 1974. The office was initially given five years to come up with policies and regulations for federal procurement, and then was given a four-year extension (until October 1983) to develop a comprehensive procurement system. A first draft proposal for a uniform system was submitted to Congress in October 1980, superseded by the draft plan put forth in October 1981 and then submitted in final form in the winter of 1982.

The proposal was designed to create a simplified, streamlined contracting process, to set up a trained, professionalized contract management workforce, and to establish control systems to ward off problems before they occur and to get feedback to a greater degree on contractor performance. The proposed new system was also designed to eliminate such "persistent problems" as a lack of competition for contracts; wasteful, hurried-up spending at the end of every fiscal year; a morass of burdensome regulations on contractors; a lack of accountability for results on contracts; and excessive delays, changes, and cost growth in the procurement of new defense systems.

Unquestionably, the system needs standardizing and simplifying, and the proposal, despite some flaws, was a serious attempt to bring some order out of chaos. Two major statutes have for years covered government contracting and the authority for agencies to issue their own regulations governing contracting. These are the Armed Services Procurement Act of 1947, which applies to procurement activities of the Defense Department and the National Aeronautics and Space Administration, and portions of the Federal Property and Administrative Services Act of 1949, as amended, which covers the contracting practices of civil agencies. These two basic statutes are backed up by more than 4,000 other legislative provisions covering some aspect of contracting, as well as a number of circulars issued by the Office of Management and Budget over the years. On top of this, the Office of Federal Procurement Policy, in a survey of nineteen agencies, found in 1978 and 1979 that 485 federal offices regularly issue procurement regulations; that there are 877 different sets of contracting regulations covering 64,600 pages; that more than 21,000 new or revised pages of regulations are issued each year.

In calling for a simplification of this mind-boggling array of statutes and regulations, the Office of Federal Procurement Policy noted in its final proposal: ". . . the government should be able to acquire products or services much as any private citizen would, consistent with the public interest. This is not possible today."

To unscramble these various cumbersome procurement systems, the Office of Federal Procurement Policy proposal called for legislation creating a generally uniform procurement system for the entire government, coupled with a series of Executive Branch actions to upgrade the contract management force and simplify the contracting process. The proposal also recommended the creation in each agency of procurement executives with over-all responsibility for contracting practices. The Office of Federal Procurement Policy would continue to have the limited role of overseeing contracting policy and developing more professionalism in the various agencies' contracting forces. However, it would have no authority to enforce any of the standards it helps promulgate, which means the standards could be ignored just as past rules have been. President Reagan approved the proposal for the uniform procurement system in March 1982.

The biggest obstacle to putting the draft proposal into final form legislation appeared to be the Defense Department, which has long opposed any uniform procurement system. With support from its allies on the House and Senate Armed Services Committees, the Pentagon has defeated past efforts to put the Defense Department into a common system. Defense officials have argued that it should not be part of a uniform system because the Pentagon has unique, special needs and problems in providing for national security and defense that other agencies do not have. Common rules, they say, could hamper Pentagon efforts to obtain exactly what they need, when they need it. The counter-argument is that much of the Pentagon's procurement is in everyday items—food, paper clips, office supplies, clothing, guard services, maintenance, and repair work—about which there is no life-and-death immediacy, and for which no separate procurement system is needed. For those items that wouldn't fit into a uniform system, the procurement proposal could be tailored to give the Defense Department flexibility. The Office of Federal Procurement Policy proposal, in fact, originally called for "dual conforming statutes" for the Pentagon and civilian agencies, so that the Defense Department would abide by the same procurement rules as civilian agencies, but under a parallel system that would "recognize traditional jurisdictional patterns."

However, after receiving congressional, contractor, Pentagon, and other federal agency feedback, the Office of Federal Procurement Policy revised the initial proposal. On February 26, 1982, the office submitted to Congress its final proposal, which pulled back from the concept of new "dual conforming statutes" and instead called for revision of the existing Armed Forces Services Procurement Act and the Federal Property and Administrative Services Act to accomplish the uniformity it desired. The revised proposal was a recognition that the initial measure could get bogged down indefinitely in the congressional committee system, with Armed Services committees in each house working to keep the Pentagon system separate, and government operations committees pushing for uniformity.

As of late 1982, the proposal was still being studied in Congress. Some members of Congress were unhappy that the proposed system didn't call for total uniformity in one statute, or at least "dual conforming statutes." Others were concerned that the proposal did not give the Office of Federal Procurement Policy enforcement powers. Passage of the measure seemed a long way off. Nevertheless, LeRoy J. Haugh, associate administrator for regulatory policies, of the Office of Federal Procurement Policy, said in August 1982 that 50 percent of the proposal—including the professionalization of the contracting staff, improvement in monitoring and feedback, and similar managerial initiatives—were being implemented without legislation. Haugh said the procurement policy office estimated that the system, if fully implemented, could save taxpayers $2 billion to $9 billion annually.

In its proposal for the more uniform system, the Office of Federal Procurement Policy had included a number of points that seemed certain to please contractors. One significant point was both the draft and final proposal's recommendation that no limits be set on the profit or fee a contractor may earn. "Any statutory limitation on contractor profit or fee," the initial report stated, "should only be applicable to noncompetitive procurements, and should be reserved for wartime or emergency conditions when many normal procedures are bypassed." The report stated there was no need for profit or fee limitations because "techniques of negotiation, use of cost and price analysis, and contract audit, plus the Truth in Negotiations Act, are adequate safeguards against paying excessive prices under normal conditions." Given past government-wide problems with contractors making, and winning, excessive contract claims against the government, this part of the proposal doesn't offer much hope of protecting the public against contractor excesses.

Also, the proposal provided for reduced monitoring by the government of certain types of contractors "whose costs are largely controlled by the competitive environment of the commercial marketplace." Government monitoring would be "reserved for business locations that operate mainly under large negotiated cost-type contracts." Again, such a proposal should be looked at with some skepticism, given the documented record of past abuses.

Another key aspect of the proposal is its revision of the government's standard concept of competition away from advertising with rigid specifications for products and services, and toward a system with less rigid specifications permitting more consultation with prospective contractors before a contract is awarded. The rationale for this is that rigid requirements often scare off prospective contractors thereby lessening competition for a contract. Also, in some cases, it causes contractors to tailor their bids deliberately low so they can win the contract and then later attempt to make up for their low bid with overrun claims. By permitting more consultation, government officials would be able both to determine not only a company's cost proposals, but also the firm's level of competence and ability to do the job. The danger is, of course, that too flexible a system will produce more arbitrariness in contract awards, possibly resulting in a favored few getting the contracts rather than producing an expanded contractor base.

In another proposal, which would have the effect of shielding the activities of contractors from the eyes of Congress, the Reagan administration in its second year recommended legislation to allow it to eliminate certain periodic reports on contracting it was required to make to the Senate and the House. Among the reports it wanted to scrap were ones requiring the Defense Department to list the functions it wanted to turn over to contractors, the Nuclear Regulatory Commission to show how it uses contractors, the Small Business Administration to list annual dollar value of all federal contracts awarded to businesses classified as small, disadvantaged, or owned by women, the Interior Department to monitor the potential conflicts of interests of agency personnel who handle, among other matters, management and sale of public lands, Outer Continental Shelf oil leasing, and mining in national parks. The proposal would also eliminate more than 150 other reports and scale down 46 others, many of which have nothing to do with contracting. These include, for example, a Defense Department report to give Congress notification of planned closure, realignment or expansion of military bases, and a Labor Department report detailing the health and safety records of federal agencies.

Another major pro-contractor initiative attempted by the Reagan administration was an effort, apart from the uniform procurement system just discussed, to lower the wages government construction contractors are required to pay their workers. Under the Davis-Bacon Act, which was enacted in 1931 and then modified in 1935, construction contractors on projects built with federal funds are required to pay their workers the local prevailing wage, which, in heavily unionized areas, is the union wage scale. Contractors have complained over the years that the law required them to pay too much in labor costs and have attempted to have it repealed or modified. Labor unions have successfully fought any efforts at repeal, so when the Reagan administration came in, it attempted a different approach to undercut the law—namely, to change the regulations adopted by the Labor Department to back up the law.

The Labor Department thus proposed that the definition of "prevailing wage" and the means of determining the prevailing wage in a community be changed so that contractors could generally pay lower wages and use more semi-skilled, lower-paid workers on federally funded projects. The new regulations would also have eliminated the requirements that companies submit weekly payroll records to the Labor Department—a provision that had been required partly to determine if kickbacks were being paid on a project. *New York Times* columnist Tom Wicker said the proposed changes "give the construction industry most of what it wants."

To block what it saw as an attempt to circumvent Congress and to hurt the wage scales of persons working on federally funded projects, the American Federation of Labor and Congress of Industrial Organizations (AFL-CIO) went to court and in late July 1982 got a federal judge to block the implementation of the new regulations. U.S. District Court Judge Harold H. Greene in Washington, D.C., noted that the prevailing wage law had been in effect for forty-seven years under eight Presidents and fifteen secretaries of Labor, but that the Reagan administration was attempting to change it without trying "to show that the earlier understanding of the statute was wrong or that experience has proved it to be defective." Lacking proof to the contrary, Greene said, a judge has to give "very substantial weight" to the consistent administration of the law over the last forty-seven years.

Also pending in 1982 was a similar Labor Department proposal to change provisions of the 1965 Service Contracts Act, which was designed to protect workers under federal contracts in generally low-paying jobs, such as janitors, security guards, and general laborers. The Service Contracts Act requires companies with federal contracts to pay service workers at least the minimum wage, or an amount equal to the prevailing wage in a particular locale if the prevailing wage is higher. Under the existing regulations, the secretary of Labor had authority to exempt a service contractor from the act if there were strong evidence to show that the exemption "is necessary in the public interest." The proposed new regulations would permit more exemptions to the act so that contractors could pay less than the prevailing wage.

The Labor Department had also attempted to ease federal regulations barring race and sex employment discrimination by government contractors. However, after consulting with the White House—which had been under increasing criticisms from civil rights groups concerned by a number of administration policies regarding rights of minorities—the Labor Department in July 1982 withdrew the proposal and said it would be rewritten, but gave no indication whether the new version would be as favorable to contractors as the initial draft.

The Reagan administration also took a soft position on the "revolving-door" issue. Although the movement of officials from high federal posts to business and industry, or from the business community into government (as in the Bechtel situation), has created a number of potential conflicts of interest and problems with federal policies and contracts over the years, the Reagan administration announced in mid-1982 that it planned to seek repeal of the law that requires top government personnel to make public their financial interests. Administration officials contended that the Ethics in Government Act of 1978 had hampered the recruitment of people for federal positions.

A more likely reason for administration concern over the act was that information contained on the disclosure forms and then published in the press had involved some of the members of the administration in controversy. For example, Labor Secretary Raymond J. Donovan had been the target of some congressional and editorial criticism after his disclosure that after he joined the government he received up to $150,000 in loans from his former construction firm employer. Attorney General William French Smith also came under fire over his disclosure that he had received a $50,000 severance payment from a California steel firm eleven days before he became attorney general and had invested it in two oil and gas drilling tax shelters. Under criticism, Smith subsequently returned the $50,000 "to dispel unfounded concerns" over "even a possible appearance of impropriety." And Central Intelligence Agency Director William J. Casey received some unwanted publicity after he reported that he held shares in a company that was part of a consortium seeking loan and price guarantees from the U.S. Synthetic Fuels Corporation.

White House counsel Fred Fielding said that the disclosure provision "has inhibited recruitment; talented individuals otherwise willing to serve have concluded that public disclosure is too high a price to pay." Supporters of the Ethics in Government Act disagreed. Ann McBride, of the public-interest group Common Cause, said that polls of federal officials leaving government showed that more than half listed low salaries as a main reason for going into the private sector, while only 8 percent listed the Ethics in Government Act as a reason for leaving.

President Reagan, during his successful campaign for the presidency and afterward, referred constantly to "fraud, waste, and abuse" in government and his plans to eradicate it. When Reagan used the terms, however, he would often follow up with an anecdote about someone cheating on welfare, or using food stamps to buy expensive food, or he would attack some byzantine bureaucratic procedure or regulation that was hurting business or costing the taxpayers money. But by mid-1982 one could search the public record in vain for similar criticisms by Reagan of "fraud, waste, and abuse" by government contractors, even though reports over the last twenty years from Congress and the General Accounting Office show strongly that this is the most fertile field of all for uncovering monetary losses.

In his first eighteen months in office, Reagan and his subordinates took a number of steps based on the premise that holding down the number of civil service employees, per se, limits the cost of government. These steps included hiring freezes, layoffs of federal workers, and establishment of personnel ceilings.

The basic problems with hiring freezes, layoffs (called RIFs, for reductions in force), and personnel ceilings is that unless they are accompanied by reductions in an agency's workload and budget, agency managers have to resort to other means to get the work done. In an early 1982 report, the General Accounting Office noted this problem with the Reagan administration personnel ceilings and reductions in force, indicating that projected savings from the program would, as in the past, prove to be illusory. The reason for this, the accounting office said, is that agency managers likely would "compensate for ceiling reductions by awarding contracts or using overtime to perform separated employees' functions." If contracts or overtime were not used to compensate for the lower in-house employee level, the accounting office said, the result would be "significant program problems"—work just wouldn't get done.

Reagan's April 1981 budget proposal to the Congress called for reducing federal personnel ceilings by 43,000 positions, a move the Office of Management and Budget projected would produce total savings of $1.6 billion for fiscal years 1981 and 1982. (While civilian agencies' personnel ceilings were being reduced by 63,000, the Defense Department received a 20,000 personnel increase.) However, the General Accounting Office found that the Office of Management and Budget estimate of savings was "optimistic" by as much as $1 billion because it failed to take into account severance pay, unemployment compensation and lump-sum annual leave payments to laid-off workers, pension costs for workers who decided to retire early, and the loss of government income that would result—such as a reduction of $182 million in the tax revenues collected and assessed by the Internal

Revenue Service because of personnel cuts in that agency. The estimates also failed to take into account the use of contractors by agencies to take the place of laid-off employees.

The report said that in the Department of Energy, for example, officials had reported limitations on their in-house work force "prevents the agency from hiring the people it needs," with the result that agency officials turn to contracts with private firms, or grants to nonprofit institutions, to accomplish their various missions. The General Accounting Office noted the self-defeating nature of this situation, stating, "Although contract employees providing such services are not included in personnel ceilings or counted as part of the federal work force, they are paid with federal funds and are generally doing the same type of work as federal employees." This use of personnel ceilings also "reinforces the misconception held by many in government and in the general public that constraining the staffing level of the federal work force controls the cost of government."

By reducing the number of government employees through personnel ceilings and reductions in force, the Reagan administration was thereby able also to reduce the amount of regulation of private businesses. As Robert W. Hartman, a senior fellow at the Brookings Institution, observed, "In some of the areas, they're using reductions as a policy weapon. With fewer people to enforce regulations and laws, it means weaker enforcement." This certainly seemed to be the case in the Energy Department.

As has been discussed in a previous chapter, the Department of Energy is second only to the Pentagon in terms of inappropriate and costly contracting policies. The evidence strongly suggests that contractors, rather than in-house personnel, have been controlling or heavily influencing agency operations in the areas of fossil and synthetic fuels, solar energy, and regulatory activities. In his campaign for the presidency, Ronald Reagan called for the abolition of the Energy Department and followed up on this with a proposal for its dismantlement after he came into office. The Reagan plan, with its emphasis on eliminating in-house personnel, seemed certain to increase the use of contractors in future energy programs.

In calling for the department's abolition, Reagan contended the agency has imposed "the heavy hand of government and government regulations" on energy production. In none of his statements can there be found any concern about the department's costly, questionable contracting practices. Reagan said that his plan to dismantle the agency and shift its functions elsewhere, mostly to the Department of Commerce, would "simply change the role of government from controlling the activities of energy industries to complementing them." With energy-related contracts already eating up to 80 to 94 percent annually of the Energy Department's budget, Reagan's pledge to free the industry from the shackles of government could give scant comfort to those concerned about contractors' waste and abuses in the energy area.

The abolition of the Energy Department also seemed unlikely to save much money, especially in the contracting area. Various Reagan administration officials have publicly stated that the reorganization of energy activities could save anywhere from $250 million to $2 billion over a three- or four-year period. The Congressional Budget Office in early 1982 had put the savings at a more modest $3 million in the first year but said this would be offset by $3 million in costs resulting from personnel transfers and severance pay for dismissed federal employees. In August 1982, the General Accounting Office concluded the administration had not verified even $250 million in savings, saying it had overlooked "numerous" expenses involved in the changeover.

When the administration's proposal came up for a June 1982 hearing before the Senate Governmental Affairs Committee, members expressed serious reservations and outright opposition to the plan. One of their main concerns was the administration's philosophy, as Senator Thomas Eagleton expressed it, "that energy is no longer a special problem." Eagleton, a Missouri Democrat, said the Energy Department, "For all its flaws . . . symbolizes our recognition of the problem which hangs over our prosperity and our national security like Damocles' sword. We should be doubling our efforts to free ourselves from our dependence on foreign oil, not offering blithe assertions that we have turned the corner or spied the light at the end of the tunnel."

Other Democratic and Republican committee members were concerned that the reorganization would further reduce research and development for solar power, conservation, and renewable resources, while emphasizing nuclear power. Given the amount of opposition in the Senate, and the even more vigorous opposition to the reorganization in the House (where no bill had even been introduced by August 1982 because of a lack of a willing sponsor), both administration representatives and congressional aides said there appeared little chance of passing the measure until well after the new Congress came into office in 1983.

Although Congress was slow to respond to Reagan's plan to dismantle the Energy Department, the agency itself was attempting to do the same thing through administrative action in 1981 and 1982 chiefly by terminating in-house employees and hiring more contractors. In the fossil fuels division, which had already been largely taken over by contractors in the years prior to the Reagan administration, 173 members of the division's staff of 213 received notices of firings or reassignments in the summer of 1982, leaving contractors to take up the slack. In July 1982, the Agency's Economic Regulatory Administration disclosed its intention to eliminate jobs of 173 enforcement employees who, among other things, audit and investigate oil companies accused of overcharging. The agency's chief, Raymond Hanzlick, had pledged to shut down the office entirely by September 30, 1982.

Other areas of the Energy Department were similarly affected. The General Accounting Office reported in July 1982 that the cutbacks in in-house personnel, and subsequent hiring of contractors to take up much of the resulting slack, had severely reduced the agency's ability to manage programs designed to promote energy conservation and the development of renewable energy resources. The accounting office said that the hiring of contractors to replace the lost in-house personnel was not the right approach to enable the government to retain effective control over its programs.

As an example, the accounting office cited the department's Office of State and Local Assistance Programs, which oversees five nationwide programs to encourage energy conservation. Headquarters staff for the program was cut from 73 to 54 persons—of whom 24 were newly assigned and lacked experience—as of April 30, 1982; all seven branch chiefs were replaced, and field staff directly involved in administering the state and local assistance programs was reduced to 109 persons, a cut of 52 percent. The infusion of inexperienced personnel presented a major problem in retraining, which was made more serious by the loss of all the branch chiefs and the cutbacks in field personnel.

The Energy Department, for its part, saw no problems with the personnel cuts and the increased use of contractors. Barbara Fleming, of the agency's public information office, said that cutbacks in conservation and renewable energy programs were justified "because we feel we're in a position where private industry can pick up" and, in fact, "has picked up on a great deal of work that was done" in-house.

In one of several actions designed to give comfort to the sagging nuclear energy industry and its contractors, the Energy Department in early 1981 rewrote a 1980 agency report that claimed the nuclear industry had received $40 billion in federal subsidies over a thirty-year period. The new report downgraded the subsidies figure to $12.8 billion.

The author of the earlier report, economist Joseph Bowring, immediately charged that the revision of the subsidies' figure was due to pressure from the nuclear power industry and from pro-nuclear aides to Energy Secretary James B. Edwards. He called the revised report "garbage." Bowring's study had contended that, without the subsidies, the cost of nuclear power would have been twice as much over the years. In downgrading the subsidies' amount, the revised report attempted to make the case that nuclear power was competitive in price with electricity produced by coal and oil energy.

It wasn't that Bowring's math was bad. Rather, the Reagan administration achieved the lower figure by not counting certain things Bowring had included or by reducing some of his figures—for example, listing only $7.3 billion, instead of $23.6 billion, for research and development; excluding $4.4 billion in other research and development on the grounds that it was for military, rather than commercial, uses of nuclear power; and excluding $1.3 billion for nuclear industry safety research and $2.5 billion for uranium market promotion.

Later, in October 1981, President Reagan gave nuclear power a further boost by announcing plans—which could eventually add billions of dollars more to taxpayers' support of the nuclear industry—

to emphasize that form of energy to help make the nation less reliant on foreign sources. With nary a mention of the way government had shored up the nuclear industry in the past, Reagan maintained that the woes of the industry were due to a federal "regulatory environment" that was "forcing many utilities to rule out nuclear power as a source of new generating capacity." Disregarding the near-meltdown at Three Mile Island in 1980, and the closures and near closures of numerous other nuclear plants in recent years because of safety problems, Reagan said that "nuclear power has become entangled in a morass of regulations that do not enhance safety but that do cause extensive licensing delays and economic uncertainty."

With this in mind Reagan, among other things, said he was directing Energy Secretary Edwards to come up with ways to speed the regulatory and licensing process for new nuclear power plants so that the planning and construction of them would take six to eight years instead of ten to fourteen years, as had been the case; was proceeding swiftly to build a nuclear waste repository; was seeking a study of the feasibility of obtaining plutonium through contracts with private utilities, rather than relying solely on government-owned facilities, thereby lifting a ban President Carter imposed in 1977 on the reprocessing by utilities of spent fuel; and was planning to proceed with completion of the controversial and costly Clinch River Breeder Reactor in Tennessee. The estimated cost of finishing the Clinch River project had escalated from $669 million in 1973 to $8.5 billion in 1982. A House Energy and Commerce Committee hearing in 1981 disclosed that Atomics International, a Rockwell subsidiary, had in 1975 been awarded a noncompetitive federal contract to supply eleven steam generators to the project at a cost of $56.9 million. By 1981 the contractor had provided just two steam generators at an estimated cost of $143 million, committee investigators reported.

Representative Richard L. Ottinger, D-New York, chairman of the committee's Subcommittee on Energy Conservation and Power, found no little irony in Reagan's nuclear power announcement. "This is nothing more than a Chrysler-type bailout that will cost taxpayers billions of dollars," Ottinger said, in a reference to the federal plan to assist the financially troubled automobile manufacturer. "If it is time to get the federal government off the backs of business, as President

Reagan likes to say, then it is also time to get the nuclear business off the back of the American taxpayer." Other critics suggested the industry was terminally ill because of safety and economic—rather than regulatory—problems.

While Reagan took the position that the nuclear industry needed subsidies, other energy programs, such as solar power and conservation, would have to fend more for themselves. Mark Hertsgaard, a fellow at the Institute for Policy Studies, a left-oriented think-tank, said Reagan's talk of streamlining the licensing process was a "euphemism for slashing safety regulations so that nuclear plants can be built faster and more cheaply." While cutting federal spending for solar power by 45 percent and for conservation by 63 percent, the Reagan administration was increasing funds for nuclear plants and reactors by 6 percent for fiscal year 1983. This led Hertsgaard to wonder why nuclear energy was an exception to the Reagan administration rule that "market forces should and will solve the nation's energy problems."

The Reagan administration also provided a major subsidy to the Union Oil Company in July 1981 by signing a contract for the first commercial-scale synthetic fuels plant. Democrats on the House Government Operations Committee had complained that the Energy Department had gone ahead with the contract with Union without first determining whether the oil shale plant, planned for western Colorado, would have been built without the government subsidy. The price and purchase guarantee contract provided for the government to pay Union Oil up to $400 million more than the market value of the synthetic oil produced by the plant.

Before the contract was signed, the committee had demanded that Energy Secretary Edwards provide it with appropriate documents so it could determine whether the Energy Department was negotiating too generous a price guarantee in the contract. When Edwards refused to comply, the committee threatened him with a contempt of Congress citation. The contempt vote was avoided when Edwards agreed to turn over the documents—on the same day Reagan gave his approval to the contract with Union Oil and Edwards signed it. David Stockman, Reagan's budget director, had opposed the subsidy to Union Oil as unnecessary, saying that some private companies were then considering building synfuels plants without such assistance.

By early 1982, the Reagan budget cuts in nondefense areas were beginning to have an impact on individual federal agencies' spending, which meant there was less money for all aspects of an agency's operations. Thus, for many agencies, unless substantial personnel cuts were made, there was not a lot of extra money to be spent on contractors' services. So, although contracting continued at a high level in many nondefense agencies, it suddenly was not experiencing the growth it had been in previous years.

Doug McDaniel, staff aide on the Senate Governmental Operations Committee, said in early 1982 that the effect of the Reagan budget cuts had been felt most severely by consulting and management support services firms whose expertise lay outside the defense field. He said that, in light of the defense buildup called for by the Reagan administration, many management support firms had switched over to defense specialities in an effort to get Pentagon contracts; some of the best of the other firms managed to survive on their nondefense work, while some other companies were forced to close down or scale back their operations for lack of government work.

Typical of those firms reaping benefits from Reagan policies was Evaluation Research Corporation, a management and technical support firm located in the Virginia suburbs of Washington, D.C., which had more than $13 million in revenues in 1981. The firm's primary business since its inception in 1976 has been evaluating government programs and weapons systems. With 59 percent of its business from defense contracts and subcontracts in 1981 and only 8 percent from commercial customers (with most of the rest from other federal agencies), Evaluation Research saw opportunities in the Reagan defense buildup "to expand our defense markets in 1982 to include support to additional military field activities."

The company's president and board chairman, Jack E. Aalseth, noted in the company's annual report that he had headed the industry trade group, the National Council of Professional Services Firms, during 1981, "which, in spite of its turbulence, was a milestone year for the professional services industry as a whole." Aalseth clearly was pleased with Reagan administration contracting practices, saying, "Of primary significance was the administration's restatement of our country's traditional policy of utilizing private enterprise as its principal source of government goods and services. This policy is clearly in the national interest, and the professional service industry's long-term prospects are secure and its opportunities unlimited."

Because of the varying definitions of the term "consultant" that are used by federal agencies, it was still impossible in 1982 to get a full picture of the extent of consulting and management support services in government. The Office of Management and Budget's limited figures, however, suggested that consulting in defense areas was expected to increase in fiscal year 1982 by about 14 percent over fiscal year 1981, while consulting services in nondefense areas were expected to decline by 7 percent during the same period.

A *Washington Post* survey in mid-1982 of firms in the Washington, D.C., area that provide consulting and management support services found that companies involved in defense work were prospering, but firms such as Wapora, Inc., which had specialized in preparing environmental impact statements for the Environmental Protection Agency, had been badly hurt by cutbacks in environmental and social programs. The reduction in contracting by a less environmentally oriented EPA under Reagan had caused Wapora to trim its staff from 200 to 100. The company also experienced its first financial loss in a decade in 1981.

Mike McCullough, president of the seventy-member trade group, the Professional Services Council, said that the cuts had hurt many firms. However, McCullough, who also headed the Washington, D.C., office of Booz-Allen & Hamilton, the influential management consulting firm, said that the future looked good because "everything that has been said [by the Reagan administration] has been favorable to the private sector," including recommending the hiring of outside firms to perform government work.

Other Reagan initiatives seemed likely also to increase the amount of federal work for management support services and consulting firms. Given the complexity of the shifts of responsibilities embodied in Reagan's "new federalism" proposals, both the federal and state governments will face difficulties making the transition to the new system if Congress decides to approve the program. And there are those who stand to profit from those difficult times. "As soon as I heard President Reagan announce the 'new federalism,' I thought, 'what a bonanza this is going to be for the consulting industry,' " said Senator David Pryor, D-Arkansas. Pryor, of course, had in mind the management consulting firms' work over the last three decades at the federal, as well as at the state and local levels, in setting up new bureaucracies, revamping old ones, or integrating new programs into existing agencies. The Reagan proposal is an illustration of the principle that whenever new federal programs are introduced, or old ones discarded, contractors stand a chance of cashing in.

In the defense area under the Reagan administration, contractors of all types were continuing to thrive under the president's plan to spend $1.6 trillion over a five-year period on the military. In addition to providing a bonanza for honest contractors, the sheer size and complexity of some of the programs embodied in the program increased opportunities for fraud and waste. Joseph H. Sherick, assistant to the secretary of Defense for review and oversight, said in late 1981 that the Pentagon recognized this problem and had mobilized some 18,000 personnel from various audit, inspection and criminal investigative units within the Defense Department to deal with contract fraud and other white-collar crimes. He also cited the creation of a new organization, the Defense Criminal Investigative Service, as evidence of Defense Secretary Weinberger's intention to get tough with contract and other types of abuses.

Sherick said that ever since the Revolutionary War, "one of the problems that has consistently been with us is people ripping us off" and that "as the increased procurement programs in the Department of Defense come along, it will even get to be a bigger problem." The Pentagon, he said, may lose as much as $1 billion a year in the sole area of contractors supplying overpriced and shoddy goods—to say nothing of the other types of contract problems.

With the increased emphasis by the Reagan administration on certain types of contracting and on business's role in government, there were bound to be problems. In the first eighteen months of the Reagan administration, there had been no major contracting scandals —aside from the usual Pentagon boondoggles—but there had been plenty of questionable incidents, including one that involved the president's son, Michael Reagan.

The younger Reagan gained attention in May 1981 when it was disclosed that, in his capacity as vice president of a California company, he had used his father's name in connection with an effort to solicit defense contracts and subcontracts for his firm. The company, Dana Ingalls Profile, Inc., manufactured small machine tool parts for missiles and aircraft. The younger Reagan had written letters two months earlier to procurement officials at eight to ten military installations and to the Martin Marietta Company, a major defense contractor. In one of the letters, to Tinker Air Force Base, he stated the company's interest in doing business with the military and also called attention to his famous family member, saying, "I know that, with my father's leadership at the White House, this countries [sic] Armed Services are going to be rebuilt and strengthened."

President Reagan's initial reaction to his son's gaffe was hardly exemplary. His deputy press secretary, Larry Speakes, contended that Michael Reagan was not "trying to trade on the family name." The younger Reagan, he said, was merely "a private citizen" who had a right to make a living and that the president hoped a lot of press criticism wouldn't come up "every time he tries to do business." Displaying his lack of knowledge of the fact that the majority of defense contracts are awarded noncompetitively, Speakes maintained that Pentagon contracts were awarded on the basis of competitive bids, and that it was, therefore, difficult to "trade on the family name" in seeking such awards. Speakes also said, "I don't think the president has any problems with the way Michael is doing business."

President Reagan obviously had second thoughts about the matter. Speakes subsequently issued a new statement, saying that White House counsel Fred Fielding would provide informal guidance to all four Reagan children to help them avoid problems in any of their future business dealings. "In the president's view," Speakes's statement said, "this precautionary step is the best way to ensure that his children can continue to exercise their full rights as private citizens while also observing their special responsibilities as members of the first family, thus avoiding even the appearance of any impropriety."

In response to the growing controversy, Michael Reagan angrily resigned the Ingalls post, which he had held only since January 1, three weeks before his father took office. "It's just so silly," he said.

"Somebody else can write a letter to the military bases or to anybody and say, 'hey, I think Ronald Reagan's a great president.' I write a letter and say my dad's a great president and I have the press on my doorstep."

Problems related to government contracts also brought about the early departure from the Reagan administration of high-level Energy Department aide Armand C. (Rock) Reiser. Reiser, who left the department after Reagan had been in office just two months, had run into difficulty because of questions relating to two sets of financial disclosure forms he had filed. In the first set, Reiser had listed "none" under the income section, but then, when congressional investigators learned that Reiser's consulting firm had obtained $450,000 worth of Energy Department contracts between October and December 1980 before Reiser assumed the energy agency post, Reiser submitted an amended form. This new version listed $100,000 in income from the federal contract under which Reiser's company was to determine the attitudes of the public and legislators in seventeen states regarding nuclear waste disposal.

The Reagan administration had another brush with a contracting controversy in 1981 when it was disclosed that top Treasury Department official Norman B. Ture was being investigated by the department's inspector general's office for his part in arranging a noncompetitive, $230,000 government contract for an economic forecasting model in which he had held a financial interest.

Ture had developed the economic model in 1976 while working at his own consulting firm, Norman B. Ture, Inc. The model was developed with financial help from the Coopers & Lybrand accounting firm, which in return was given the right to use and market it. Ture was appointed by President Reagan to be under secretary of the Treasury for Tax and Economic Affairs and went on the government payroll on January 21, 1981. On January 28, Ture took the step that embroiled him in controversy: he suggested that the Treasury Department's procurement office consider awarding Coopers & Lybrand a noncompetitive contract to use the model.

The inspector general's subsequent report in October 1981 noted that Ture, five days before he began working at the Treasury Department, had agreed orally to sell Coopers & Lybrand the rights to his economic model for $60,000. It wasn't until February 2 that a formal agreement on the sale was reached.

In what was obviously a close call, the inspector general reported that the key issue was whether Ture "had a financial interest in the model at the time he participated in the contracting process." Because he still held a financial interest in the model when he initiated the contracting process on January 28, "he was arguably in technical violation of the [conflict-of-interest] statute." Nevertheless, the report found that Ture had completed his negotiations of terms with Coopers & Lybrand by January 28, and had not in any way profited from Treasury's subsequent contract with Coopers & Lybrand.

"Nonetheless, the report stated, "Dr. Ture's failure to disclose formally his corporation's ownership of the economic model is open to question and to legitimate criticism." The report went on to recommend more stringent compliance by agency employees with financial disclosure laws and establishment of an information program to make employees more aware of the provisions of the law. Ture, one of the Reagan administration's leading supply-side economic theorists, resigned his Treasury post in the summer of 1982—a move in no way related to the contract controversy.

The Reagan administration also was involved in another type of controversy with disclosures in May 1982 that the Department of Housing and Urban Development (HUD) was planning to sell seven housing projects, without competitive bidding and at extremely favorable terms, to a company that involved two well-connected Republican supporters of Reagan. The company, First American Housing Preservation Corporation, included among its principals Sheila Rabb Weidenfeld, former press secretary for First Lady Betty Ford, and her husband, Edward L. Weidenfeld, who also served on the Reagan transition team's advisory panel on housing and historic preservation.

The Weidenfelds owned 20 percent of the company's stock. The projects, involving 1,146 apartments, included subsidized low-income units as well as luxury buildings. They were among more than 250 properties taken over by HUD because of defaults by owners on their government-backed mortgages.

A subsequent investigation of the proposed $11 million transaction, by Housing and Urban Development Inspector General Charles L.

Dempsey, found that the agency ignored its own guidelines on competitive bidding for such projects, required the purchasers to put up too small a down payment, and had underpriced the properties. The report also stated that, under the terms set down by HUD, the First American firm could be expected to make an after-tax return on investment of as low as 18 and as high as 35 percent a year, rather than the 10 percent that HUD had stated would be the limit. Senator William Proxmire, D-Wisconsin, said the report confirms "that it is who you know, not what you are willing to pay, that determines how HUD disposes of its residential properties."

Sheila Weidenfeld defended the proposed transaction as "a pretty straight deal. I'm not in a position to do anyone a favor or have a favor given to me." Upon release of the report, HUD said it still planned to go ahead with the sale but would accept other proposals. It said a competing firm had made a better offer than the Weidenfeld group. Still, HUD officials defended the original plan, saying that at the time, after considering all aspects of the deal, they saw nothing to be gained by soliciting other bids.

Another controversy over Reagan administration disposal of federal property occurred in July 1982 with the disclosure that the head of the General Services Administration (GSA) had speedily approved a deal that would benefit the Republican-connected Marriott Corporation. (Various Marriott officials, members of the Marriott family and the company's political action committee had contributed almost $150,000 to Republican candidates for federal offices between 1979 and mid-1982.)

The transaction was approved in November 1981 by GSA administrator Gerald P. Carmen after he had met with Martin Artiano, attorney for Marriott. Carmen's decision was contrary to the views of five levels of professional personnel in his agency who had recommended against the transaction. The deal involved the sale of federal land to the City of San Francisco, which in turn planned to lease the site to Marriott for a hotel as part of a major redevelopment project.

Adding to the speculation by some members of Congress that Carmen's decision was politically motivated was a November 3, 1981, letter to Carmen from Frederic (Fred) V. Malek, a Marriott vice president and former special assistant to President Nixon. Malek is a Reagan supporter, having contributed $1,000 to his 1980 presidential campaign. In the letter, Malek stated that the proposed property sale would benefit "not only the City of San Francisco but also President Reagan." (Malek, it should be noted, headed the Nixon White House's "responsiveness program" under which contracts, grants, and other machinery of the federal government were used to obtain political contributions and support in the 1972 presidential election campaign.) In 1982 President Reagan nominated Malek to serve on the Postal Service board of governors, and also appointed him to the Private Sector Survey on Cost Control, which was to look for ways to reduce federal operating costs. A spokesman for Marriott said the Malek letter's reference to a benefit to Reagan meant there would be a reduction in the government's surplus property inventory.

Also raising questions was Carmen's decision to waive the usual General Services Administration procedure under which other federal agencies are given thirty days to state whether they have any need for property that GSA deems excess. GSA property experts favored having the agency either tear down two buildings on the property and then build a new federal building, or else trade the property to the city for a comparable tract. By agreeing to sell the property to the city, said Jack Galuardi, former GSA Public Building Service acting head, GSA was left with no site for a new federal building.

Carmen said he had not been in any way politically motivated in his decision. He acknowledged meeting with the Marriott attorney and two other individuals whose names he couldn't recall prior to making his decision, but said neither that meeting nor the letter from Malek had influenced his subsequent action. He said he had asked both the agency's inspector general and its ethics counsel to attend the meeting, and they had.

Joseph A. Sickon, the agency's inspector general, said in July 1982 that he was undertaking an internal review of the events leading up to Carmen's decision and would report on it later in the year. Likewise, the House Public Works Committee said it would investigate the matter. In August 1982, Carmen denied at a House hearing that there was any impropriety or political influence involved in the San Francisco transaction. He said he had not been influenced either by the Malek letter or by his meeting with Marriott representatives, and that the proposed sale was in the best interests of the government, the City of San Francisco, and the United States taxpayers.

Besides being criticized for purportedly using government machinery to help its friends, the Reagan administration was also accused of sometimes using contracts as a weapon. In one such instance, the Reagan administration used federal contracts to try to punish those universities whose law schools refused to allow army recruiters on campus. A number of institutions—including Harvard, Yale, Columbia, Wayne State, University of California in Los Angeles, and New York University—were warned by letters from Major General Hugh J. Clausen in May 1982 that they would face the loss of future defense contracts because of their policies of barring campus recruitment by employers who discriminate on the basis of sexual orientation. The issue in this case centered around the army's exclusion of homosexuals from service and, therefore, from the Judge Advocate General Corps, the army's legal branch.

Clausen, the judge advocate general of the army, wrote that in addition to denying the universities future contracts, there was also the possibility that army officers would not train at the universities and that Reserve Officer Training Corps (ROTC) programs would be removed from the institutions. Clausen defended the army's ban on homosexuals and said, "We will not submit to recruiting in a clandestine fashion like a second-class entity."

By July 1982, some of the universities said they were reviewing their policies with an eye toward possibly making an exception for the army from their anti-discrimination policies. With the six universities having more than $41 million in Pentagon research and development and other contracts in fiscal year 1981, much was at stake in the battle between the army and the campuses. The growing acceptance of military contracts by colleges and universities had already stirred some controversy on many campuses by 1982 (just as it had more than a decade earlier), and the army's attempt to use contracts as a weapon to dictate university policy seemed likely to escalate the campus debate over the potential threats to academic freedom that are posed by a reliance on defense money. As Barbara Bruno, assistant dean of placement at

Wayne State University in Detroit, said, the army's threats were "annoying and scary." But, she told the *National Law Journal,* "with the job market as tight as it is, we have to think very hard about any policy that prevents potential employers from interviewing students."

One unusual initiative by the Reagan administration in the contracting field concerned the hiring by Budget Director David Stockman of the Claremont Economics Institute to handle economic forecasting for his office. The California-based institute provided the basic outline for Reagan's first economic report to Congress and was to provide economic forecasts for the president's entire first term in office.

By hiring Claremont, Stockman took an end-run around his own experts at the Office of Management and Budget, as well as the economic planners at the Treasury Department and the Council of Economic Advisers. Claremont director John Rutledge, touting his organization's expertise, said that the government's in-house economic planners "don't understand or sympathize with our model, and they couldn't help write a report if we wanted them to." The Claremont model was based on assumptions of expansion of federal revenues along with a healthy growth in the economy. This would make it possible to pay for the rising costs of defense, while still allowing for tax cuts and a balanced budget by as early as 1983. In his 1980 quest for the presidency, Republican (and later third-party candidate) John B. Anderson had said that such a situation could be achieved only "with mirrors." By mid-1982 Anderson and the other critics appeared to be correct as the economy was still stagnating and the projected $100-billion-plus deficit for fiscal year 1983 made any early chance of a balanced budget a pipedream.

The Reagan White House was not alone in drawing on private firms for its economic planning. Increasingly, federal agencies were also turning to outside economic experts. Four major economic forecasting services—Chase Econometrics, Data Resources Inc., Wharton Econometric Forecasting Associates Inc., and Merrill Lynch Economics Inc.—received $1.8 million on contracts with various federal agencies in fiscal year 1978 and had boosted this to $3.3 million by fiscal year 1980, with further gains anticipated in future years. Senator Lloyd Bentsen, D-Texas, wondered why it was necessary for the agencies to contract-out for such services instead of drawing on governmental resources, such as the President's Council on Economic Advisers. "There appears to be a lot of room for Congress to make a substantial cut in spending here," Bentsen said.

The Reagan administration came under fire in 1981 on the contracting front for the way it spent most of the $50 million that Congress had allocated for relief for victims of the November 1980 earthquake in southern Italy, which killed 3,000 people and left many hundreds of thousands homeless. More than 80 percent of the money was to go to United States companies under contracts, drawn up by the State Department's Agency for International Development, to build twelve earthquake-proof schools by 1985. Private relief organizations assailed the plan as one that would be of more help to American business concerns than to the Italian earthquake victims.

"The government ought to follow the humanitarian way," said Leon O. Marion, executive director of the American Council of Voluntary Agencies, a coalition of private organizations that supervises overseas disaster relief. "As much money as possible should be given to the people themselves." Marion noted that many private organizations had installed permanent prefabricated community centers for less than $100,000 each, and that it had been hoped that the Agency for International Development would have made the $50 million stretch further.

The Italian relief distribution program typified the Reagan administration's approach to the handling of overseas aid. In mid-1981, the Agency for International Development established a new unit, the Bureau for Private Enterprise, to enable American companies to benefit from aid distributed overseas. In its first year of operation, the bureau reported that 65 percent of the money spent for overseas aid programs had been paid to United States firms and institutions for contracts for goods and services.

Because the Reagan administration had as its stated goal the reduction of fraud, waste, and abuse in government, it is difficult to understand some of Reagan's dealings during his first eighteen months in office with the chief watchdogs over federal waste (the offices of inspector general in nondefense agencies).

On his first day in office, Reagan fired all fifteen inspectors general and their deputies. Three months later, the posts were still vacant, and

Reagan had forwarded no names of successors to the Senate for confirmation. Finally, five months after the mass firings, nominations for all but one of the inspectors general had been submitted to the Senate, and three had been confirmed. Five of the inspectors general fired by Reagan won reappointment.

The wholesale firings at the watchdog offices sparked much congressional criticism. Representative L.H. Fountain, D-North Carolina, chairman of the House Government Operations Committee's Intergovernmental Relations Subcommittee and a sponsor of the legislation that created the inspectors general, requested an investigation by the General Accounting Office and scheduled hearings on the matter. Despite the accounting office's best efforts, the White House ignored the agency's request for information for almost two months.

Finally, in an April 1, 1981, hearing before Fountain's subcommittee, Dr. Edwin Harper, deputy director of the Office of Management and Budget, testified that the administration had not reviewed the performances and qualifications of the inspectors general before firing them. He also said that members of Congress and heads of the affected agencies were not advised in advance of the mass removals. The decision to fire them, the accounting office later quoted OMB officials as saying, "was based on the principle that it is each new president's prerogative to terminate the predecessor's appointees to posts in the executive branch." The committee, however, disagreed, saying Reagan had violated the intent of the law establishing the inspectors general by engaging in the "abrupt and disorganized" mass firings.

Under the Inspector General Act of 1978 and subsequent legislation, the inspectors general are responsible for conducting and supervising audits and investigations of agencies' programs and operations, with an eye toward promoting efficiency and economy and preventing and detecting fraud and abuse. The inspector general, whose findings can be referred to the Justice Department for possible prosecution, also report to the agency heads and to Congress on problems and deficiencies in agency operations, and suggest corrective actions. Their jurisdiction covers both contract and in-house operations. Given the important responsibilities of the inspectors general, it scarcely made sense for President Reagan to leave vacant the top post in most of these offices during the first half-year of his administration.

It also seemed particularly short-sighted on Reagan's part when in late 1981 he ordered an over-all 12 percent reduction in the original $301 million budget proposal for the inspectors general, which he had submitted the previous March for fiscal year 1982. Congressional critics of the cuts contended that the reductions would make the offices less able to uncover waste and abuse and were contrary to Reagan's pledge of the previous March when he set up the President's Council on Integrity and Efficiency. The council's goal, Reagan said, was "to follow every lead, root out every incompetent, and prosecute any crook we find who's cheating the people of this nation." The council consisted of the inspectors general plus representatives of the Federal Bureau of Investigation, the Office of Management and Budget, the Office of Personnel Management, and the departments of Defense, Justice, and the Treasury.

The OMB's Harper, who also served as chairman of the President's Council on Integrity and Efficiency, commented in a late 1981 press conference that the personnel and spending limitations on the inspectors general had not harmed those offices' operations. Harper said that "people and dollars . . . really shouldn't be the criteria. What should be the criteria are results. And I think clearly the results that we've experienced . . . with the resources we've allocated, indicates that we've had some real successes." Harper said it was "mindless" to think that "more is always better, whether it's dollars or people." He attributed what successes the inspectors general had had under Reagan to "increased productivity" and the "over-all strengthening and support the program has gotten" from the Reagan administration.

To the contrary, Representative Fountain said, the cuts "would aggravate an already bad situation and have a devastating impact." Others in Congress commented that the cuts were especially ill-advised because most of the inspectors general offices usually recovered much more money than they spent. At about the same time, the General Accounting Office lent support to Fountain's concerns, reporting that the chief problems in the inspectors general offices were a shortage of money and personnel.

Despite the inspectors general's problems, the Council on Integrity and Efficiency reported in the spring of 1982 that the watchdog offices had saved taxpayers some $8 billion over the past year by uncovering and helping reduce fraud and abuse in government programs. However, these purported savings drew some skepticism on Capitol Hill and, in June 1982, the General Accounting Office questioned earlier administration claims of substantial savings for part of 1981.

The GAO reported that the actual saving by the government for the six-month period ended September 30, 1981, was far less than the $2.1 billion figure cited by the administration. The accounting office said that the President's Council on Integrity and Efficiency had wrongly attributed $538 million in savings on program changes in air force weapons systems to Reagan's term, when the savings were actually achieved in fiscal year 1980 during President Carter's term in office. The report also stated that "some agency figures were double counted," and that there was a lack of uniformity in data collection methods and an absence of standard definitions that made it difficult to verify the accuracy of some of the council's figures. Representative John D. Dingell, D-Michigan, who had asked for the GAO study, said the report "demonstrates that the administration statistics are misleading because they are based on incomplete and inconsistent data." Joseph H. Wright, Jr., of the Office and Management and Budget, acknowledged that there were problems with some figures but stood by their over-all accuracy.

The Reagan administration also took other steps that caused problems for some of the inspectors general offices. For example, funding problems at the Department of Health and Human Services in July 1982 came close to forcing an almost complete summertime shutdown of the agency's inspector general's office. The office had had its operating expenses reduced by the Reagan administration by 16 percent the previous December and lacked necessary funds to continue at full strength through the last three months of the fiscal year. A shutdown was averted when Health and Human Services Secretary Richard S. Schweiker obtained funds for the office from elsewhere in his agency's budget; shortly thereafter, Congress approved a supplemental federal budget providing funds for the office.

Just as President Reagan has repeatedly turned to the private sector to hire executives to head major federal agencies, he also established in early 1982 a business-dominated private sector study group that was to report by mid-1983 on ways to reduce government operating costs by eliminating "overlap, duplication, and nonessential administrative activities." One of the panel's 35 task forces was to deal with procurement, contracts, and inventories. The panel, officially called the Private Sector Survey on Cost Control, was headed by J. Peter Grace, chairman and chief executive officer of W.R. Grace & Company, a diversified multinational firm with interests in chemicals, natural resources, and consumer services. The group was to be funded by companies represented on the panel and by other business groups. Reagan also named more than 1,000 other leading business executives to serve on the panel as unsalaried volunteers.

In agreeing to head the panel, Grace said that he was "a natural optimist. I'm sure I'm going to fall flat on my face nineteen times, but I'm also sure we're really going to come up with something quite meaningful. Fresh minds and imaginative, resourceful people can always do this." It didn't take Grace long to fall on his face. Less than three months after his appointment, Grace told a Dallas meeting of the American Feed and Grain Manufacturers' Association that the federal food stamp program "is basically a Puerto Rican program." And, he added, "I've got nothing against Puerto Ricans, but this is a little much."

Grace's speech produced immediate outrage and demands for his resignation from the Reagan panel by Representative Robert Garcia, D-New York, chairman of the Congressional Hispanic Caucus; Resident Commissioner Baltasar Corrada, who represents Puerto Rico in Congress; New York Lieutenant Governor Mario Cuomo; New York City Council President Carol Bellamy; and a number of Spanish-language and general circulation newspapers. Garcia commented that Grace's statement "may play well" in Dallas, but "it is as racist as anything I have ever heard in my seventeen years of elective office."

The outcry against his speech prompted Grace to apologize. Still, he insisted he was "factually correct" in stating that many Puerto Ricans in New York were receiving food stamps, but that calling it "basically a Puerto Rican program" and suggesting that most Puerto Ricans were receiving food stamps "were oratorical mistakes for which I apologize." White House spokesman Larry Speakes said Grace's apology was sufficient and that Grace would not be dismissed.

The cost control survey group itself encountered controversy in late

1982 when the House Post Office and Civil Service Committee initiated an investigation into potential conflicts of interest involving panel members who were studying policy matters from inside the government.

Given the business dominance of the panel, it seemed unlikely that it would come down too heavily on waste relating to contractors' practices, especially when many of the companies represented on the panel were federal contractors. Still, there was plenty for the panel to look into—both in the official bureaucracy and in the contractors' bureaucracy. This was made apparent in a study released in April 1981, which showed that 45 percent of federal employees surveyed claimed they had personally witnessed instances of fraud, waste, or mismanagement in their agencies over the past year. The study was conducted by the United States Merit Systems Protection Board, which was created in 1978 to protect that minority of federal employees (known as "whistleblowers") from reprisals from superiors when they report instances of fraud, waste, or mismanagement in their agencies. About 8,500 federal employees in fifteen federal agencies responded to a questionnaire that had been distributed to about 13,000 government workers. Seventy-three percent of those who responded that they had witnessed questionable activities said they did not report them because they felt nothing would be done about them. Nineteen percent said they did not report the questionable activities for fear of reprisals.

One would expect, therefore, the Reagan administration to be taking extra steps to encourage "whistleblowers" to come forward to report problems involving both in-house employees and contractors. However, such apparently was not the case. In May 1982 Representative Patricia Schroeder, D-Colorado, who worked to create the office of special counsel in the Merit Systems Protection Board in order to give whistleblowing federal workers extra protection against retaliation by agency managers, called for the abolition of the counsel's office. She said the office was failing to protect the rights of whistleblowers and that federal employees should take their complaints directly to the merit board or to the courts, rather than going through an unsympathetic counsel's office.

The reason for the unhappiness of Schroeder and other members of Congress was that since June 1981, when Alex Kozinski became special counsel, until May 1982, the office had initiated no disciplinary action against any federal manager for a merit system abuse. Also, it had filed no new requests for "corrective actions," such as rehiring someone who was illegally fired or transferred. Also, the office had submitted fewer than five requests to halt employee firings, compared with twenty filed in 1980, the last year of the Carter administration.

Kozinski defended his performance, saying that he had shifted the emphasis of the office away from being an advocate for federal employees and toward a more conciliatory approach. He said that his office had been able to settle sixty cases through conciliation without having to go to the formal complaint stage. Schroeder remained unconvinced. She said the office was "a fraud on the American taxpayer" with its cost of $4 million a year "to fund an office which is not doing the job Congress gave it, to fight waste, fraud, and abuse." Kozinski resigned his post—for reasons he said were unrelated to the congressional critricism—in August 1982 to become a commissioner for the United States Court of Claims.

Considering all of the Reagan administration's efforts to help business through contracts, leases, tax breaks, subsidies, deregulation, and other incentives, perhaps the most far-reaching and controversial of all of its contract-related actions in its first two years in office was its plan announced in early 1982 to sell off as much as 35 million of the 700 million acres of United States land under government control. The program was touted by Reagan as a way to raise money to offset huge federal deficits. The administration hoped to raise $1.3 billion by such property transactions in fiscal year 1983, and $4 billion annually in following years. The *New York Times* said the land program "could be the most extensive transfer of public property and resources to private control in recent American history."

And the man who was going to be playing a leading role in the program was the man whose agency controlled the most federally owned land: Interior Secretary James G. Watt, the bane of environmentalists throughout the nation.

7 · Watt: Giving Away the Store

James Gaius Watt, President Reagan's secretary of the Interior, has probably been the most controversial Cabinet officer in the last fifty years.

As the point man for President Reagan's program to sell, lease, or contract the maximum amount of federal land and resources to private interests, Watt in his first two years in the Cabinet was under constant fire from environmental organizations, news media editorialists and commentators, liberal politicians, and even many moderate and conservative Republicans who felt he was violating a trust, begun in the Theodore Roosevelt era, to safeguard the nation's wilderness areas, national parks, and resources. With a free-market approach to federal land and resources, coupled with a fundamentalist Christian philosophy that it is God's will that land and resources be used extensively, Watt established himself as a throwback to the Robber Baron days when the leading industrialists quoted Scripture to justify their exploitative tactics.

Watt, in the words of *New York Times* columnist John Oakes, is an "extremist ideologue" and a "fanatical believer in the maximum development of resources in even the most protected of public lands." Watt's predecessor as interior secretary, Cecil D. Andrus, branded Watt "one of the most reckless Cabinet members ever appointed in the history of our country" who is pursuing a "fanatical philosophy" that will "wreck our wilderness and destroy our wildlife." Russell W. Peterson, the former Republican governor of Delaware, who in 1982 was president of the National Audubon Society, charged that in the Reagan administration "an anti-environmental wrecking crew led by Interior Secretary James Watt has begun to wipe out the hard-won gains and safeguards put in place by a generation of active and caring citizens." And the St. Paul *Pioneer Press* observed editorially, "Watt represents confirmed exploiters who look at majestic redwoods, for example, and see nothing but dimension lumber."

From Watt's viewpoint, his critics were "environmental extremists" who "just weren't credible." They were reacting, he said, to his efforts to bring some balance into a system of "forty, fifty years of bad government" at the Interior Department—a period that it should be noted included such Republican presidents as Eisenhower, Nixon, and Ford who had not generally been regarded as "environmental extremists."

Because of Watt's many controversial actions during his first two years as interior secretary, conservation groups said they were experiencing great growth in contributions, memberships, and citizen activism. While extremely unpopular in some quarters, Watt was a much sought after speaker in his first year in office by state and local Republican organizations, which said Watt was the best crowd-drawer and fund-raiser among administration figures. By Watt's second year, some Republicans, concerned over an environmentalist inspired backlash against Watt, were shying away from joint appearances with the interior secretary. Wherever Watt went, he was likely to be greeted by conservationist demonstrators.

Yet in many areas of the western United States where resentment runs deep among the developer class over the federal government's ownership of so much land, Watt is just as likely to be met with "We Love You Jim" signs. The so-called "Sagebrush Rebellion" of economically and politically influential westerners who oppose federal control of land and resources viewed Watt as their primary champion within the Reagan administration. His speeches' one-liners were especially popular with pro-business audiences. For example, on endangered species, Watt said there was no need to worry because "we can't even get rid of the cockroach." As for environmentalists' concerns that the national parks were becoming overcrowded, Watt commented, "We can learn a great deal from Walt Disney's crowd management principles"—suggesting to environmentalists that Watt equated the national parks with Disney World.

Whatever other emotions Watt may inspire, apathy is certainly not among them. To friendly audiences, Watt showed a sense of humor, even a self-mocking sense of humor. To congressional Democrats, Watt was often uncooperative and evasive. To news media interviewers, Watt would often answer tough questions with *non sequiturs* and a big grin.

In contrast to Watt's failings in the eyes of environmentalists and many members of Congress and the press, his life from boyhood until he became a Cabinet officer has been marked by one success after another. He was raised in the small farming community of Wheatland on the plains of eastern Wyoming and was an excellent student, graduating from high school at the head of his class. He was chosen by the local American Legion post to go to Wyoming Boys' State, an annual gathering of youth leaders who set up a mock legislature and debate issues. Watt was elected "governor" at the conclave. In 1957, at age nineteen, while a freshman at the University of Wyoming, he married his high school sweetheart, Leilani Bomgardner.

At college, Watt was a fraternity man but, unlike many of his brothers, he was also a teetotaler. An outstanding student, he received his degree from the university's College of Commerce and Industry in three years, graduating with honors. He then entered the university's law school, where he edited the law journal and received his law degree in 1962. With his conservative political philosophy clearly emerging, Watt went to work for former Wyoming Governor Milward L. Simpson as a personal assistant in his U.S. Senate election campaign. After Simpson was elected, Watt served him as legislative assistant, speechwriter, and counsel from November 1962 to September 1966 before accepting a lobbying position with the United States Chamber of Commerce. In that post, Watt was responsible, and served as Chamber spokesman, for activities relating to mining, energy, public lands, water, and environmental pollution. He lobbied against the Senate effort to draft the nation's major water quality legislation. In his personal life, Watt became a born-again Christian in 1964.

Upon Richard Nixon's election as president in 1968, the Chamber recommended Watt to serve on Nixon's transition team in the Interior Department. Watt was given the major assignment of preparing Interior Secretary-designate Walter Hickel for what proved to be a stormy confirmation proceeding because of environmentalists' concerns over Hickel's background in land development. In May 1969 Watt was appointed deputy assistant interior secretary for water and power resources. In that development-oriented post, Watt directed seven agencies that marketed electric power and water and also designed, built, and operated water distribution systems, reservoirs, and electric power transmission systems.

From that post, Watt moved in July 1972 to become director of the Bureau of Outdoor Recreation (which later was named the Heritage Conservation and Recreation Service—an agency Watt abolished after he became interior secretary). During his almost three and a half years in that post, Watt managed a $300-million-a-year fund for federal agencies to acquire and develop land and facilities for recreation purposes. Watt's major duty, in 1973, was to produce a nationwide outdoor recreation plan that by then was almost five years overdue. Although Watt later during his interior secretary confirmation hearings held out the plan as evidence of his concern for proper uses of the outdoors, environmentalists contended it was largely a boiler-plate document that merely restated all of the ongoing recreation programs and policies of various Interior Department agencies.

At the Bureau of Outdoor Recreation, Watt also instituted the Interior Department's first management-by-objectives and financial management systems. In a move that later caused him some political embarrassment, Watt—despite warnings from aides that he might be violating civil service hiring rules—awarded two consulting contracts to an old college friend, Don Thoren, who specialized in management-by-objectives systems.

In 1975 Watt was appointed by President Ford to serve on the Federal Power Commission, which regulated the interstate aspects of the natural gas and electric power industries. During Senate Commerce Committee confirmation hearings, Watt acknowledged that he had erred in awarding the Bureau of Outdoor Recreation contracts to a friend. Watt said he was "embarrassed by it because I violated my own standard," but said he had done it because he was "trying to get results" rapidly. His confirmation to the Federal Power Commission was held up for almost a year while Senate investigators looked into the contracts.

Once on the commission as a member, and later vice chairman for seven months in 1977, Watt sided with the industry position more than 90 percent of the time and led the commission's successful effort to permit a tripling of the allowable price for newly discovered natural gas—the largest increase granted in the history of the commission.

In a preview of the types of allegations that would surface again when Watt became interior secretary, a House Commerce Committee subcommittee investigated charges that Watt and another Federal Power Commission member had taken retaliatory personnel action against commission staff attorneys. The alleged retaliations came after the lawyers had testified in congressional hearings that some major companies were withholding natural gas from the market. Although the subcommittee made no determination as to whether any federal laws were violated, it did conclude that there was evidence to show "discriminatory promotion and personnel assignment practices, the illogical reshuffling of gas pipeline and electric rate regulation and unjustified transfer of several of the Office of General Counsel's most experienced natural gas attorneys." In his interior secretary confirmation hearings, Watt stated, "[I have] never taken and I will never take action against an employee simply because of the expression of views contrary to my own."

With Jimmy Carter's election in 1976 and the subsequent creation of the Energy Department, which swallowed up the Federal Power Commission, Watt was out of a job in July 1977. He then moved on to his most controversial private-sector position: president and chief legal officer for the Mountain States Legal Foundation, a pro-business public interest law firm.

With the Mountain States Legal Foundation, the bespectacled, balding Watt was a familiar figure before pro-development audiences. He regularly gave a speech, "Environmentalists: A Threat to the

Ecology of the West," also dubbed the "Green Speech." In it, he railed against "narrow special interest groups"—i.e., environmentalists—who would lock up the west's treasure house of oil, natural gas, and minerals. He also questioned their patriotism, asking: "What is the real motive of the extreme environmentalists, who appear to be determined to accomplish their objectives at whatever cost to society? Is it to simply protect the environment? Is it to delay and deny energy development? Is it to weaken America?" The issue, Watt said, is "our freedom, our right to use the land for productive purposes."

While conservationist critics have assailed the Mountain States Legal Foundation as a front for development interests, the foundation describes itself as a tax-exempt, nonprofit, public interest law firm seeking to counterbalance "those who are using our judicial system to restrict economic growth"—that is, the "extreme environmentalist groups and no-growth advocates." Another purpose of the foundation is to defend "individuals and the private sector from excessive bureaucratic regulation [with] responsible representation in our judicial system." The foundation was established to be a conservative, pro-business alternative to Ralph Nader–style public interest litigators.

The foundation and six others like it in other regions of the country are affiliated with the National Legal Center for the Public Interest, based in Washington, D.C. The Mountain States affiliate was established in 1976 through a $50,000 contribution from the National Legal Center and $25,000 from Joseph Coors, the Colorado beer magnate who was also a major contributor to the national foundation. Coors, a close friend of President Reagan, has frequently helped to finance conservative projects, including the Heritage Foundation, the think-tank that exerted much domestic policy influence in the first year of the Reagan administration's efforts to slash spending for social programs. From Mountain States' relatively humble beginnings with a $194,000 budget in its first year, its annual budget had grown to $1.3 million by the time Watt left to take over at the Interior Department. Among those recommending Watt for the Cabinet post was Joseph Coors.

The contributors to the foundation included many of the major oil, mineral, timber, utility, and other development-oriented corporations. Although the foundation's list of contributors is not publicly available, names of the organization's 1978 contributors were obtained by various congressional and environmental organizations' offices. The 1978 list showed major contributions from such conservative foundations as the Scaife Family Charitable Trusts, $55,000, and the Adolph Coors Foundation, $35,000, and from such oil company foundations as Phillips Petroleum Foundation, $5,000; Amoco Foundation, $2,500; and Cities Service Foundation, $2,500. Among the contributors of $500 or more were such energy and mineral giants as Amax, Inc.; Chevron U.S.A., Inc.; Exxon; Fluor Oil and Gas Corporation; Husky Oil Company; Gulf Resources & Chemical Corporation; Shell Oil; Morrison-Knudsen; Northwest Pipeline Company; Occidental Oil Shale; Pacific Power and Light Company and numerous other utilities; as well as such other significant corporations as Sears, Roebuck & Company; Boise Cascade Corporation; and Johns-Mansville Corporation. A number of gambling interests—Bally Distributing Company, Harrah's, Harvey's Wagon Wheel, Sahara Nevada Corporation, and Union Plaza Hotel & Casino—also contributed to the foundation. In 1979 the foundation assisted the gambling interests by filing a suit challenging an Environmental Protection Agency requirement that the sewage system on the Nevada side of Lake Tahoe be improved before new sewer connections could be granted. Both Harrah's and Harvey's Wagon Wheel had plans to expand their casino operations and would have been adversely affected by such a ban.

In 1980 the foundation's major contributors included many of the same donors as the earlier list: Exxon, $5,000; Shell, $3,000; Chevron, $10,000; Arizona Public Service Company, $6,000; Consolidated Coal, $2,000; Gulf Oil, $1,000; Boise Cascade, $7,500; Amax, $5,000; Burlington Northern, $4,000; and Phillips Petroleum, $2,500. The Adolf Coors Foundation kicked in another $35,000, and the Amoco Foundation contributed $10,000.

Despite its classification as a public interest legal organization, the Mountain States Legal Foundation draws the heavy majority of its cases from issues affecting resource development corporations and other major business interests—most of which were contributors to the foundation or whose officers served on the foundation's board of directors.

To cite just one of many examples, the Mountain States Legal Foundation intervened on the side of the states of Virginia and Indiana in a suit involving the Interior Department, concerning compliance with the Surface Mining Control and Reclamation Act. The intervention, on December 19, 1980, came just three days before President-elect Reagan formally announced his selection of Watt as interior secretary. The foundation alleged that certain portions of the strip-mining act were unconstitutional. Among the other parties to the suit was the Amax Coal Company, a foundation contributor, which was represented by the law firm of David Kennedy, who was a member of the foundation's board of litigation. Another party to the suit was the Peabody Coal Company, which was represented by Stanley Hathaway, a foundation board of litigation member.

The Mountain States Legal Foundation also intervened in two state cases involving the Mountain Fuel Supply Company and the Utah Public Service Commission. One was a case to determine how Mountain Fuel's assets should be figured during a sale of its oil and natural gas assets to a subsidiary; the other concerned an effort to prevent the Public Service Commission from opening its meetings to the public. Mountain Fuel also was a contributor to Mountain States, and its president and board chairman sat on the foundation's board of directors. Also, former Utah Governor Calvin Rampton, who sat on the foundation's board of litigation, was a member of a law firm that represented Mountain Fuel Supply.

In another case, the foundation intervened on the side of Amoco and Marathon Oil in their effort to prevent the Jiscarilla Apache Tribe from levying a severance tax. Both the Amoco Foundation and the Marathon Oil Foundation were contributors to Mountain States.

In a nonresources case, the foundation joined in a suit by the Associated General Contractors of Wyoming against the U.S. Secretary of Commerce in opposition to a minority business subcontracting program on federal contracts. The contractors' organization was also a contributor to the foundation.

The foundation has also represented other major corporations and organizations, such as the Rocky Mountain Oil and Gas Association, Independent Petroleum Association of the Mountain States, Montana Power Company, and the Idaho Cattlemen's Association. Critics of the foundation's choice of cases contend it should not have a tax-exempt status because the Internal Revenue Service has ruled that for a firm to be designated "public interest" and to be entitled to tax-exempt status it must first of all handle cases that would not be economically feasible for its clients to undertake through a private firm. In fact, in its filing for tax exempt status, the foundation said it would represent the broad public interest, rather than private interests. Mountain States consistently became involved in cases where its clients clearly could have hired private law firms.

Certainly, Mountain States and its affiliated foundations have turned the concept of public-interest—defense of the underdog or of the public at large—on its head. One of its earlier cases, filed in three states, sought to eliminate natural gas discounts that utilities were granting to low-income, elderly, and disabled customers. The foundation's stated rationale was that it was attempting "to protect residential natural gas customers who are not low-income, elderly, and disabled."

In another case, the foundation sought abolition of a program at the University of Colorado Law School whereby a certain number of disadvantaged minority students would be allowed to enroll even though their grades were too low to qualify them otherwise for admission. Watt personally contended that such programs for lawyers, doctors, and other professionals would produce inferior minority professionals. Of course, admission to a university does not guarantee a degree; the student still has to earn that. Nevertheless, Watt made it appear that a lot of unqualified lawyers and doctors were going to be unleashed on the world. In a remark that later brought him criticism at his Interior Secretary confirmation hearing, Watt in 1977 was quoted as saying: "As a white man, in ten years . . . I'm going to be very hesitant to allow a black doctor to operate on me because I'll always have the feeling that he may have been carried by the quota system." Watt sidestepped questions about the remark at his confirmation hearing, saying the quote should be looked at in the context of his overall statement in opposition to discrimination and quota systems. The foundation itself had no quota system of any kind. Its 30 directors and 24 members of the board of litigation in 1981 were all white—and all male. All 54 were from 10 western states, and most were executives or attorneys for oil, mining, utility, ranching, banking, and other business interests. The all-male foundation had, incidentally, filed a legal action against the Equal Rights Amendment.

Many of Watt's critics in Congress, in the press, and in conservation organizations contended that Watt's former position with the Mountain States Legal Foundation presented him with innumerable possibilities of conflict of interest with his Interior duties. Senator Dale Bumpers, D-Arkansas, who opposed Watt's nomination as Interior secretary, noted that "sixty to eighty percent of the people who contributed to the Mountain States Legal Foundation are either in the oil business, the mining business, or the timber business." Bumpers said at the time of the Senate vote on Watt's nomination that there were 58 cases pending against the Interior Department filed by contributors to the Mountain States Legal Foundation, plus administrative decisions estimated in the "thousands" Watt would be required to make on matters in which foundation contributors and board members have interests. In addition, Watt would have before him issues on which, in his post at the foundation, he had been involved in suits against the Interior Department.

Watt agreed not to participate in any Interior Department proceedings in which his former foundation was a party, but did not similarly pledge to withdraw from making decisions affecting contributors to the foundation. Despite Watt's promises, though, in his first year as Interior secretary, he did participate in matters in which the Mountain States Legal Foundation, under his direction, had been involved.

One such matter involved the administrative appeal, filed in the spring of 1980 by the foundation, to allow motorized boats and rafts to continue to operate on the Grand Canyon segment of the Colorado River. Watt and the foundation labeled Interior's 1979 effort to phase out and then ban the craft "an elitist policy."

Despite his earlier involvement in the suit on the side of motorized craft concessioners, Watt, as Interior secretary, in December 1981 overturned the 1979 ban on such craft. Ed Norton, of the Wilderness Society, said that Watt's decision not to withdraw from making this decision was "a distinct conflict of interest" because of his previous legal action on this issue on behalf of the foundation.

Another such matter involved the foundation's intervention in the summer of 1980 on the side of a mining company in an administrative appeal to the chief of the Forest Service. The mining company wanted to explore for oil and natural gas by exploding 250,000 pounds of dynamite in areas covering 200 miles of seismic lines in Montana's Bob Marshall, Scapegoat, and Great Bear Wildernesses. National and state conservation organizations contended that this "bombing of the Bob Marshall" was unnecessary, as well as potentially detrimental to a pristine area, because much of Montana's national forest land was already covered by oil and gas leases yet to be explored, and there thus was no need to move into yet another area. Forest Service regional officials had denied the company's application because the firm had not obtained the proper leases.

In connection with his confirmation hearings, Watt had pledged specifically to withdraw "from participation in any aspect of litigation in federal or state court and any administrative proceedings . . . involving the adjudication or decision of a specific matter such as an application or appeal within the Department of Interior or any other department or agency of the federal government, when the Mountain States Legal Foundation is a party or represents a party." Nevertheless, on the Bob Marshall matter, Watt as Interior secretary decided to issue oil and gas leases sought by industry. At the urging of conservation groups, the House Interior Committee voted in May 1981 to tell Watt to withdraw the Bob Marshall area from mineral leasing. Watt questioned the committee's constitutional authority to issue such an instruction, but he complied with it on June 1. Both the Pacific Legal Foundation, a pro-business law firm, and Watt's old organization, Mountain States Legal Foundation, immediately filed lawsuits to overturn Watt's action.

Although there may have been some irony in Watt's old employer suing him, conservation organizations didn't think so. Rather, they charged that Watt was in collusion with these two foundations to get his own decision overturned. Particularly arousing the suspicions of attorneys for the Wilderness Society and other organizations was a July 22, 1981, letter from Ronald A. Zumbrun, director the Pacific Legal Foundation, to Alfred Regnery, deputy assistant attorney general in the Justice Department's Land and Natural Resources Division. Attorney General William French Smith, whose department defends executive branch agencies against lawsuits, had (as had the two plaintiffs in the suit against Watt) asked that the court invalidate the House committee's resolution as an unconstitutional intrusion on the executive branch's prerogatives. The tone of Zumbrun's letter was that of an ally—but an ally unhappy with the tactics Justice was using in the case.

Zumbrun's letter stated, among other things, "We were informed that the filing of this lawsuit was received with favor by the involved officials of the Executive Branch because there was a belief that the House Committee had overstepped its authority and intruded into the authority of the Secretary of the Interior." But, Zumbrun went on, the Justice Department was not pursuing a strategy designed to put forward the best possible version of Watt's desire to open the Bob Marshall. "Quite frankly," Zumbrun wrote, "we are at a bit of a loss to comprehend the line of strategy which is being followed in the case in order to achieve the objectives of the Secretary. The Justice Department actions . . . are not consistent with what we believe to be a strategy which would make the Secretary look good . . ." and lead to a quick, favorable resolution of the case. The letter invited Justice to work with the plaintiffs in developing a common strategy in the case.

Zumbrun's letter indicated a copy was also sent to William H. Coldiron, Watt's solicitor in the Interior Department. Court papers later disclosed that Coldiron had originally informed Zumbrun of Watt's decision to comply with the House committee resolution, and had said there was an "unusual" legal basis for the action and that perhaps Zumbrun "might be interested in the matter."

To the conservation organizations, Zumbrun's contract with Coldiron and his subsequent letter to Regnery provided evidence of possible collusion between Watt and the two legal foundations. In fact, Regnery had responded somewhat testily to Zumbrun's letter, stating: "We are not aware of the source of your information regarding the reaction to your lawsuit by the defendants. It is not this administration's practice or policy to encourage or welcome suits against it or its decisions." Noting another suggestion in Zumbrun's letter, Regnery said it would be "highly irregular" for the Justice Department to "participate in the formulation of discovery questions to be directed" to Watt.

While the suit was pending, Watt agreed to a six-month moratorium on leasing in wilderness areas. Then, in what at first appeared to be a shift in position, he proposed in early 1982 that leasing federal wilderness land for commercial purposes be delayed until the year 2000. However, Watt's proposal also called for setting a deadline date after which Congress could no longer place wilderness lands under protection from development. Democrats as well as Republicans denounced the proposal. Representative John F. Seiberling, D-Ohio, chairman of the House Subcommittee on Public Lands and National Parks, called the Watt proposal an effort to "gut the nation's wilderness system." Seiberling said the proposal had loopholes in it "as big as the whole wilderness system." Representative Richard Cheney, R-Wyoming, said in March 1982 that he had received more than one thousand letters expressing fears that there could be gas and oil development in his state's Washakie Wilderness area. Those writing were not only the environmentalists who always write, Cheyney said, but also "ranchers, farmers, snowmobile advocates, hunting and fishing guys as well as a lot of folks in the oil patch who are eager to develop resources but who believe a certain part of the state ought to be off limits."

In August 1982, the House overwhelmingly approved, 340 to 58, legislation to prohibit permanently oil, gas, and mineral exploration and extraction in the nation's wilderness areas, except when Congress and the president agreed there was an "urgent national need" for exploration or development. Pending at the time of the House vote were some 1,000 applications for developers to drill in some three million acres of federal wilderness. The Senate was unable to vote on the measure before its December adjournment, so the issue was expected to be debated further in 1983.

As has been indicated, Watt's previous service with the Mountain States Legal Foundation made it virtually impossible for him not to be encountering potential conflict-of-interest situations almost daily in his work at the Interior Department. As Alexander Cockburn and James Ridgeway observed in *The Village Voice* shortly after Watt took office, "It is hard to fathom how he can conceivably disentangle himself from the network he helped to construct and remain an effective Secretary of the Interior."

At the time Watt took office, more than forty major contributors to the Mountain States Legal Foundation had pending or ongoing dealings with the Interior Department. For example, the Adolph Coors Company (the brewery, which also had ceramics and energy operations) owned 106 oil and gas leases on 97,005 acres of federal land in Colorado. The company also owned two coal mines, one of which was awaiting approval for its strip-mining plan from Interior's Office of Surface Mining.

Exxon, through the parent company and its subsidiaries, had a number of dealings with the Interior Department. In Colorado alone, Exxon had 262 oil and gas leases on 226,378 acres, as well as thousands more oil and gas leases in offshore areas on the east and west coasts and off Alaska. The company also had many federal coal leases on federal land in the West and was operating two coal mines and seeking approval of a permit for a third, in Wyoming. Exxon also had pending with Interior an oil shale leasing program on federal lands in western Colorado, as well as a proposal to exchange numerous scattered tracts of unneeded land that it owned for 10,000 acres of federal lands in Colorado that were believed to be rich in oil shale. Also pending with the department was Exxon's application for a shale oil pipeline right-of-way in Colorado.

Amax, which along with its subsidiary, Climax Molybdenum, had contributed to the foundation, had, at the time Watt assumed office at Interior, federal coal leases in Wyoming and was operating strip mines regulated by Interior's Office of Surface Mining in Illinois, Ohio, Wyoming, and Indiana. The corporation was also planning to open a coal mine on a Washington Indian reservation—an action that could require Bureau of Indian Affairs approval—and its Wyoming mine had an application pending before the Office of Surface Mining. In addition, the company had plans for a molybdenum mine, which would need right-of-way permits from Interior's Bureau of Land Management.

Potential conflicts similar to those just described also existed concerning other major foundation contributors, such as Burlington Northern Railroad, Consolidated Coal Company, Arizona Public Service Company, Nevada Power Company, Fluor Oil and Gas Corporation, Gulf Resources and Chemical Corporation, Utah Power & Light, Occidental Oil Shale, Montana Power Company, Northwest Pipeline Company, Phillips Petroleum, Marathon Oil, Chevron, and Amoco.

Of the 550 coal leases the Interior Department had at the time of Watt's confirmation by the Senate, 232 were held by contributors to the Mountain States Legal Foundation. Citing this and the numerous cases in which the foundation had filed suits or intervened on behalf of its contributors, Senator Bumpers noted during debate over Watt's confirmation that Watt had testified the foundation had only on one occasion "brought a lawsuit in the interest of conservation or preservation."

"Is that a balance?" Bumpers asked. "Is that somebody who is really concerned about preserving the people's common treasure? His total identification with the oil, timber, and coal interests literally invites a potential for conflicts of interest, or at least, a very grave appearance of conflicts of interest." Bumpers also wondered why Watt was "so red hot to produce more coal out there when the biggest problems in West Virginia and Kentucky are closed mines and idle mines with almost 100 million tons of surplus coal on the market?" The same question applied to oil and gas exploration "when only 1.3 percent of the lands that are leased for oil and gas now are being drilled?" Bumpers said he was "proud of the progress we have made in clean air and clean water in this country. It has come at a price. . . . I really do not think Mr. Watt is sensitive to that. I think he is a developer at any price." Further evidence of this, Bumpers said, was Watt's service on the Federal Power Commission during which he opposed the position of the applicant—usually a natural gas company or public utility—in only three of the seventy-six cases that came before him. Said Bumpers, "surely the gas companies and the public utility companies were wrong in more than three out of seventy-six cases."

Senator Howard Metzenbaum, D-Ohio, also raised the conflicts issue. Noting Watt's filing in late December 1980, on behalf of the foundation, a brief challenging enforcement of the federal strip-mining act (three days before his nomination to the Interior post) Metzenbaum asked whether the public could "believe that he will enforce the law aggressively now that he has filed a court suit to challenge the basis of that law?"

Watt's defenders, such as Senator William L. Armstrong, R-Colorado, argued that Watt, rather than believing in development at any price, was really a moderate who was trying to strike a balance between preserving the nation's natural heritage as well as providing for the nation's self-sufficiency in the production of oil, natural gas, coal, and minerals. Armstrong said Watt, in contrast to "the extreme environmentalists," was "an environmentalist, but he is also a realist who recognizes that America needs the energy and minerals that underlie our public lands; that the international situation and America's national security demand that these domestic fuel and nonfuel materials be found and developed . . . and that exploration and development can be accomplished without significant adverse impacts on the environment—but only if the activities proceed in a timely, orderly fashion, before a major socioeconomic crisis overtakes us."

With Watt's critics, assurances by the secretary's supporters carried less weight than the words of Watt himself. Such sentiments as, "I will err on the side of public use versus preservation," and that the Interior Department must be "the amicus for the minerals industry in federal policy," were hardly comforting to environmentalists.

From the day Watt took office, environmental organizations found themselves engaged in a nonstop battle to combat various actions taken by the Interior secretary. The Wilderness Society, in a voluminous "Watt Book" published during Watt's first year in the Cabinet, documented scores of decisions by Watt they said endangered federal wilderness lands, national parks, fish, wildlife, and other valuable resources.

For example, the organization noted that Watt had imposed a total moratorium on the acquisition of additional parkland, "a move that would lead to the loss of critical areas to development, increase crowding at national parks, and ensure heavier purchase costs" at a later date when the congressionally approved parkland is eventually acquired. Watt had also proposed giving national parks in metropolitan areas to generally fiscally strapped state and local governments, a shift that "would result in an increased financial burden on those governments, and the probability that these parks would not remain well-maintained or provide a broad range of visitor facilities." In addition, Watt had moved to allow environmentally disturbing snowmobiles in Yosemite and other California parks, motor-powered craft on the Grand Canyon portion of the Colorado River, airboats in the Everglades National Park, and greater access for dune buggies to the national seashores.

In the area of energy and minerals, Watt in his first 18 months in office took a number of environment-threatening actions, including gutting strip-mining legislation by rewriting regulations to accommodate industry's wishes and slashing the enforcement powers and personnel (by 70 percent) of the Office of Surface Mining. Also, Watt had expressed his intention to open additional wilderness areas to mining; announced plans to offer almost the entire Outer Continental Shelf under United States jurisdiction for oil and gas leasing—including the nation's richest fishing grounds in Alaska; and, in Alaska, called for a speedup of oil and natural gas leasing on 100 million acres of wildlife refuge and other federal lands "without providing for congressionally intended studies to assess the impact of such actions on sensitive lands."

In addition, Watt had suspended rules covering acreage limits for recipients of federal water projects, thereby benefiting primarily large agribusinesses; had called for disestablishment of certain national wildlife refuges; had suspended the listing of species under the Endangered Species Act and severely cut the program's funding; frozen regulations designed to protect a variety of highly endangered marine mammals; authorized, despite the provisions of the Endangered Species Act and a 67-nation treaty aimed at protecting endangered species, a private group to capture and import the endangered peregrine falcon; pushed for abolition of the Council on Environmental Quality (which, in fact, did have its staffing, funding and authority reduced); and fired 51 members of his department's solicitor's office—the office, coincidentally, which had defended the department against the pro-industry lawsuits brought by the Mountain States Legal Foundation.

As this list of decisions shows, when it comes to Watt, the reality measures up to, and in some cases, exceeds the editorial page and comic strip caricatures of the secretary as the man who killed Bambi, or whose hobby is raising gypsy moths.

Looking at some of Watt's programs in detail, environmental organizations and congressional critics were especially disturbed by Watt's plans to open up one billion acres on the Outer Continental Shelf for offshore oil and natural gas exploration and development. The critics saw this proposal as being especially reckless and detrimental to the environment and the public interest. To put Watt's proposal in perspective, it should be noted that the federal government owns just over one billion acres of offshore submerged lands on the Outer Continental Shelf, which meant that Watt wanted to make almost all offshore land available for leasing. Since the enactment of the Outer Continental Shelf Lands Act in 1953, the Interior Department until 1980 had leased about 27 million acres for oil and natural gas exploration. In the final year of the Carter administration, the department proposed the most ambitious leasing program up to that time by calling for the amount of leased offshore acreage to be doubled by 1986. By the time Watt came into office, approximately 40 million offshore acres had been offered for lease.

Watt, with his proposal to lease up to one billion acres, wanted to multiply the previous amount of leased acreage 25 times over, rather than merely double it. Both Watt and Energy Secretary James B. Edwards, in announcing the plan in April 1981, said that the unprecedented offshore program was needed to reduce the nation's dependence on foreign oil imports. "This administration, with its commitment to relieve America of the stifling economic and strategic burden of imported energy, is determined to do all that it can, with appropriate environmental safeguards, to make these safe and secure domestic resources available for all the people," Watt said.

Reaction to the proposal was swift in coming. California Governor Jerry Brown, whose state's entire coastline, including the spectacular Big Sur area, was included in the proposal, charged that the accelerated offshore program would "despoil our scenic and natural resources." The state, fearing disastrous oil spills, damage to fish and wildlife, and a loss of tourism, filed suit. A federal judge enjoined lease sales off northern California because of Watt's failure to consult with the state before proceeding with his plans.

Nonetheless, Watt was undaunted. In May 1982 he again proposed leasing areas off northern California, including tracts within three miles of the Big Sur coastline. The department withdrew from consideration the tracts that had been the subject of the previous year's controversy, but made available other tracts surrounding the earlier controversial ones. This did little to appease the critics. Senator Alan Cranston, D-California, said the new proposal was "another Watt version of a Trojan horse," which once again showed that Watt "is an advocate for an extreme pro-oil, industry position, not the impartial arbiter of competing public interests that his position demands." In July 1982 Watt released the final version of his plan, again calling for the leasing of up to one billion offshore acres over the next five years. In the Big Sur area, according to the *New York Times,* "some old-timers are saying that people along the coast have not been so aroused by anything since a Japanese submarine surfaced off Santa Barbara in 1942 and lobbed a few shots toward shore before disappearing."

In addition to being concerned about the potential ecological damage of offshore drilling, the environmental organizations also contended that such a massive offering of offshore leases would cheat citizens "of a fair return for the sale of the public wealth." The wholesale lease offerings would result in depressed bids, the National Wildlife Federation noted, due to the "industry's lack of financial resources to bid competitively on all leases" because of "reduced competition as smaller companies drop out of the bidding process." The organization said, "uncertainty of tract value due to lack of geological and biological information" would also hold down the dollar value of the bids. "The result is that the public will get only the price industry chooses to pay in a flooded market, at a time of an energy glut, when the economy is in a recession, and when production is suffering an absolute decline," the federation said. "This is not the time to put virtually our entire inventory of off-shore wealth on the auction block." Some smaller oil companies apparently agreed with the environmentalists' criticism that the program would benefit major oil companies. Said Robert S. Friedenberg, president of Seahawk Oil International of California, "It's a game for the very cash-rich, high-hitter companies."

Watt, for his part, defended the plan as providing revenues to help balance the budget, as being environmentally sound and, what's more, a deterrent to war. Responding to a letter from twenty-eight House and Senate Democrats criticizing his program, Watt wrote: "America must be prepared. It is much easier to explain to the American people why we have oil rigs off our coasts than it would be to explain to the mothers and fathers of this land why their sons are fighting on the sands of the Middle East as might be required if the policies of our critics were to be pursued."

Big oil companies, after initial caution and even criticism that the program was overblown, eventually welcomed it, in the words of the American Petroleum Institute, as "the most progressive ever adopted in the 28-year history of federal leasing on the Outer Continental Shelf." In the initial sale offered under the program, in August 1982, oil companies' high bids on 40 of the 554 tracts offered for sale were described as the lowest per acre in the 28-year history of Outer Continental Shelf leasing. In more than 250 other lease sales in Watt's second year in office, the department, as an "incentive," had reduced the standard 16.67 percent royalty rate, which is the federal government's share of profits, to 12.5 percent. A coalition of environmental organizations said Watt's leasing policies were giveaways equivalent to "Napoleon selling the Louisiana Territory to pay for his wars."

Watt also reflected his pro-industry bent in his agency's lenient attitude toward strip mining—an activity that historically has produced damaged farmland and unreclaimed lands, water pollution, erosion, floods, slope failures, loss of fish and wildlife resources, and a decline in natural beauty. In Watt's first year in office, his department's Office of Surface Mining reduced its strip-mine inspections by one-half, decreased enforcement actions against coal operators by 40 percent, and failed to assess and collect more than $40 million in mandatory reclamation fees owed the government by coal operators. In addition, Watt's department had allowed states to adopt weaker strip-mine programs environmentalists claimed inadequate to protect the environment and to require sufficient reclamation of strip-mined land. At the same time, the Office of Surface Mining eliminated its five regional offices, reduced its number of job slots from 1,010 to 650, and proposed eliminating federal inspectors' major enforcement powers, thereby barring effective oversight of state programs. Watt's Office of Surface Mining, in the words of one journalist, was headed by "a new team led by former coal industry consultants and coal state officials."

Also, Watt, through proposed surface-mining rules changes, in mid-1982 was attempting to open up some 1.2 million acres of national forests and wildlife refuges to strip-mining. Other proposed changes would, according to Norman L. Dean, staff attorney for the National Wildlife Federation, "allow mining next to many vacation homes, on certain privately owned lands that have been given the status of public parks and on privately owned lands that are listed in the National Register of Historic Places." Watt, "in a particularly insensitive proposal, has redefined 'cemetery' so that mining will be permitted in family burial plots." Interior in June 1982 agreed to consider an industry proposal to strip-mine new areas of Death Valley National Monument and five other national parks where such activities had been permitted until a moratorium was declared in 1976.

Dean also outlined a chilling picture of what would be the effects of Watt's various proposed strip-mining rules changes. "Responsibility for compliance with many of the new standards would be assigned to certified engineers selected and paid by mining companies. It does not take an expert in human nature to predict that those engineers will be beholden not to the public interest but, rather, to the companies that butter their bread." Also, Watt proposed to "delete specific requirements to protect the migratory routes of wildlife, to protect eagles and other birds from electrocution in power lines, and to protect wildlife from toxic-waste ponds. Major loopholes would be provided in the requirements that coal miners restore the land to its original contour after mining. Existing restrictions on the use of persistent pesticides by miners would be lifted. Explosives could be used at night and within 1,000 feet of homes and public buildings. Individuals would be permitted to explore for coal under certain circumstances without first informing the government." In addition, the "public's right to participate in the control of strip-mining would also fall victim under the Watt program. Hunters, fishermen, hikers, and others who use but don't own environmentally sensitive lands would lose their existing right to petition to have them declared unsuitable for strip-mining."

Watt's effort to weaken strip-mining standards came despite a shameful historic record by strip-mining operations that have ruined more than 10,000 miles of streams by acid drainage or siltation, that have destroyed thousands of acres of valuable midwestern farmland, and that have left many more thousands of acres unreclaimed. Federal inspectors who had reputations for being tough with strip-mine operators, and with state officials who were too close with the coal companies, suddenly found themselves moved out of the field and into office posts where they could not threaten Watt's deregulation program. As one such federal inspector, Bruce Boyens, told the *Washington Post* after he quit government service rather than be kicked upstairs to a Washington, D.C., desk job: "I have to say I think they're gutting the program. They got people anxious. They took their job security. They made speeches about getting the Office of Surface Mining zealots off industry's back. You start to go home at night and ask yourself, what does this administration want from me. . . . Some of our regulations were bad. Some of them needed changing. But an across-the-board attack is wrong. We had a strong program. We had industry complying. This could be a signal to operators that they could do what they want now."

The Interior Department's coziness with the coal operators prompted charges in July 1982 by congressional Democrats that the agency may have deliberately undervalued the coal in conducting its biggest sale in history of leases to mine coal on federal lands. The leases were for an April 28, 1982, sale for some 1.6 billion tons of coal in the Powder River Basin of Montana and Wyoming. Just before the sale, Interior had changed the rules for bidding to reduce the minimum allowable bids to $42.5 million below the minimum value the agency's mining management field staff had placed on the leases. Under the old rules, the bidders were required to file "minimum acceptable bids"; under the new rules, bidders were required to submit merely an "entry level" bid at a minimum price of $25 an acre. The result was that the minimum acceptable bid total for the Powder River Basin sale was reduced from $94.7 million to $52.2 million.

Senator Dale Bumpers, D-Arkansas, charged that the department's "abrupt decision to lower the minimum bid total . . . raises obvious questions about possible industry involvement in that decision to change the bidding process." Bumpers and Democratic Representatives Edward J. Markey, of Massachusetts, and James D. Santini, of Nevada, the chairman of a House Interior Subcommittee, argued that the department may have violated federal standards requiring the government to receive fair value for resources turned over to private interests. Santini wondered whether fair market value and competitive bidding were "sacrificed so as to avoid the embarrassment of an unsuccessful sale."

Markey noted that at a time of $100 billion federal deficits, "the public has a right to know that our coal is not being sold off at rock bottom prices. Does it make sense to auction off federal resources using a system which calls for starting the bidding at the bottom, which much more often than not means there is only one bidder, without first testing the market? Who can blame the energy companies for offering only 3.6 cents a ton if that is all the department asked for?"

At a July 15 hearing of Santini's subcommittee, various witnesses indicated that it wasn't a case of there being an emergency in which Interior had to sell leases at lower prices. At the current rate of extraction of resources, these witnesses maintained, enough coal leases had been sold on federal lands to last two hundred years. David C. Russell, deputy director of the Interior Department's Minerals Management Service, responded to the critics' allegations by saying that his department was "confident that its procedures resulted in a successful sale, meeting the statutory obligation to obtain fair market value." Despite many pressing questions from subcommittee members, Russell said he had no documentation to show how the calculations for the lower minimum bids were made. In Watt's first two years in office, Interior had sold eight times as many coal leases as it did in the final two years of the Carter administration.

Even the national parks, which Watt himself had said were sacrosanct as far as development activities were concerned, apparently were not so safe after all. An August 25, 1982, memorandum written by Richard H. Briceland, associate director for science and technology for the National Park Service, warned that possible rules changes pending before the Office of Surface Mining could result in strip mining in 26 units of the national park system. The proposal, environmentalists charged, was contrary to Congress's intention to prohibit any mining in national parks.

Perhaps best symbolizing the Reagan/Watt philosophy of turning over public land and resources to private interests was a controversy in the early months of the Reagan Administration over a speech Watt gave to the Conference of National Park Concessioners. In that speech, on March 9, 1981, Watt gave every indication that he intended to depart from the traditional method of allowing a limited role for concessioners in national parks by turning park operations over to the concessioners.

Private concessioners are an important and necessary presence in the national park system. By 1982 there were more than 500 private contractors providing a variety of services—primarily operating hotels, gift shops, restaurants, and gas stations—as well as providing other services environmental groups say are harmless in themselves but inappropriate in national parks, detracting from the parks' natural beauty. Such activities include downhill skiing (which requires mechanized equipment); motorboating on park lakes and rivers; managing tennis courts, golf courses, and swimming pools; and operating convention facilities. The concessioners, ranging in size from units of giant conglomerates such as TWA Services and MCA Corporation, to small businesses that rent canoes or guide visitors on river and lake trips, were grossing more than $300 million annually by the early 1980s.

Watt told the concessioners in his 1981 speech, "[You are] going to play a tremendously important role and a growing role in the administration of our national parks, and we were going to reach out to involve you in some areas . . . that you haven't been allowed to be involved in before." Watt said he had "a bias for private enterprise. . . . We believe concessioners can do the job." To those already fearful of Watt's initiatives in other areas, added to the past efforts by some major park concessioners to create more of a Disneyland-like atmosphere in the national parks, the Watt speech conjured up visions of Park Service rangers, who greet visitors and conduct nature tours, being replaced by contractor personnel; of private companies performing security functions; of expansion of service—i.e., tennis courts, miniature golf courses, convention facilities—within the park to attract more visitors for whom the outdoor experience isn't enough; of contractors actually managing and doing the planning of the parks.

Watt also told the concessioners that his agency wanted "an aggressive program with the private entrepreneurs who are willing to invest and manage resources in the National Park Service for people." If anyone in the Park Service attempted to thwart these goals, Watt said, the person would be fired. If the concessioners ran into problems with park programs, Watt invited them to contact him or National Park Service Director Russell Dickenson, or Ray Arnett, assistant secretary for fish, wildlife, and parks. "If we need to change personnel under Russ to accomplish a more aggressive concessioners' program," Watt said, "we will change the people. . . . If a personality is giving you a problem, we're going to get rid of the problem or the personality, whichever is faster." To underscore this, Watt noted that he had already "fired every person in the Department of Interior that was a presidential appointee. I mean we've cleaned every one of them out and then we started appointing good people." Primarily, he said, the department and other government agencies had in them a lot of "old-time liberals that don't want change" and were attempting to "frustrate we [sic] conservatives who want change every chance we can."

The speech, remarkable in its candor concerning the administration's goals for private enterprise in the national park system, was also significant for the disdain Watt expressed toward the wild areas of the country. Recalling a trip he took on a motorized craft down the Colorado River in Grand Canyon the previous September, Watt said that the first day on the trip "was spectacular . . . an exciting, thrilling day. The second day started to get a little tedious, but the third day I wanted bigger motors to move that raft out. There is no way you could get me on an oar-powered raft on that river. I'll guarantee you that. On the fourth day we were praying for helicopters, and they came." Later in the meeting, in answer to a question, Watt noted that he brought "much controversy and flack" to the Interior Department post because, "I don't like to paddle and I don't like to walk"—two activities much pursued by persons Watt has characterized as "environmental elitists" because they want the parks kept in as pristine a state as possible.

Watt's tale of tedium in the Grand Canyon prompted former Assistant Interior Secretary Nathaniel P. Reed, a Republican, to remark: "Can you imagine? We have a secretary of the Interior who is bored by the Grand Canyon! If he had his druthers, he'd probably run the lower Colorado by hovercraft. This is a man who was nominated for his job in part because he is a westerner, and yet his insensitivity to the beauty and adventure of the West is appalling."

Despite the environmentalists' criticisms, Watt's comments to the concessioners fell upon a most receptive audience. Some concessioners followed up with proposals to allow them to replace the park rangers in the operation of park entrance stations, in giving interpretive talks to visitors, and in managing campgrounds. One major proposal, made by a subsidiary of the giant Music Corporation of America, which runs the concessions at Yosemite National Park, called for the company's employees, rather than park rangers, to meet visitors at the entrances and give them orientations.

Faced with criticism by environmental groups and by some members of Congress who had been concerned about past concessioner abuses in national parks, Watt's eventual proposal for greater contractor participation in park management—while still objectionable to the critics—fell short of their worst fears. The proposal, on July 18, 1981, called for no immediate turning of additional activities over to contractors, but did ask the National Park Service "to investigate proposals for concessioner-operated campgrounds [including providing campground security], the feasibility of shared maintenance and storage facilities, and coordinated planning efforts." The proposal also benefited concessioners by recommending that the Park Service "explore the need for longer concession contracts in areas where large investments are needed to upgrade services."

The proposal also waived the franchise fee normally charged concessioners, in an effort "to spur increased concessioner creativity" in improving visitor services. Watt's statement noted that "in these tight budget times, we must seek the maximum cooperation of private enterprise" to improve park visitor services. "Through these initiatives," he said, "I am trying to make it easier for the National Park Service and the private sector to work together in upgrading the quality of our parks and the services offered within them."

Ronald Tipton, national parks specialist for the Wilderness Society, a major private environmental organization, said in an interview that when he first heard of Watt's speech to the concessioners, "I envisioned a situation where the National Park Service might go and grant a large number of longterm contracts and have all the concessions locked in until the year 2010. Or that concessioners would be given authority to operate entrance stations. I had visions of the Yosemite concessioner greeting visitors with a spiel about a discount being offered on their nine-hole pitch 'n' putt golf course in the park."

Tipton said that perhaps more than any other government service, the national park system has an extremely positive image in the minds of citizens who have visited the parks. And the symbol of the national park system is the ranger, noted for his or her courtesy and knowledge of all facets of the park. The greeting, the field trips, the nature walks and talks conducted by the rangers "should not be turned into a commercial enterprise," Tipton said, because "it would take away the things that made the national park system what it is today." Also, he said, private contractors would not be as responsive as the rangers to visitors' needs.

T. Destry Jarvis, director of federal activities for the National Parks and Conservation Association, another major organization concerned with the national parks system, said that putting contractors into activities carried out by park rangers would not only "erode the historic good image" of the parks, but would also undoubtedly mean greater costs for park visitors. Concessioner-run campgrounds would cost more so that the contractor could make a profit, and concessioners also likely would charge separate fees to visitors for the interpretive programs now provided free of charge by the rangers.

Tipton said putting concessioners in the campground operations would answer the concerns of private campground operators outside the parks who often complain that they are being undercut by the prices charged for ranger-run parks. Concessioners surely would raise the in-park campground fees to the level of those outside, he said.

Tipton said that Watt wanted contracts of up to thirty years for park concessioners but that environmental groups, concerned over past abuses, feared that this would lock some inadequate contractors into long-term deals that would harm the park system. Watt's department wanted to award a new thirty-year concessioner contract for Yellowstone National Park, even though the concessions are in a government-owned, rather than contractor-owned, facility. Under pressure from environmental groups, the Park Service eventually awarded a five-year contract to TWA Services.

Tipton in early 1982 felt that Watt still wanted to turn over major functions in the park system to contractors, but was proceeding cautiously because "they want to change the policy without getting a lot of flak." So emotionally charged is the issue of the concessioners' role in the parks that, according to Tipton, had Watt moved rapidly "to give concessioners the kind of control he was talking about, it would have knocked him right out of the Cabinet."

Despite Watt's contentions that national park concessioners were being thwarted, a number of congressional hearings and investigations during the 1970s reached just the opposite conclusions. Instead of keeping concessioners under tight control, according to a 1976 joint report by the House Committees on Government Operations and on Small Business, the "National Park Service administration of concessions has been inadequate and ineffective," and the concessioners "have, in effect, been allowed to do business with little overall control or supervision by the National Park Service." The report also found that the concessioners had "undue influence" over parks management and policies; that concession contracts were "vague, ambiguous, and generally do not adequately protect the government's interest"; that concessions' policy "discourages competition for concessions and encourages large corporations to take over an increasing number of concession operations at the more profitable areas . . . , to the detriment of small business"; and that the public was "rarely consulted" as to its needs and desires regarding management of the national park system.

The investigation also determined that the Yosemite Park and Curry Company, a subsidiary of the Music Corporation of America, which was the largest concessioner at Yosemite, paid a lower than normal franchise fee to the government of just three-fourths of 1 percent on gross receipts exceeding $20.9 million, even though the National Park Service itself had determined that a fair fee would be almost twice that amount. The study also determined that the MCA subsidiary was charging lodging rates of up to $12 higher than for nine comparable lodging facilities outside Yosemite.

Another serious problem unearthed by the investigators was that the long-term contracts of twenty years and more favored by the Park Service reduced the agency's ability to manage the concessioners effectively and also discouraged bids for concessions by small businesses. Small firms were unable to make the capital investments required in these long-term contracts, while larger businesses were happy to do so because it meant attracting more visitors to the parks, which spelled larger profits for them in the long run.

Perhaps more serious than many of the problems unearthed was the use of park facilities for purposes other than that of enjoying nature. The General Accounting Office determined that many of the concessioners were heavily promoting the national parks as convention centers. In 1974, for example, the concessioner-run Ahwahnee Hotel in Yosemite had 19 percent of its rooms occupied by conventioneers and other persons attending group meetings during the prime tourist months of May through September. For 1975, there were 51 more conventions and group meetings scheduled at Yosemite. Several other national parks concessioners also held conventions, with most of these during the peak tourist season. The concessioner at Mammoth Cave National Park—National Park Concessioners, Inc.—even ran advertisements offerings its park hotel for "banquets, wedding parties, bridge parties, group meeting facilities, and special occasion dinners."

MCA was, in fact, aggressively marketing Yosemite as a convention site with promotional literature and a brochure entitled, "Yosemite the Unconventional Convention." At the time of the 1976 congressional committee report, MCA had already scheduled conventions and group meetings as far ahead as 1980, as well as hosting such events as the Ahwahnee Winter Wine Festival in 1975. The joint report expressed concern that these various conventions and other events were preventing people who had come to enjoy the park's beauty from obtaining convenient rooms and other services within the park. The report concluded that the Park Service should not permit any conventions or other meetings within national parks unless it could be "satisfied that they will not prevent the concessioner from accommodating individual visitors."

Finally, the joint report noted that MCA—but not the public—had been deeply involved in 1974 in preparing five working drafts of a master plan for Yosemite. "Indeed," the report stated, "the concessioner involvement was so great that it prompted one Interior Department official to remark in September 1974 that they [the drafts] appear 'to have been written by the concessioner.' " While concessioners would certainly opt for increased concession activities in the parks, the joint committee report called for eliminating at Yosemite certain types of facilities that would be readily available nearby outside the park: such as golf courses, tennis courts, a bank, service stations and garages, barber and beauty shops, and nineteen places for the sale of liquor. The report said that such facilities "certainly provide conveniences to the park visitors" but hardly met the "necessary and appropriate" test which is supposed to prevail in the provision of concession services in national parks.

Perhaps the most publicized controversy involving concessioners in the parks was a 1974–75 incident in which the MCA Corp., the parent of the major Yosemite concessioner, filmed the television series "Sierra," within the park, thereby infuriating conservationists. To aid in the filming, MCA painted some rocks in Yosemite and also proposed, unsuccessfully, to put an aerial tramway in the park.

Some conservationists noted that many of the parks contracts are relatively small change to some of the major enterprises which operate concessions. Still, as Ron Tipton, parks expert for the Wilderness Society, noted in early 1982, there has been "a major shift in recent years from the mom and pop type concessioners to subsidiaries of conglomerates." The Park Service likes the big corporations because it feels they can follow through on capital investments that smaller operators are unable to make. A concessioner such as TWA can make some money off concessions, but better yet "can package fly-drive vacations in conjunction with the national parks," which enables them to earn profits from airline tickets as well as from hotel accommodations. Also, Tipton said, "it's good public relations" for the major corporations to be connected with the national parks "because the park system has such a good image." Basically, he said, while some concessions such as those at Yosemite and Grand Canyon South Rim are lucrative, many of the others are not big money-makers because of the short seasons they are open. Yellowstone, for example, has only a 75-day season for concessioners.

"Our contention," Tipton said, "is not that there have been a lot of ripoffs, but rather that there must be a proper philosophy as to the appropriate role of concessioners in the national parks. Certainly, they must provide services that the visitors need, but it is fundamentally wrong to give them any sort of control over park operations and planning, as Watt apparently wants to do."

Another issue that aptly symbolizes the Reagan/Watt public lands philosophy was the proposal to sell to private interests over a five-year period some 35 million of the more than 700 million acres of federally owned land, as well as some government-owned property. The 35 million acres represents an area about the size of Iowa, or the combined sizes of Massachusetts, New Hampshire, and Vermont. Potential offerings for sale included areas in cities, suburban areas, and rural areas. Specific offerings included a 17-acre section of Fort DeRussy on Waikiki Beach, Hawaii, a lighthouse with a lofty view of California's spectacular coastline 100 miles south of San Francisco, and the Treasury Department's Assay Office near Wall Street in New York City. Helping identify prime pieces of federal land and property for the administration was the National Association of Realtors. Reagan, Watt, and other administration officials said the land sales would allow the government to get rid of unneeded land and buildings and to reduce the mounting federal debt. The goal was to raise $17 billion over five years under the program. As steward over the most federal land, Watt' was the key to the program.

Watt emphasized in mid-1982 that the government would not sell any wilderness areas, national parks, wild and scenic rivers, Indian trust lands, wildlife refuges, or national recreation areas. White House officials also said the government would not sell lands having coal, minerals, and geothermal resources.

Seen in combination with the Reagan administration's accelerated mineral, oil, and natural gas leasing programs on and offshore, the land-sale program was seen by its critics as being part of an over-all giveaway of public resources. Coming as the land sale did during a recession, the number of potential buyers was limited, which meant, in the phrasing of Representative John F. Seiberling, D-Ohio, chairman of the House Public Lands Subcommittee, that the federal holdings would be sold to business interests and speculators for "fire sale prices" far below their real market value. The *Washington Post,* in questioning the program, noted that history showed many "examples of land sales to raise quick cash," which "in retrospect . . . look like pretty terrible deals"—i.e., Napoleon's sale of the Louisiana Territory for $15 million and Czar Nicholas's sale of Alaska for $7 million.

Although well-to-do westerners had long pushed for a transfer of federal lands to the states or private interests, many of them did not like the Reagan/Watt plan. Real estate people were concerned the federal sales at low prices would depress land prices generally in their region; ranchers who used federal lands for animal grazing were disturbed that such lands would fall into private hands and would no longer be available to them. Environmentalists said the sales were being pursued at such a rapid pace that there was no real time to study adequately the potential environmental impact of such sales.

In addition to the land sales to private interests Watt, in his first year as Interior secretary, implemented a "Good Neighbor Policy" under which the government sold or leased some 10,000 acres of federal lands to local governments. In the first year, the government sold or leased land at $28.8 million below its fair market value—the figure representing a loss to the taxpayers. Local governments in Oregon, for example, paid just $1,750 for four parcels with a listed market value of $1 million. William L. Turnage, executive director of The Wilderness Society, said the administration was "pirating the public treasure for private benefit."

Helping Watt implement his controversial policies were a number of agency appointees who came largely from the ranks of industries regulated by, or having contracts and leases with, the department. A late 1981 study by Common Cause, the public interest organization, found that of the top sixteen Interior Department appointees (most of whom were white, middle-aged, male westerners), ten had potential conflicts of interest because of employment or investment connections with specific corporations, partnerships, or other organizations. Also, six of the sixteen "reported stock holdings in companies engaged in extensive oil, gas, and mining operations on public lands."

For example, Interior Undersecretary Donald P. Hodel had his own energy consulting firm before joining the department. His major clients included utilities "with extensive operations on federal land leased from the Interior Department." Among the firm's clients were Montana Power Company, which, with its subsidiaries, leased 76,600 acres of federal land from the department, and Pacific Power and Light Company, which, with its subsidiaries, leased 34,100 acres from the department. Hodel had also been the attorney for Georgia-Pacific Company, a major purchaser of timber from federal lands. In addition, Hodel at the time of his confirmation hearings had financial interests in a number of energy, timber, and other firms holding Interior Department leases or otherwise having business pending before the department.

Another appointee, Robert F. Burford, who headed the department's Bureau of Land Management, which administers some 328 million acres of federal land, primarily in western states and in Alaska, had pushed for legislation to turn these lands over to the states to dispose of them. James R. Harris, selected to head the Office of Surface Mining, had as an Indiana state senator contended that the strip-mine law—administered by the Office of Surface Mining—was unconstitutional. This followed the Reagan administration pattern of appointing to top positions in various agencies people who were hostile to what the agency stood for. *New York Times* columnist Anthony Lewis argued that Reagan, by using this approach, was "without the benefit of legislation . . . turning policy upside down." And, he added, "The blithe way in which such appointees propose to turn their offices inside out is like something out of Orwell."

The same sort of patterns prevailed on the various advisory panels selected by Watt to provide advice on Interior Department policies in a number of areas. For example, in early 1982 Watt chose a National Public Lands Advisory Council dominated by people with mining, oil, natural gas, timber, and ranching interests—the very interests that have long sought greater private control of, and access to, federal lands under the domain of the Bureau of Land Management. A survey by the *Washington Post* found that of the 21-member panel, 3 members had ties to the oil and gas industry, 3 had mining connections, 7 had current or former ranching interests, 1 was the owner of a logging company, and 1 was an attorney whose firm's clients included corporate mining interests. As with most Interior appointees, the panel was made up entirely of westerners.

Characteristically, the Bureau of Land Management press release announcing the appointments attempted to pass of many of the appointees as disinterested, public-spirited citizens, rather than as people who had a decided financial interest in how BLM lands were used. For example, Calvin Black was referred to as chairman of the San Juan, Utah, County Commission, but there was no mention of his presidency of Markey Mines or his directorship in an oil company. April Westbrook was listed as a Hobbs, New Mexico, "civic leader," but conspicuously missing was other more pertinent biographical data —such as that she was also co-owner and director of the V.H. Westbrook Oil Company; an officer of Badger Industries and Badger Rentals, which provide equipment for drilling sites; and treasurer and director of TUSCO, an oil equipment firm.

At the time of the appointments, the Bureau of Land Management was considering regulatory changes that would have severely lessened the amount of public participation in the decision-making process for planning for the use of BLM-administered lands. Thus, a panel heavily weighted toward development interests would be certain to go along with efforts to curtail public participation in the process. Nevertheless, Bureau of Land Management spokesperson Tim Monroe contended that the panel's makeup was justified, especially considering the matters of energy planning and range management that would be brought before it. "We think we've met the criteria of balance," Monroe said. "Just because we might talk to them about matters of land-use planning doesn't mean we have to have land-use planners on the council."

Watt has also stirred controversy for occasionally letting his fundamentalist religious beliefs spill over into the area of Interior Department policymaking. He has been characterized as someone who believes that he "has been called on a religious mission by the Lord, Jesus Christ." William Hines, of the Chicago *Sun-Times,* wrote that Watt, "like other true believers from St. Paul to Ayatollah Ruhollah Khomeini . . . seems confident that God is on his side, which—by a process of elimination—places those with differing views in the camp of the devil."

Watt's most widely quoted statements in this regard were ones that he made early in his term. Regarding his duties at the Interior Department, Watt said, "my responsibility is to follow the scriptures, which call upon us to occupy the land until Jesus returns"; his other widely quoted statement: "I do not know how many future generations we can count on before the Lord returns." To his critics, these and similar statements showed clearly that Watt not only was a pro-development zealot, but that he saw a religious basis for his department's public policy and that he wanted to speed up the process of development because the Second Coming might be just around the corner.

Colman McCarthy, a columnist for the *Washington Post,* said Watt appeared "to regard Christianity as the state religion." And, noted McCarthy, "If I get the drift of Watt's pastoral vision, the land of milk and honey overseen by the Department of the Interior—770 million acres of publicly owned land—is now under divine mandate to be bulldozed, leveled, drilled, mined, and leased down to the last holy square yard. Jesus might return and be displeased that federal regulations prevented the strip-mining of Appalachia, or that the coastline of northern California was kept free of oil rigs, or that national parks had too many backpackers worshipping false gods and not enough timber companies clear-cutting the hills." McCarthy made it clear that Watt was entitled to his private religious beliefs, but that he was not entitled to use these to shape public policies. "Watt is paid to be a public official upholding the Constitution, not a public evangelist holding up his Bible."

Watt insists that some of his religious quotes have been taken out of context. He notes that the sentence following his statement about the Lord returning was: "Whatever it [the time left] is, we have to manage with skill to have the resources needed for future generations," which he said showed that he meant to be a prudent steward of the national resources. Yet as late as August 1982, Watt told radio interview show host Larry King that his earlier religious statements were made in the context of his desire to restore a "balance" to the policies of the Interior Department. And, to Watt, who believed that the department's policies in the past had been "way out in left field" and had overregulated industry, "balance" was a code word for giving business more control over federal lands and resources.

Stories also abound in Washington of Watt even telling people he was firing that it was the Lord's will. Roy Wood, who served under Watt in the Bureau of Outdoor Recreation during the Nixon administration, was quoted in the 1982 book, *Reagan's Ruling Class*, as saying Watt asked him to pray with him moments after Wood was fired. Said Wood: "Watt said, 'Let's pray about it' and down on our knees we went. We prayed on our knees, and I could feel that steely knife twisting in my backbone." Watt then contacted Wood's wife, Matilda Wood, and reportedly told her "he had talked with the Lord and the Lord felt we should return to Georgia." Wood repeated the same story to this author.

Watt, in addition to his warning that wholesale drilling on the Outer Continental Shelf was a deterrent to war in the Middle East, has on other occasions ventured into the foreign policy realm. Watt's most controversial foray into foreign policy surfaced in July 1982 (in the same week he defended the Outer Continental Shelf program as a war deterrent) when it was disclosed that he had written Israeli Ambassador Moshe Arens the previous month that U.S. support for Israel might be weakened if "liberals of the Jewish community join with other liberals of this nation" in opposing the Reagan administration's efforts to develop new domestic energy resources. Watt wrote that "the friends of Israel" should support the administration's energy policies "if they really are concerned about the future of Israel."

A number of Jewish leaders and organizations, as well as some members of Congress, responded angrily that Watt was attempting to blackjack Jews into supporting administration policies by holding up the threat of a decrease in U.S. support for Israel. Senator Daniel Patrick Moynihan, D-New York, called for Watt to "resign immediately for this act of bare-knuckled bigotry" or for Reagan to fire him. If Watt were to leave office, Moynihan said, perhaps his departure might "awaken the country to the fact that ideologues of the radical right have taken over whole areas of American government," and thereby provide "some gain from this latest episode of bigotry and bullying." Bertram H. Gold, executive vice president of the American Jewish Committee, commented that Watt needed "a refresher course on the American political system, for he seems to question the right of Americans that hold opinions different from his."

Watt denied that the letter threatened anyone and said he was "proud" of it—even though a White House statement had termed the letter "unfortunate." Watt said the letter was really part of his effort to reach out "to every identifiable group in America, whether unions, the black community, East, West, North, South, Catholics, Protestants, Jews, gentiles" to win support "to make America strong." Within a few days, though, Watt met privately with Jewish leaders and reportedly admitted he had "made a mistake" in sending the letter. Reagan, at a press conference, restated his faith in Watt and said, "He shouldn't be fired." When Jewish organizations said they were satisfied with Watt's apology, members of Congress who had pushed for Watt's removal over the letter backed away from their efforts.

In early 1983, Watt's tongue brought him more controversy. His environmentalist critics, Watt said, were moving toward "centralized planning and control of the society" in the manner of Nazi Germany and the Soviet Union. On another topic, Watt said, "If you want an example of the failure of socialism, don't go to Russsia. Come to America and see the Indian reservations." After major Indian organizations called for his resignation, Watt apologized to them.

Other aspects of Watt's personal attitudes drew fire in his handling of the department. As secretary, Watt achieved a reputation for being secretive, vindictive, and destructive of employee morale, according to a number of interviews and published accounts. Several published reports said that Interior, under Watt, had "put out the word" that the department would not hire "politically undesirable" lawyers and consultants who had connections to environmental organizations or to past Democratic administrations. *Legal Times,* a Washington, D.C., publication, listed four examples in which organizations having dealings with the Interior Department switched attorneys or consultants in order to project the correct political image the department indicated it wanted. In one case, Kenneth Berlin, counsel and legislative director for wildlife programs at the National Audubon Society, said he had contacted an outside attorney about doing some work for the society on a matter before the Interior Department. Berlin said the lawyer agreed to do it, then called back and said that "because of pressures some Interior people had put on his clients, he couldn't do it. They were painting him as an extreme environmentalist, so he decided it wouldn't help his situation if he was identified with us."

One especially noteworthy example of Watt's purported method of operation was the case in which a gas company lobbyist was fired by his employer after a top Watt aide complained that the lobbyist had questioned Watt's remark that U.S. political life was composed of "liberals and Americans." Watt had used the phrase in a November 1981 speech in which he said, "I never use the words Republicans and Democrats. It's liberals and Americans." When reporters questioned him about the remark later, Watt, typically, tried to laugh it off with such comments as, "some of my best friends are liberals"—and then naming Senators Jesse Helms, R-North Carolina, and Strom Thurmond, R-South Carolina, who are known to be among the most conservative members of Congress.

When Timothy L. Donohue, the lobbyist for Ensearch, a Dallas-based natural gas company, saw the comment, he wrote Watt and asked him to "kindly furnish a further clarification of your remarks . . . which could be construed as questioning the patriotism of certain individuals." Donohue added that he was "an American and a liberal. And the Washington lobbyist for a $3 billion energy concern." Donohue received no response from Watt, but in early January 1982 he was told by his boss that he was being fired for his "lack of judgment" in sending the letter. His boss showed him a copy of a letter sent by Stanley W. Hulett, a top Watt aide and director of the department's congressional affairs office, to William C. McCord, chairman and chief executive officer of Ensearch. Hulett's letter stated, among other things, that Watt "is, frankly, surprised at Mr. Donohue's representation in the attached letter," and that Watt's statement "was part of a joke the secretary told at a political fund-raiser and is certainly not meant to question the patriotism of anyone."

But some people, including such usual defenders of Watt as Representative Charles Wilson, D-Texas, weren't laughing. Donohue had worked on Wilson's staff for seven years before coming to Ensearch in 1980. Wilson noted that Hulett had "taken the trouble to track down" Donohue's boss and then had sent a letter to the company's board chairman, instead of to Donohue. This action, he said, "represents the smallness, the pettiness and the hatefulness people have been accusing Watt of. I have been a defender of Watt, but this represents a kind of vengefulness I hate to see." The Interior Department said Hulett had written the letter on his own, without consulting Watt.

In late 1981, Watt also issued an order to his top aides not to meet with officials of national conservation organizations. Douglas Baldwin, Watt's chief spokesman, said Watt did not want Interior officials "wasting government money by talking to national conservation leaders" who were really concerned with politics, not natural resources.

Watt has also been accused of vindictiveness in his handling of departmental employees. In his first two months in office, Watt fired 51 employees in the solicitor's office, among whom were 28 attorneys —some who had been on the opposite side during many of the Mountain States Legal Foundation's lawsuits against the department. Watt contended that the firings were not in retaliation for his past disputes with the solicitor's office; instead, he said the Carter administration had exceeded the department's hiring freeze and had illegally hired too many people. However, two months later Interior moved to hire 6 attorneys and was offering the new employees salaries twice that of most of the fired lawyers. Department officials said it had not rehired any of the fired employees because they lacked the skills the agency most needed. However, critics noted that among the new attorneys hired was one whose background was in child custody and personal injury cases, and not in natural resources. Later in the year Watt ordered transfers for 13 more attorneys in the solicitor's office, amid charges this was another move to get rid of political undesirables— that is, as one of the lawyers put it, "anyone who was there" when the Reagan administration took over from the Carter administration.

By early 1982, Watt had also decided to fortress himself against what he perceived to be a hostile press and a hostile Congress. In February, the department said it would cut back drastically on the number of news releases it sent out, supplying such releases only when there is a "major story." It also said reporters would no longer be able to obtain information over the telephone, but would personally have to come in to pick up any data deemed releasable. Reporters' interviews with Watt were virtually eliminated. At about the same time, Watt informed a House Interior subcommittee that he would no longer allow agency staff aides to discuss departmental issues informally with congressional investigators. Rather, Watt said, he would cooperate with "formal, on-the-record inquiries." The subcommittee chairman, Representative John F. Seiberling, D-Ohio, angrily denounced Watt as unconstitutionally disregarding Congress's right to inquire into matters concerning the Executive Branch. He said Watt's action "appears to be based on a total misunderstanding, or even a studied disregard, of both the law and tradition." Watt similarly refused to allow his aides to talk with some other committee staffs.

Watt's most publicized clash with Congress brought him to the brink of being cited for contempt of Congress in early 1982. In fact, the House Energy and Commerce Committee voted 23 to 19 in March 1982 to cite Watt for contempt, after the secretary had refused the previous August to turn over to the ·committee subpoenaed documents relating to Canada's new energy policy. Some United States business interests felt the policy was discriminatory because of restrictions it imposed on U.S. companies holding Canadian mineral leases.

The White House finally avoided a House vote on the contempt issue by agreeing to let members of the committee review the documents. Originally, the White House had contended the issue of "executive privilege" was involved in its refusal to allow Watt to turn over the documents. Representative Marc L. Marks, R-Pennsylvania, the only Republican committee member to vote for the contempt citation, said after seeing the previously withheld documents that there was nothing sensitive in them. "Watt could have given over the papers had the White House not intervened. They were being obstructive just to be obstructive. . . . Politically, this is one of the most asinine things they've pulled to date."

Watt also raised congressional hackles by his evasiveness and outright refusal to answer questions at some hearings, and by his chiding of some members at hearings that they were not paying attention to what he was saying. He also earned no credit with House Democrats when he boasted to the press that he had Representative Morris Udall, D-Arizona, a leading congressional environmentalist, under control because Udall wanted a particular water project, over which Watt had authority, for his district. Udall angrily denounced Watt's contention.

So apparently unpopular had Watt become in his first year in office that former Republican officials in the Interior Department and GOP members of Congress called for his ouster; the Sierra Club in October 1981 submitted more than one million signatures on petitions calling for the removal of Watt as Interior secretary; the National Wildlife Federation, the nation's largest and also considered the most conservative of the conservation organizations (its 4.5 million members voted by a two-to-one margin for Reagan over President Carter in 1980), called for Watt's firing in July 1981. Conservative Pennsylvania Representative James K. Coyne in September 1981 expressed the feelings of many of his fellow Republicans who were embarrassed or politically threatened by Watt's performance: "I'd love to see Watt resign. I think he's doing a poor job. He's a disgrace to the administration." Senator Alan Cranston, D-California, the Senate assistant minority leader, expressed the prevailing Democratic sentiment in the summer of 1981, terming Watt a "puppet of the exploiters and destroyers," an "extremist," and a "radical" who was "the champion of narrow special interests." Editorialists and broadcasting commentators, from small as well as major outlets, from liberal as well as conservative areas of the country, branded Watt as the tool of private economic interests. Many of them castigated him as the worst Interior secretary the nation has ever had. The Springfield, Missouri, *Leader & Press,* in a typical press commentary, said in August 1981 that Watt "is a burden neither the Reagan Administration—nor the United States— can afford" and called for Watt either to resign or for Reagan to fire him. The *Kansas City Times* labeled Watt "that great mischief-maker" whose trademark is the "desecration of the earth." The Ogden, Utah, *Standard Examiner* said in June 1982 that Reagan was rapidly losing support in the West and that the one way for him to regain some popularity in a region that had backed him heavily in 1980 was "to announce that he has fired James Watt as Interior Secretary."

By the end of his first year in office, editorial support among major United States publications was virtually nonexistent. Nevertheless, he did have his supporters. The *Wall Street Journal* in October 1981 assailed "radical" environmentalists who were out to "get" Watt, and praised the secretary as "a western conservationist and multiple land use advocate, a natural choice for an administration seeking to respond to a changing set of national priorities." An oil company magazine, *Cities Service Today,* praised Watt as being "devoted to preserving the environment. But he also realizes for our country's long-term economic survival, we must develop the abundant resources on our federal lands."

With all the focus on Watt and to a lesser degree on Anne Gorsuch, the pro-business administrator of the Environmental Protection Agency, President Reagan himself was largely escaping criticism for environmental and wilderness policies in the first year of his administration. Many of the calls for Watt's resignation that were addressed to Reagan seemed based on the premise that Reagan somehow didn't know what his Interior secretary was doing—or, perhaps for political reasons, ignored Reagan's support for Watt in the face of fierce criticism. Typical in this regard were the May 1981 comments of Nathaniel P. Reed, former assistant secretary of the Interior Department under President Ford. Reed, a lifelong Republican said, in a scathing indictment of Watt's performance, that his "quarrel is not with Ronald Reagan," who, he said, "will be a good president and a notable environmentalist." Rather, he said Watt and some other anti-environmentalist appointees in the administration "have broken faith with the Republican party and betrayed their president." Likewise, Dan W. Lufkin, another lifelong Republican and chairman of the Task Force on the Environment, an advisory committee established by Reagan, wrote the president in the summer of 1981 that he knew Reagan supported the environmental ethic, but that Watt and some of his other key people were pursuing a course "that will be totally destructive to the political and philosophical goals you have so admirably set out to achieve." Lufkin, however, pulled no punches as he termed the administration's record in environmental affairs "crazy" and its policies "retrogressive, catapulting us back to the days of grab and plunder"—a "meat ax approach to gutting programs."

Friends of the Earth, a major environmental organization, harbored no illusions about Reagan's relationship with Watt. In a lengthy statement in February 1982, the organization noted that environmentalists were reluctant to criticize Reagan in his first year in office, concentrating instead on Watt. "But," the organization continued, "let's face it, Mr. Reagan is the real James Watt. . . . Our president is taking apart nearly every institution that protects planetary and human health. His actions and his rhetoric are consistent: destructive, disdainful, and uncomprehending of environmental values." Friends of the Earth noted that, like Watt, Reagan had equated much of the environmental movement with "extremism" and that, in response to the more than one million signatures on petitions asking for Watt's firing, Reagan had said that Watt was his favorite Cabinet member.

William Hines, of the *Chicago Sun-Times,* likewise saw Watt as having considerable job security under Reagan. "Why should Reagan get rid of him?" Hines wrote in late 1981. "Not only is Watt doing the job the President appointed him to do, but also, in acting as flak-catcher, he serves a valuable purpose for the President. Like Richard Nixon in Dwight Eisenhower's time and Spiro Agnew in Nixon's, Watt is the house ogre. He keeps Reagan looking good by comparison." Initially, Budget Director David Stockman served the same function. Thus, in the Reagan strategy, it was "Stockman's budget" that was causing all the slashes in social programs (the bad news), while it was Reagan's tax cut (the good news). And, it was Watt's strip-mining and Outer Continental Shelf oil exploration proposals (the bad news), while it was Reagan expressing his love for the outdoors at his California ranch or at Camp David (the good news). The result of this successful deflecting of the blame for controversial programs is that, according to many polls, most voters by mid-1982 still were not holding Reagan accountable for many of his administration's most controversial actions and noteworthy failures.

Nevertheless, Watt himself has made it clear that he is Reagan's man. Reagan, said Watt, understands the Interior Department better than any recent president and "when I said, 'I want to do this I want to do that, he replied, 'Sic' em.' " Certainly, Reagan's rhetoric on environmental issues is similar to Watt's. As Reagan said when campaigning for the presidency in April 1980, "I think we're in the hands of what I call some environmental extremists. The best way to describe them is that they wouldn't let you build a house unless it looked like a bird's nest." In truth, Reagan and Watt are ideological soulmates.

True to his word Watt, in his first eighteen months in office had used his wide discretionary powers and the budget system as "the excuse to make major policy decisions." Summing up his first year as

Secretary, Watt said the actions he took were "to restore America's greatness" and to end "50 years of bad management" of federal lands in the West. When he became secretary, he said, the department was engaged in a "war on the West," and its policies were "in far left field," and he had begun moving the pendulum back to the center to achieve "a balance that is necessary for a strong and vibrant America."

But a governor from a "Sagebrush Rebellion" state, Richard D. Lamm, of Colorado, saw it differently. Watt, rather than shifting the pendulum, was attempting "to take the pendulum off the clock."

8 · Prospects for Change

Two decades ago, author and legal scholar Arthur S. Miller wrote that "Democratic government is *responsible* government—which means *accountable* government—and the essential problem in contracting-out is that responsibility and accountability are greatly diminished [his emphasis]." The use of contractors by the government, Professor Miller wrote, had placed "the influence over, and sometimes even control of, important decisions one step further away from the public and their elected representatives."

The widespread use of contractors to perform basic functions of government marks a radical departure over the last forty years from the American tradition of accountability of power. The policy did not come about suddenly, rather, gradually and on an ad hoc basis. No great public debate as to the desirability of such a policy accompanied the growth of the contract bureaucracy. No law was passed by Congress authorizing contractors to control or influence the operations and costs of government.

This makeshift policy, in addition to giving contractors a greater voice in the running of the government, has also produced since World War II, one failure, problem, and scandal after another: overcharges, cost overruns, the undermining of the civil service system through contract patronage, the loss of government in-house expertise, bribery, political influence, the "revolving door" between government and private firms, the individual and organizational conflicts of interest among contractors, the awarding of duplicative or useless contracts, and the dumping by agencies of their unspent money in the last weeks of a fiscal year on unnecessary contracts.

Because of these various inefficiencies, frauds, and abuses, un-counted billions in taxpayers' dollars are wasted every year. With some 18 million government contracts for goods and services costing more than $150 billion annually, and with Executive Branch and congressional control over the contracting process woefully inade-quate, there are substantial opportunities for improprieties to occur. Although no one inside or outside of government has any authorita-tive figures as to the amount of monetary waste on federal contracts, some contracting critics have tried to make informed estimates. For example, the *Chicago Tribune* in 1981 put the amount of federal contracting waste at $15 billion annually. Some other critics think the true figure may be much higher, because possibly $15 billion is wasted on just the noncompetitive contracts alone—with billions more wasted in other ways.

But whatever the figure, it is a sad fact that, in an era of taxpayers' revolts epitomized by California's tax-cutting Proposition 13, con-tracting-out is one of the best-kept secrets of government. While much attention has been focused by President Reagan and other politicians, as well as by many editorial writers and tax-revolt leaders, on both the real and imagined shortcomings and cost of social programs mainly benefiting the disadvantaged in our society, there has been no corresponding hard look by those same forces at the various govern-ment benefits for the nation's business interests: everything from tax breaks and subsidies to costly, and oftentimes unnecessary, govern-ment contracts. This lack of meaningful congressional or Executive Branch monitoring of government contractors is perhaps the most serious defficiency in the federal budgetary and fiscal review process, yet it arouses scant public interest.

Although this chapter will propose several steps that can be taken to curtail the waste and loss of accountability in the present federal contracting system, all such proposals will be useless unless there is heightened public awareness of the costs involved in the present sys-tem. For those interested in economy and accountability in government, it makes no sense to assail the visible civil service bureaucracy, while at the same time overlooking the far more costly and more pervasive contractors' bureaucracy. Only an examination of the *total* bureaucracy—by the president, Congress, the press, and the public—can help to produce cost-effective as well as accountable government.

Most supporters of contracting reform see a difficult road ahead. The problem, said Arkansas Senator David Pryor in an early 1982 interview, is that contracting "is not a sexy issue, like Social Security or food stamps" that directly affects citizens. This makes it harder to bring contracting reform to the forefront of national issues even though "there's lots of bucks there to be saved."

Like many other contracting critics, Pryor said that most contractors are honest and do high quality work. Often, the contracting abuses are the fault of the federal agency and not the contractor. Any reforms that occur must be aimed not just at the contractors, but at the government contracting agencies, which often foster, or wink at, fraud, waste, and abuse. Regardless of where the blame lies in specific cases, though, the overwhelming weight of evidence reveals persistent and widespread abuses getting worse by the year as the volume of federal contracting increases.

Pryor said it is vital to reform the system, because "Today, the passage of each new law, the emergence of each new 'crisis,' the creation of each new program, is the cause for wholesaling the basic work of government to an ever-growing contractor work force that, by default, is fast becoming the intelligence of government." The "basic questions of government that command the attention of us all," Pryor said, "include the sheer invisibility of a large and growing portion of the federal work force, the related lack of accountability of that work force, and the failure to apply to that work force even the minimal codes of ethics and disclosure that apply to 'officials' at virtually every level of American government."

L.M. Pellerzi, former chief counsel for the United States Civil Service Commission who later held the same position for the American Federation of Government Employees (AFL-CIO), the largest federal workers' union, also sees an urgent need for reforms. Pellerzi is the author of the Civil Service Commission's "Pellerzi Standards," which outlined the proper use of contracting for government services.

With the increasing use of contractors for functions previously performed by career employees, Pellerzi said, "the government completely circumvents the civil service laws which barred patronage, tested personal competence, precluded conflicts of interest and demanded strict personal accountability of public funds and the use of public authority." The result, Pellerzi said, "has been to hoodwink the American public into believing that the government bureaucracy is being made more efficient and reduced in size when, in fact, the opposite is happening." What is needed, he said, is for contracts and contract personnel costs to be examined in the federal budgetary process with the same detail as are the costs of civil service employees. Contracting should be limited to those situations in which Congress has approved appropriations for it. "Then," he said, "we'll get a true picture of who's costing who what in this country" in the operations of government.

Of course, despite the documented widespread abuses, not all government contracting is wasteful or unnecessary or gives too much power to contractors. Nor can federal workers alone always do whatever work needs to be done. It is obviously appropriate that most manufacturing activities, such as those for the Defense Department, be performed by private contractors—but under close government supervision of cost and quality that has often been sadly lacking in the past. Or, when a vitally needed skill is truly unavailable from the civil service work force, it is certainly advisable to turn to private contractors in such circumstances to perform specific identified tasks for a limited period of time. The problems develop when there is a continued adherence by federal agencies to an ad hoc policy that promotes unplanned, haphazard contracting with little regard given to the impact such a policy has on the costs or on the orderly functioning of government.

Solutions to the contracting problems will not come easy. The policy has gained such momentum for almost four decades that it is impossible to bring it under control all at once. But there are some steps that can be taken, if a presidential administration or Congress has the will.

As a start, the thrust of the current policy should be reversed. The present policy is weighted toward having the government contract-out as much as it possibly can, under the unproved, debatable assumption that private enterprise is inherently more efficient than the government. Any new policy must start with the assumption that basic governmental functions are to be performed by the government unless (among other things) it can be positively shown that the federal activity is in direct competition with the private sector, or that to turn the function over to a private firm would in no way disrupt the operations of government, hurt the national interest, undercut federal accountability, lead to greater costs, or add to unemployment problems. Many of these suggested steps are present to a degree in current contracting guidelines, but they are inadequately enforced and there are seldom any penalties—to contractors or agency officials—for violating these standards.

Given the widespread inattention to guidelines, any new policy should be expressed preferably through legislation, rather than through Office of Management and Budget circulars, as has been the case. OMB circulars do not have the force of law and have not been widely enforced—and often have been ignored by federal contracting officials. Any new legislation should place agency managers and contracting officials on notice that they must follow certain procedures before and after contracting for goods and services—rather than giving agency executives so much discretion as to render any voluntary guidelines virtually meaningless, as has been the case with contracting policies for almost four decades. To insure that the new policy is followed, penalties must be provided for contractors and government officials who violate it.

Any new policy should also state specifically what types of functions and services can be contracted for, and under what circumstances. It should also make clear what are essential functions and services of government, and prohibit those from being contracted-out under any circumstances. Again, penalties must be provided for violations. Activities that should be prohibited from being contracted-out include many that have regularly been placed under contract by various agencies, such as drafting agency budgets, official reports, legislation, programs and policies; reorganizing departments of government; selecting and monitoring other contractors; performing regulatory functions, and carrying out day-to-day managerial operations.

The new policy should also not emphasize cost factors to the exclusion of almost all other factors, as has frequently been the case when justifications for contracting-out have been given by contracting advocates. To cite a rather far-fetched example, it would certainly not be desirable—nor presumably would it meet with favor from the citizenry—to turn over the management of such clearly governmental functions as the Marine Corps or the Social Security System to a private company, even if it could be shown that the private firm could perform the functions well. Obviously, more is at stake in the running of the Marine Corps or the Social Security System than whether a private firm could do it efficiently or cheaply.

If there is waste or inefficiency in a program that is inherently governmental in nature, the solution is not to contract out that program. Rather, it is up to the president, the Congress, and the federal managers to do their jobs and find the source of the problems and then correct them—instead of sacrificing accountability to the pursuit of illusory savings or to some notion of getting private enterprise more involved in government operations.

In those circumstances in which the function is not inherently governmental in nature and in which contracting-out is shown to be needed, the new policy should also require some form of competition in which all qualified contractors are allowed to participate. Noncompetitive or sole-source contracts, which make up the majority of the contracts issued government-wide every year, should only be permitted in a true emergency or when it can be definitely shown that only one contractor is qualified to do a particular job or provide a particular product. As it is, sole-source contracts have been a joke and a scandal in the federal government for years.

Government monitoring of contracts should include the use of some realistic yardstick so that federal managers will have a sound idea of what the contract should cost, and not just accept the contractor's word for it. Also, contracts with fixed budgets allowing some leeway for unforeseen circumstances, as opposed to those that reimburse contractors for all costs plus allowing for a fixed profit, should be used in most circumstances. In addition, provisions for overruns, or add-ons expanding the scope of work of the original contract, or follow-on contracts and other such devices used by contractors to recoup avoidable losses or to obtain windfall profits, should be severely restricted.

Also, Congress should make programs that use contracting part of the annual budgetary review process, subject to the same scrutiny as are government-run programs and civil service personnel. To examine only the civil service bureaucracy, and not the contractors' bureaucracy, makes a sham of politicians' promises to bring the federal government under fiscal control and make it more accountable to the people.

A good starting point for reform legislation would be the unsuccessful measure to regulate consultant and management support service contractors that was first introduced in 1980 by Senator Pryor and Representative Herbert E. Harris II. To recapitulate, the legislation —which encountered fatal opposition from the United States Chamber of Commerce, contractors' organizations, and the Office of Management and Budget—would have, among other things, made lists of contracts available to the public; required a line item in the budget for contracts; mandated more contracts to be advertised in the *Commerce Business Daily,* in order to increase competition; required agencies to disclose how contractors were used in preparing official reports; defined conflicts of interest, required contractors to disclose such conflicts and given the federal agency authority to terminate the contracts if the contractor failed to disclose a conflict; and limited the amount of funds an agency could spend on contracts in the last two months of a fiscal year. The measure did not come up for a floor vote in either house of Congress.

Many other critics of contracting have commendable suggestions on how to bring about contract reform. Admiral Hyman Rickover, the father of the nuclear navy, has offered a number of sensible recommendations to cut down on waste and fraud in Defense Department contracting. Rickover has suggested that Defense not award new contracts to companies that, "through their own inefficiency, incur cost overruns, fail to meet delivery schedules or quality requirements, and try to shift these problems to the government through inflated claims and threatened work stoppages." Rickover said Congress should also pass legislation to permit the Pentagon to award contracts to other than the lowest bidder when they suspect that a contractor is deliberately bidding low to get the contract—and then is planning later to submit cost overrun claims to make up for the original low bid.

Rickover has also proposed that Congress establish a one-year statute of limitations on submissions by contractors of cost overrun claims. He said this would "foreclose the present practice of contractors waiting for several years to see how well they make out on a given contract and then submitting claims to make up for their overruns." Delays in submitting claims, he said, "obfuscate issues and frustrate government analysis of the claims." Frequently, when claims are submitted years later, "the knowledgeable people in government . . . have left, leaving the government at a disadvantage." Finally, Rickover recommended that the Justice Department, contrary to its past performance in the contracting area, "vigorously enforce federal laws which make it a crime to submit false claims against the government."

The recommendations in this chapter are by no means all-inclusive. Many persons in government, with years of experience in dealing with the contract bureaucracy, such as Admiral Rickover and the air force's Ernest Fitzgerald, are in a far better position than this author to supply the technical and legislative details needed to bring the government's runaway contracting policies under control. Various recommendations made here and by other contracting critics should, at the very least, be discussed publicly in the press, in Congress, in the Executive Branch, and by the citizens who ultimately bear the costs and feel the impact of the federal government—be it government by civil servants or by contractors.

For it is clear that unless federal contracting policies are reined in, we can only expect business to increase its influence over the operations and costs of government, and thereby alter permanently the relationship between the citizenry and their government—and further erode the traditional concept of governmental accountability.

As H.L. Nieburg put it almost two decades ago, "Business and industry have always been close to the center of political power, but never before in peacetime have they enjoyed such a broad acceptance of their role as a virtual fourth branch of government. . . ." And, he added, "it is necessary to judge the appropriateness and adequacy of national policies that increasingly raise a question concerning the relation between government and private contractor: who is serving whom?"

The question is an even more urgent one today. Government by contract is an issue that should be addressed now.

Sources

Listed below are many of the sources I drew upon for this book. I have not included all of the several thousand newspaper and magazine articles, or all of the hundreds of documents, that I used; instead, I have listed major articles and reports that provided substantial information or a special insight into an issue. Interviews are noted in the text of the chapters.

1 ▪ The Role of Contracting in Government

Books
Nieburg, H. L. *In the Name of Science.* Chicago: Quadrangle Books, 1966.

Sharkansky, Ira. *Wither the State? Politics and Public Enterprise in Three Countries.* Chatham, New Jersey: Chatham House Publishers, 1979.

Articles
Heyman, Victor K. "Government by Contract: Boon or Boner?" *Public Administration Review.* Spring, 1961.

Pincus, Walter. "New Tank Needs An Ace to Dig a Hole." *The Washington Post.* February 9, 1982.

Pincus, Walter. "Recall the MI's ACE? Now It's Got a Problem." *The Washington Post.* March 3, 1982.

Documents
"Large-Scale Production of the M1 Tank Should Be Delayed Until Its
Power Train Is Made More Durable." United States General
Accounting Office report to Congress. December 15, 1981.
"Use of Management Support Service Contracts by Defense Department."
Subcommittee on Human Resources, Committee on Post Office and
Civil Service, House of Representatives, and the Subcommittee on Civil
Service and General Services, Committee on Governmental Affairs,
United States Senate. Joint hearing. April 29, 1981.

2 ▪ How the System Works (or Doesn't)

Books
Adams, Gordon. *The Iron Triangle: The Politics of Defense Contracting.*
New York: Council on Economic Priorities, 1981.
Guttman, Daniel, and Willner, Barry. *The Shadow Government.* New
York: Pantheon Books, 1976.

Articles
Allen, Henry. "The Consultants." *The Washington Post/Potomac
Magazine.* August 26, 1973.
Aug, Stephen M. "OMB Prepares Conflict Rules for Contractors." *The
Washington Star.* September 17, 1977.
Cleemput, Diane. "I Was a Teen-age Consultant." *The Washington
Monthly.* May, 1980.
Cramer, John. "Uncle Sam Wasting Billions in Contracting-Out, GAO
Study Charges." *The Washington Star.* June 3, 1977.
Easterbrook, Gregg. "How to Make the Coming Bad Times Good Times
for You." *The Washington Monthly.* May, 1980.
Easterbrook, Gregg. "The Art of Further Study: Life in the Consulting
Cult." *The Washington Monthly.* May, 1980.
Farrier, John. "Use It or Lose It." *Inquiry.* December 29, 1980.
Gay, Lance. "The Consultant Mystery—Who Knows How Much?" *The
Washington Star.* May 23, 1977.
"Government Consultants: A Booming Industry Comes Under Fire." *U.S.
News & World Report.* August 15, 1977.
Hamilton, Martha M. "Increase in Federal Contracting Generates
Troubling Questions." *The Washington Post.* February 24, 1980.
"How Many Contractors? Nobody Knows for Sure." *Federal Times.*
August 29, 1977.

Kurtz, Howie. "Documents Say SBA Aided Favored Firms." *The Washington Star.* April 26, 1981.

Kurtz, Howie. "GSA: Buildings and Boondoggles." *The Washington Star.* Series: June 15, 16, and 17, 1981.

Kurtz, Howie. " '78 Consultants Cost HEW $10 Million." *The Washington Star.* April 7, 1979.

Kurtz, Howie. "U.S. Auditors Challenge Fees of D.C. Firm." *The Washington Star.* March 9, 1981.

Landauer, Jerry. "GSA Acts to Prevent 'Improper' Influence in Selecting Firms for Federal Contracts." *The Wall Street Journal.* June 11, 1974.

Lambro, Donald. "The GSA Ripoff." *Inquiry.* December 25, 1978.

Lambro, Donald, "After $22 Billion 'War,' 26 Million in U.S. Still Poor." United Press International dispatch in *The Washington Post.* December 8, 1977.

Love, Thomas. "Consulting for U.S. Is Big, but Just How Big?" *The Washington Star.* February 26, 1978.

Neumann, Jonathan, and Gup, Ted. "Government Out of Control: Contracts." *The Washington Post.* Series: June 22–26, 1980.

Thomas, Jo, "Congress Questions Advantage and Cost of U.S. Consultants." *The New York Times.* December 5, 1977.

Documents

Abourezk, Senator James. "Statement on Organizational Conflicts of Interest in Government Contract." Senate Committee on Governmental Affairs. June 9, 1977.

"Access to Certain Consulting Service Contract Information." United States General Accounting Office report to Representative Ralph Regula. December 2, 1981.

"Agencies Should Disclose Consultants' Roles in Preparing Congressionally Mandated Reports." United States General Accounting Office report to Senator David H. Pryor. August 19, 1980.

"Civil Servants and Contract Employees: Who Should Do What for the Federal Government?" United States General Accounting Office report to Congress. June 19, 1981.

"Congressional Oversight Hearings: The Plight of the Service Worker Revisited." Subcommittee on Labor-Management Relations, Committee on Education and Labor, House of Representatives." Report. April, 1975.

"Consultant Reform Act of 1980." Committee on Governmental Affairs, United States Senate. Hearings. August 19–20, 1980.

"Consultants and Contractors: A Survey of the Government's Purchase of Outside Services." Subcommittee on Reports, Accounting and Management, Committee on Governmental Affairs, United States Senate. Report. August, 1977.

"Contracting Out of Jobs and Services" (parts I and II). Subcommittee on Employee Ethics and Utilization, Committee on Post Office and Civil Service, House of Representatives. Hearings. March 28 and 31, 1977, and July 8, 12, 14, and 19, 1977.

"Controls Over Consulting Service Contracts at Federal Agencies Need Tightening." United States General Accounting Office report to Representative Herbert E. Harris II. March 20, 1980.

"EPA's Use of Management Support Services." United States General Accounting Office report to Senator Max S. Baucus. March 9, 1982.

"Federal Consulting Service Contracts" (parts I and II). Subcommittee on Civil Service and General Services, Committee on Governmental Affairs, United States Senate, and the Subcommittee on Human Resources, Committee on Post Office and Civil Service, House of Representatives. Joint hearings. March 27, April 3, June 24, and July 22, 1980.

"Federal Government's Use of Consultant Services." Subcommittee on Civil Service and General Services, Committee on Governmental Affairs, United States Senate. Hearing. October 12, 1979.

"Government Agencies Need Effective Planning to Curb Unnecessary Year-end Spending." United States General Accounting Office report to Representative Herbert E. Harris II. July 28, 1980.

"Government Earns Low Marks on Proper Use of Consultants." United States General Accounting Office report to Congress. June 5, 1980.

"GSA's Personal Property Repair and Rehabilitation Program: A Potential for Fraud." United States General Accounting Office report to Congress. November 14, 1979.

"Investigation Into the Small Business Administration's Section 8(a) Program." Subcommittee on Federal Spending Practices and Open Government, Committee on Governmental Affairs, United States Senate. Hearings. July 6, 7, and 8, 1977.

Mathias, Senator Charles McC., Jr., and Sarbanes, Senator Paul S. Letter to Joel W. Solomon, administrator of general services, General Services Administration. October 4, 1977.

"Request for Proposal No. E(49–18)–2213—Provide Planning; Analytical, Technical and Other Required Services." United States Energy

Research and Development Administration (Fossil Energy). October 10, 1975.

Rosa, James R., assistant general counsel for litigation, American Federation of Government Employees (AFL-CIO). Letter to Peter Marudas, office of Senator Paul Sarbanes. August 25, 1977.

"Serving Two Masters: A Common Cause Study of Conflicts of Interest in the Executive Branch." Common Cause report. October, 1976.

Staats, Elmer B., Comptroller General of the United States. "Statement on the Consultant Reform Act of 1980." Testimony. Senate Committee on Governmental Affairs. August 19, 1980.

"Status of Major Acquisitions as of September 30, 1981: Better Reporting Essential to Controlling Cost Growth." United States General Accounting Office report to Congress. April 22, 1982.

3 ▪ Ever Since Washington

Books

Hawke, David Freeman. *Paine.* New York: Harper & Row, 1974.

Macy, John W., Jr. *Public Service: The Human Side of Government.* New York: Harper & Row, 1971.

Articles

Badhwar, Indirjit. "Ford Orders More Contracting-Out." *Federal Times.* August   25, 1976.

Kurtz, Howie. "Businesses Fighting Harris on Contracts." *The Washington Star.*   March 27, 1980.

Documents

"Federal Personnel Ceilings and Contracting Activities." Committee on Post Office   and Civil Service, House of Representatives. Report. December 20, 1979.

Fettig, Lester A., administrator, Office of Federal Procurement Policy, Office of Management and Budget. "Establishment of the Federal Procurement Data System." Memorandum for department and agency officials. February 3, 1978.

Ford, President Gerald R. "Management Initiatives." Memorandum to Cabinet members and other top Executive Branch officials. July 24, 1976.

Lynn, James T., director, Office of Management and Budget. "Presidential Management Initiatives." Memorandum to Cabinet members and other top Executive Branch officials. July 27, 1976.

"Model Control System for Consulting Services." Office of Federal Procurement Policy. Draft report. 1981.

Pellerzi, L.M. "Opinion of General Counsel" to the United States Civil Service Commission. October 1967.

"Proposal for a Uniform Federal Procurement System." Office of Federal Procurement Policy. Draft report. October 29, 1981. Revised report. February 26, 1982.

4 ▪ Pentagon Contracting: The Open Money Sack

Books

Adams, Gordon. *The Iron Triangle: The Politics of Defense Contracting.* New York: Council on Economic Priorities, 1981.

Fallows, James. *National Defense.* New York: Random House, 1981.

Articles

Alter, Jonathan, and Keisling, Phil. "35 Ways to Cut the Defense Budget." *The Washington Monthly.* April, 1982.

Andelman, David A. "Pentagon Spends Millions to Save Ailing Companies." *The New York Times.* April 30, 1973.

Baker, Donald P. "Congressman Says Hill to Probe Navy Overhaul Program." *The Washington Post.* February 6, 1981.

Blumenthal, Ralph. "Lawmaker's Funds Clouded by Flaws." *The New York Times.* January 18, 1982.

Burkholder, Steve. "The Pentagon in the Ivory Tower." *The Progressive.* June, 1981.

Clines, Francis X. "Navy's Secretary Charges Supplier 'Rip-Offs.' " *The New York Times.* August 20, 1981.

Cramer, James J. "The Bar That Beats the Navy." *The American Lawyer.* March, 1981.

Cramer, James J. "Who's Who in the Contracts Bar." The American Lawyer. March, 1981.

Dumas, Professor Lloyd J. "Swords Into Plows." *The New York Times.* March 2, 1982.

Fallows, James. "America's High-Tech Weaponry." *The Atlantic Monthly.* May, 1981.

Friedman, Thomas L. "Big Defense Profits: Maybe." *The New York Times.* October 9, 1981.

Gansler, Jacques S. "Defense Spending: How About Some Real Competition?" *The Washington Post.* April 4, 1982.

Greider, William. "The Education of David Stockman." *Atlantic.* December, 1981.

Halloran, Richard. "Caucus Challenges Defense Concepts." *The New York Times.* July 12, 1982.

Henderson, James. "The Corrupt Military: A Case History." *The Washington Monthly.* September, 1977.

Jones, Thomas V. "The Flaws in Defense Contracting." *The Wall Street Journal.* November 25, 1977.

Kamen, Al. "Pentagon Whistle Blower Wins Long Fight for Job." *The Washington Post.* June 16, 1982.

Lippman, Thomas W. "U.S. Navy: Shipbuilding Industry's Lifeline." *The Washington Post,* August 30, 1981.

Love, Thomas. "Jury Is Probing Rockwell Over NASA Billings." *The Washington Star.* June 12, 1981.

Lynton, Stephen J. "Rickover Says Justice Tries to Scuttle Suits." *The Washington Post.* June 23, 1982.

Mace, Don. "Mitre Corp. Gets Still Mightier." *Federal Times.* April 10, 1974.

Mintz, Morton. "Lockheed, Pentagon Team Up to Sell C5s." *The Washington Post.* June 22, 1982.

Mohr, Charles. "Even a Trimmer Military Wouldn't Be Any Bargain." *The New York Times.* May 9, 1982.

Mohr, Charles. "Fears About Deficit Imperil Effort to Improve Weapon Acquisitions." *The New York Times.* March 14, 1982.

Noble, Kenneth B. "Boeing Pleads Guilty to Hiding Commissions." *The New York Times.* July 1, 1982.

Pincus, Walter. "Helicopter Maintenance on the Hill." *The Washington Post.* March 14, 1982.

Pryor, Senator David. "Butter for Big Guns." *The New York Times.* January 31, 1982.

Smith, Hedrick. "How Many Billions for Defense?" *The New York Times Magazine.* November 1, 1981.

Smith, Philip. "GRC Fined $30,000 in Army Case." *The Washington Post.* June 26, 1982.

Taylor, Paul. "Boeing Goes Full Throttle in Attempt to Sell 747s to Pentagon." *The Washington Post.* May 23, 1982.

Taylor, Paul. "U.S. Seeks to Cap Lobbying Reimbursements." *The Washington Post.* October 20, 1981.

United Press International. "New Study Shows Joblessness Fanned by U.S. Spending of Defense Dollars." *The Houston Chronicle.* September 30, 1981.

Weinraub, Bernard. "Military Costs Trouble Conservatives." *The New York Times.* April 19, 1982.

Wicker, Tom. "Why Build the MX At All?" *The New York Times.* October 6, 1981.

Wilson, George C. "Arms Cost Could Exceed Plan by $750 Billion, Leaders Told." *The Washington Post.* January 8, 1982.

Winslow, John F. "How the Conglomerates Get Free Money From the Navy." *The Washington Monthly.* November, 1977.

Documents

"Actions Needed to Reduce Schedule Slippages and Cost Growths on Contracts for Navy Ship Overhauls." United States General Accounting Office report to Representative Joseph P. Addabbo. March 17, 1982.

"Allegations of an Inappropriate Army Sole-Source Award for Commercial Construction Equipment." United States General Accounting Office report to Senator Carl Levin. October 15, 1981.

"Analysis of NASA's Fiscal Year 1983 Budget Request for Research and Development to Determine the Amount That Supports DOD's Programs." United States General Accounting Office report to Senator William Proxmire. April 26, 1982.

"Audit, Inspection and Investigative Operations in the Department of Defense (April 1, 1981–September 30, 1981)." United States Department of Defense, the Assistant Secretary of Defense (Review and Oversight). Report. November 29, 1981.

"Audit, Inspection and Investigative Operations in the Department of Defense (October 1, 1981–March 31, 1982)." United States Department of Defense (Review and Oversight). May 28, 1982.

"Better Management Needed in DOD to Prevent Fraudulent and Erroneous Contract Payments and to Reduce Real Property Maintenance Costs." United States General Accounting Office report to Congress. January 9, 1980.

"Better Navy Management of Shipbuilding Contracts Could Save Millions of Dollars." United States General Accounting Office report to Congress. January 10, 1980.

"Budgetary Pressures Created by the Army's Plans to Procure New Major

Weapon Systems Are Just Beginning." United States General Accounting Office report to Congress. October 20, 1981.

Cooper, Richard V. L. "Contract-Hire Personnel in the Department of Defense." Rand Corporation study for the Department of Defense. April 1977.

"Controls Over DOD's Management Support Service Contracts Need Strengthening." United States General Accounting Office report to Representative Geraldine Ferraro and Senator David Pryor. March 31, 1981.

"Defense Contractor Entertainment Practices." Joint Committee on Defense Production, United States Congress. Report. September, 1977.

"Department of Defense Food Service Program Needs Contracting and Management Improvements." United States General Accounting Office report to the Secretary of Defense. October 20, 1981.

"DOD's Beef Procurement Program Still Needs Improvement." United States General Accounting Office report to Secretary of Defense. February 17, 1982.

"Economics of Defense Policy: Admiral Hyman G. Rickover (Part I)." Joint Economic Committee, Congress of the United States. Hearing. January 28, 1982.

"Economics of Defense Procurement: Shipbuilding Claims." Subcommittee on Priorities and Economy in Government. Joint Economic Committee. United States Congress. Hearings. June 7 and 25, 1976, and December 29, 1977.

"Effect of Contracting Out Work at Naval Air Rework Facilities." Subcommittee on Human Resources, Committee on Post Office and Civil Service, House of Representatives. October 27, 1979.

"Estimated Expenditures for States and Selected Areas, Fiscal Year 1983." United States Department of Defense. 1982.

"Factors Influencing DOD Decisions to Convert Activities From In-House to Contractor Performance." United States General Accounting Office report to the Senate and House of Representatives committees on armed services. April 22, 1981.

"Final Report of the Task Force on Acquisition Improvement." Department of Defense Acquisition Improvement Task Force. December 23, 1981.

"Five-hundred Contractors Receiving the Largest Dollar Volume of Prime Contract Awards for RDT&E Fiscal Year 1981." Department of Defense. Report. February, 1982.

"Followup on the Navy's Efforts to Improve Productivity at Navy Aircraft

Overhaul Depots." United States General Accounting Office report to the Secretary of Defense. December 5, 1979.

Gould, Clifford I., director, federal personnel and compensation division, United States General Accounting Office. "Statement on the Government's Use of Consulting Service and Management Support Contracts." Subcommittee on Defense, Committee on Appropriations, House of Representatives. Testimony. June 25, 1981.

"Guidelines for Assessing Whether Human Factors Were Considered in the Weapon Systems Acquisition Process." United States General Accounting Office. Staff study. December 8, 1981.

"Hearings on Military Posture and . . . Department of Defense Authorization for Appropriations for fiscal year 1982 and . . . Department of Defense Supplemental Authorization for Appropriations for fiscal year 1981." Committee on Armed Services, House of Representatives. February 26; March 4, 5, 12, 16, 19, 23, 25, 26, and April 1, 2, 8, 9, and 29, 1981.

Horan, Donald J., director, procurement, logistics and readiness division, United States General Accounting Office. "Statement on Profit Limitation Legislation." Subcommittee on Procurement and Military Nuclear Systems, Committee on Armed Services, House of Representatives. Testimony. June 16, 1981.

"If Army Helicopter Maintenance Is to Be Ready for Wartime, It Must Be Made Efficient and Effective in Peacetime." United States General Accounting Office report to the Secretary of the Army. May 10, 1979.

"Improving the Acquisition Process." Memorandum. Deputy Secretary of Defense to secretaries of the military departments, chairman of the Joint Chiefs of Staff, under secretaries of defense, assistant secretaries of defense, general counsel, and assistants to the secretary of Defense. April 30, 1981.

Long, William A., deputy under secretary of Defense for research and engineering (acquisition management). "Statement on Sole-Source Procurement." Subcommittee on Procurement and Military Nuclear Systems, Committee on Armed Services, House of Representatives. May 4, 1982.

"Military Contractor-Operated Stores' Contracts Are Unmanageable and Vulnerable to Abuse." United States General Accounting Office report to Congress. July 8, 1981.

"One-Hundred Companies Receiving the Largest Dollar Volume of Prime Contract Awards Fiscal Year 1981 (Corrected Copy)." United States Department of Defense. February, 1982.

Pellerzi, L.M., general counsel, American Federation of Government Employees. "Contracting Out at Polaris Missile Facility, Charleston, South Carolina." Memorandum to Joseph D. Gleason, executive vice president, AFGE. September 29, 1977.

"Prime Contract Awards by Region and State, Fiscal Years 1979, 1980, and 1981." United States Department of Defense. January, 1982.

"Questionable Contracting for Mobile Field Radios by Department of the Army." Subcommittee on Legislation and National Security. Committee on Government Operations. United States House Of Representatives. Hearings. June 22, 1976.

"Retention of Unneeded Government-Owned Special Tooling by Contractors Causes Unnecessary Costs." United States General Accounting Office report to the Secretary of Defense. October 7, 1981.

"Status of Major Acquisitions As of September 30, 1981: Better Reporting Essential to Controlling Cost Growth." United States General Accounting Office report to Congress. April 22, 1982.

"The Navy Is Not Adequately Protecting the Government's Investment in Materials Furnished to Contractors for Ship Construction and Repair." United States General Accounting Office report to the Secretary of the Navy. June 9, 1981.

"The Navy Overhaul Policy—A Costly Means of Insuring Readiness for Support Ships." United States General Accounting Office report to the Committee on Appropriations, House of Representatives. December 27, 1978.

"Use of Management Support Service Contracts by Defense Department." Subcommittee on Human Resources, Committee on Post Office and Civil Service, House of Representatives, and the General Services Subcommittee, Committee on Governmental Affairs, United States Senate. Joint hearing. April 29, 1981.

"Weaknesses in Accounting for Government-Furnished Materials at Defense Contractors' Plants Lead to Excesses." United States General Accounting Office report to Congress. August 7, 1980.

5 ▪ A Company Called TRW

Books

Lindsey, Robert. *The Falcon and the Snowman.* New York: Simon & Schuster, 1979.

Nieburg, H. L. *In the Name of Science.* Chicago: Quadrangle Books, 1966.

Articles

Anderson, Jack, and Whitten, Les. "Energy Efforts Scored." *The Washington Post.* Syndicated column. July 10, 1976.

Lindsey, Robert. "Inmates Reportedly Gave Spy Help in Coast Escape." *The New York Times.* January 28, 1980.

McCombs, Phil. "Contractors, Consultants Get 87% of DOE Budget." *The Washington Post.* June 25, 1980.

Mintz, Morton, and Marcus, Ruth. "GAO to Testify on Pentagon Task Force." *The Washington Post.* July 22, 1982.

Mintz, Morton. "Conflict of Interest Question Raised on Computer Policy to Go to Justice." *The Washington Post.* July 23, 1982.

Mintz, Morton. "Computer Conflicts Are Denied." *The Washington Post.* August 5, 1982.

Munson, Richard. "Ripping off the Sun." *The Progressive.* September, 1979.

Reece, Ray. "The Solar Blackout." *Mother Jones.* September/October, 1980.

Documents

"A Company Called TRW: A Corporate History." TRW, Inc. Pamphlet. Undated.

"Comments on the Energy Research and Development Administration's Contract with TRW, Inc., for Planning and Analysis Services. United States General Accounting Office report to the chairman, Subcommittee on Energy Research, Development and Demonstration (Fossil Fuels), Committee on Science and Technology, House of Representatives, and to the chairman, Subcommittee on Conservation, Energy and Natural Resources, Committee on Government Operations, House of Representatives. September 21, 1976.

"Consultant Reform Act of 1980." Committee on Governmental Affairs, United States Senate. Hearings. August 19–20, 1980.

"Consultant Reform Act of 1980." Subcommittee on Human Resources, Committee on Post Office and Civil Service, House of Representatives. Hearings. August 25 and 28, 1980.

Denman, Scott, and Bossong, Ken. "Big Business & Renewable Energy Resources: An Analysis of the Corporate Connection." Citizens Energy Project pamphlet. 1981.

"Department of Energy Authorizations (Fiscal Years 1979 and 1980) and Energy Emergency Preparedness." Subcommittee on Energy and Power, Committee on Interstate and Foreign Commerce, House of

Representatives. Hearings. February 13, 14, 15, 22, 23, 26, and 28 and March 2, and 6, 1979.

"Department of Energy Procurement Activities." United States General Accounting Office report to Representative John D. Dingell. September 5, 1980.

"Economy in Government Procurement and Property Management." Subcommittee on Economy in Government. Joint Economic Committee. United States Congress. Hearings. May 8, 9, 10, and 16, 1967.

"Examination of the Pricing of Fuel Booster Pump Repair Kits Under Department of the Air Force Negotiated Contract AF 01 (601)—20268—with Thompson, Ramo-Wooldridge, Inc., Cleveland, Ohio." United States General Accounting Office. Report. May 10, 1960.

"Federal Consulting Service Contracts." Subcommittee on Civil Service and General Services, Committee on Governmental Affairs, United States Senate, and the Subcommittee on Human Resources, Committee on Post Office and Civil Service, House of Representatives. Joint hearings (Part I and Part II). March 27, April 3, June 24, and July 22, 1980.

"Large Businesses Dominated Awards Made Under DOE's Alternative Fuels Program." United States General Accounting Office report to Senator Thomas F. Eagleton, et al. May 15, 1981.

"Need for Improvements in Controls over Government-Owned Property in Contractors' Plants." United States General Accounting Office. Report. November 24, 1967.

"Objectivity of the Defense Science Board's Task Force on Embedded Computer Resources Acquisition and Management." United States General Accounting Office report to Represenative Jack Brooks. July 22, 1982.

"Organization and Management of Missile Programs (Eleventh Report)." Subcommittee on Military Operations. Committee on Governmental Operations. United States House of Representatives. Hearings. February 4, 5, and 6 and March 2, 3, 5, 13, and 20, 1959.

"Oversight of the Structure and Management of the Department of Energy." Committee on Governmental Affairs and its Subcommittee on Energy, Nuclear Proliferation and Federal Services, United States Senate. Hearings. November 2, 14, and 28, and December 13, 1979.

"Oversight of the Structure and Management of the Department of Energy." Committee on Governmental Affairs, United States Senate. Staff report. December, 1980.

"Potential for Savings and Improvements Needed in DOE Contracting for

Moving and Storage Services." United States General Accounting Office report to the Secretary of Energy. February 20, 1980.

Ryan, Representative Leo J. Press release. October 26, 1976.

"Small Business Participation in the Department of Energy's Solar Energy Programs." United States General Accounting Office report to Senator Gaylord Nelson. September 29, 1980.

"The Department of Energy Needs Better Procedures for Selecting a Contractor to Operate Argonne National Laboratory." United States General Accounting Office report to Congress. June 8, 1981.

"The Department of Energy's Practices for Awarding and Administering Contracts Need to Be Improved." United States General Accounting Office report to Representative John D. Dingell. November 2, 1979.

"The Department of Energy's Use of Support Service Contractors to Perform Basic Management Functions." United States General Accounting Office report to Senator James A. McClure. September 14, 1981.

"The Relationship Between the Department of Energy and Energy Industries." Committee on Energy and Natural Resources, United States Senate. Hearings. June 16 and July 10, 1978.

"The Subcontracting Practices of Large Department of Energy Contractors Need to Be Improved." United States General Accounting Office report to Senator James A. McClure. April 22, 1982.

"TRW Fact Sheet." TRW, Inc. Undated.

"TRW Inc. Annual Reports" (and other documents required to be filed with the Securities and Exchange Commission). 1975 through August, 1982.

6 ▪ Reagan: Business As Usual

Articles

Anderson, Harry, et al. "Reagan Readies the Ax." *Newsweek.* February 16, 1981.

Bredemeier, Kenneth. "Hard Times Hit (Nondefense) Consultants." *The Washington Post.* June 21, 1982.

Dowie, Mark. "The Bechtel File." *Mother Jones.* September/October, 1978.

Earley, Pete. "Wholesale Firings Hit Advisory Councils." *The Washington Post.* May 7, 1982.

Friedman, Saul. "Reagan's Ideological Principles Dictate His Policies." *Philadelphia Inquirer.* October 4, 1981.

Greider, William. "The Education of David Stockman." *Atlantic.* December 1981.

Greve, Frank. "With Industry Experts Placed in the Top Spots . . . The Regulated Have All but Captured the Regulator." *Philadelphia Inquirer.* July 26, 1981.

Hershey, Robert D., Jr. "Energy Dept.'s End Proposed." *The New York Times.* May 25, 1982.

Hershey, Robert D. Jr. "Reagan Outlines Plans for Revival of Nuclear Power." *The New York Times.* October 9, 1981.

Hoffman, David, and Cannon, Lou. "Men with a Mission, at the Midterm: The Reagan Cabinet (Part I)." *The Washington Post.* July 18, 1982.

King, Seth S. "U.S. Official Cleared on Role in $230,000 Contract Award." *The New York Times.* October 12, 1981.

Kurtz, Howie. "Plan to Abolish DOE Offers Little Saving." *The Washington Post.* October 2, 1981.

Lippman, Thomas W. "Designating Shultz as Next Secretary Adds to Bechtel's Strong Administration Ties." *The Washington Post.* June 26, 1982.

Marcus, Ruth. "Army, Law Schools in Showdown on Gay Rights." *The Washington Post.* July 24, 1982.

Omang, Joanne. "Nuclear Energy Subsidy Estimate Slashed by DOE." *The Washington Post.* April 8, 1981.

Pauly, David, and Lubenow, Gerald C. "Master Builder . . ." *Newsweek.* August 29, 1977.

Reid, T.R. "Protection for Nation's Largest Consumer." *The Washington Post.* October 30, 1981.

Shandler, Philip. "The Federal Column: OMB Is Pushing Contracting-Out of U.S. Work." *The Washington Star.* April 1, 1981.

Shribman, David. "U.S. Easing Rules on Discrimination by Its Contractors." *The New York Times.* July 25, 1981.

The Associated Press. "Judge Blocks a Plan to Ease Wage Law in Building Projects." *The New York Times.* July 23, 1982.

United Press International. "U.S. Agency Chief Admits Meeting on a Land Deal in San Francisco." *The New York Times.* July 24, 1982.

Walsh, Edward. "Michael Reagan to Quit Jobs in Dispute." *The Washington Post.* May 15, 1981.

Documents

"Addressing Fraud, Waste and Abuse: A Summary Report of Inspectors General Activities." President's Council on Integrity and Efficiency. December 7, 1981.

"Bechtel Briefs." Bechtel Group. December, 1977.

"Facts About Bechtel." Bechtel Group. 1977.

Harper, Edwin, chairman, President's Council on Integrity and Efficiency. Transcript. Briefing for reporters. December 7, 1981.

Henderson, Laura. "Statement on S. 719, the Proposed 'Consultant Reform and Disclosure Act of 1981'." Subcommittee on Federal Expenditures, Research and Rules, Committee on Governmental Affairs, United States Senate. Testimony, for the National Council of Professional Services Firms. September 18, 1981.

"Loss of Experienced Staff Affects Conservation and Renewable Energy Programs." United States General Accounting Office report to Senator Mark O. Hatfield. July 19, 1982.

"Proposal for a Uniform Federal Procurement System." Office of Federal Procurement Policy. Draft report. October 29, 1981. Revised report. February 26, 1982.

Pryor, Senator David. Letter. To David A. Stockman, director of Office of Management and Budget. September 18, 1981.

Reagan, President Ronald. "President's Private Sector Survey on Cost Control in the Federal Government: Executive Order 12369." June 30, 1982.

"Recent Government-Wide Hiring Freezes Prove Ineffective in Managing Federal Employment." United States General Accounting Office report to Representative Geraldine Ferraro. March 10, 1982.

"Review of Circumstances of the Mass Removal of Statutory Inspectors General." United States General Accounting Office report to Representative L.H. Fountain. July 9, 1981.

"Savings From 1981 and 1982 Personnel Ceiling Reductions." United States General Accounting Office report to Representative Geraldine Ferraro. January 15, 1982.

Stockman, David A., director, Office of Management and Budget. Letter. To Senator David Pryor. October 22, 1981.

"Validity and Comparability of Quantitative Data Presented by the President's Council on Integrity and Efficiency on Inspectors General Activities." United States General Accounting Office report to Representative John D. Dingell. May 18, 1982.

7 · Watt: Giving Away the Store

Articles

Adler, Jerry, et al. "James Watt's Land Rush." *Newsweek.* June 29, 1981.

Andersen, Kurt, et al. "Always Right and Ready to Fight." *Time.* August 23, 1982.

Anderson, Jack. "Secretary Watt and His Promise." *The Washington Post.* May 4, 1981.

Broder, David S. "Gas Company Lobbyist Fired for Questioning Watt Remark." *The Washington Post.* January 26, 1982.

Cockburn, Alexander, and Ridgeway, James. "James Watt, Apostle of Pillage." *The Village Voice.* January 28–February 3, 1981.

Dean, Norman L. "Mining the Law." *The New York Times.* August 8, 1982.

Drew, Elizabeth. "A Reporter at Large: Secretary Watt." *The New Yorker.* May 4, 1981.

Gailey, Phil. "Democratic Lawyers Finding Interior Cold." *The New York Times.* February 2, 1981.

Hines, William. "James Watt: The Man They Love to Hate." *Chicago Sun-Times.* Reprinted in *Public Citizen.* Fall, 1981.

Horton, Tom. "On Many Issues, Interior Nominee Fought Department He Will Now Control." *The Baltimore Sun.* January 6, 1981.

Horton, Tom. "Watt's Unyielding Nature Seen as Barrier to His Effectiveness as Interior Secretary." *The Baltimore Sun.* January 7, 1981.

Jones, Robert A. "Concessionaire Proposes Expanded Role at Yosemite Park." *Los Angeles Times.* April 3, 1981.

Klein, Jeffrey. "Man Apart." *Mother Jones.* August, 1981.

Lange, Timothy. "New Tactic for the Right Wing: Public Interest Legal Foundations, Just Like the Left Has." *Straight Creek Journal.* October 6, 1977.

Lufkin, Dan W., chairman, President-elect Reagan's Task Force on the Environment. Letter to the editor. *Connecticut Magazine.* September, 1981.

McCarthy, Coleman. "James Watt and the Puritan Ethic." *The Washington Post.* May 24, 1981.

Pasztor, Andy. "James Watt Tackles Interior Agency Job With Religious Zeal." *The Wall Street Journal.* May 5, 1981.

Pasztor, Andy. "Reagan Mine Choice Had Profitable Deals With Coal Operators." *The Wall Street Journal.* March 18, 1981.

Peterson, Cass. "Watt Gets Public-Lands Advice in Private." *The Washington Post.* Undated (early 1982).

Rountree, Russ. "Oilmen's Interest in Legal Foundation 'Growing.' " *Western Oil Reporter.* February, 1978.

Russakoff, Dale. "The Unforcer: Strip Mining Agency Falls Victim to Reagan's Reforms." *The Washington Post.* June 6, 1982.

Shabecoff, Philip. "Watt's Oil Lease Plan: Benefits and Dangers Seen." *The New York Times.* August 10, 1982.

Sinclair, Ward. "Firms Backing Watt's Foundation Have Stake in Rulings by Interior." *The Washington Post.* January 23, 1981.

Stoler, Peter, et al. "Land Sale of the Century." *Time.* August 23, 1982.

Taylor, Stuart, Jr. "Nature Groups Accusing Watt of 'Collusion.' " *The New York Times.* August 20, 1981.

The Associated Press. "Watt Sends Congress Plan to Open Most of U.S. Coastline to Drilling." *The New York Times.* May 15, 1982.

Wolf, Ron. "New Voice in the Wilderness." Rocky Mountain Magazine. March/April, 1981.

Documents

"James G. Watt Nomination." Committee on Energy and Natural Resources, United States Senate. Hearings. January 7–8, 1981.

"Marching Backwards: The Department of Interior Under James G. Watt." National Wildlife Federation. Staff analysis. April 29, 1982.

"Mountain States Legal Foundation Annual Report." 1979–80.

"National Park Service Concessions—Oversight." Subcommittee on Parks and Recreation, Committee on Interior and Insular Affairs, United States Senate. Hearing. March 10, 1976.

"National Park Service Concessions Policy." Subcommittee on Parks, Recreation and Renewable Resources, Committee on Energy and Natural Resources, United States Senate. Hearings. March 29, April 23 and 27, 1979.

"National Park Service Policies Discourage Competition, Give Concessioners Too Great a Voice in Concession Management." Committee on Government Operations and Committee on Small Business, House of Representatives. Joint report. March 3, 1976.

"Nomination of James Gaius Watt, of Colorado, to be Secretary of the Interior." *Congressional Record.* United States Senate. Debate. January 22, 1981.

Reed, Nathaniel P., Address to the Sierra Club's 1981 annual meeting, San Francisco. May 2, 1981.

Regnery, Alfred S., deputy assistant United States attorney general.
Letter. To Ronald A. Zumbrun, president and legal director, Pacific
Legal Foundation. July 24, 1981.

"Ronald Reagan, the Health of Humans & the Natural World." Friends of
the Earth advertisement. *The New York Times.* February 2, 1982.

"Secretary James G. Watt: The First Six Months." National Wildlife
Federation. Report. July 10, 1981.

"Secretary Watt Urges Park Service to 'Get Back to Basics' in Park
Management." Department of the Interior. Press release. July 15,
1981.

"Special Report: The Results of the National Wildlife Federation's
Associate Membership Survey and Affiliate Leadership Poll on Major
Conservation Policies." National Wildlife Federation. July 14, 1981.

"Ten Secretarial Initiatives That Threaten the Health of Our Natural
Heritage." National Wildlife Federation. Report. July 14, 1981.

"The Watt Book." Wilderness Society. July, 1981, and subsequent
revisions.

"Update of Staff Analysis of James G. Watt's Performance as Secretary of
the Interior." National Wildlife Federation. Report. August 11, 1981.

Watt, James G., "Environmentalists: A Threat to the Ecology of the
West." Speech frequently given by Watt before he became Secretary of
the Interior.

Watt, James G., "Management of the National Park System."
Memorandum. To Russell Dickenson, director, National Park Service.
July 6, 1981.

"Watt Seeks Improved Services for National Park Visitors." Department of
the Interior. Press release. June 18, 1981.

Watt, James G. Transcript of speech and discussion with audience. Before
Conference of National Park Concessioners, Washington, D.C. March
9, 1981.

Watt, James G. Speech. 52nd Annual Colorado Transportation
Conference, Denver, Colorado. October 30, 1979.

"Who's Minding the Store? A Common Cause Guide to Top Officials at
the Department of the Interior." 1981.

Zumbrun, Ronald A., president and legal director, Pacific Legal
Foundation. Letter. To Alfred S. Regnery, deputy assistant United
States attorney general. July 22, 1981.

8 ▪ Prospects for Change

Books
Nieburg, H. L. *In the Name of Science.* Chicago: Quadrangle Books, 1966.

Articles
Miller, Arthur S. "Administration by Contract: A New Concern for the Administrative Lawyer." *New York University Law Review.* May, 1961.

Documents
Staats, Elmer B., Comptroller General of the United States. "Statement on the Consultant Reform Act of 1980." Committee on Governmental Affairs, United States Senate. Testimony. August 19, 1980.

Index